ENLIGHTENMENT, RIGHTS AND REVOLUTION SERIES

REVOLUTIONS IN LAW AND LEGAL THOUGHT

AUP titles of related interest

CONTEMPORARY RESEARCH ON TERRORISM
edited by Paul Wilkinson and A M Stewart

US AND THEM
A Study in Group Consciousness
W A Elliott

PRODUCT ADULTERATION AND EXTORTION
edited by Paul Wilkinson

SELF EXPRESSION AND SELF DETERMINATION
edited by W J Allan Macartney

ENLIGHTENMENT, RIGHTS AND REVOLUTION SERIES

ENLIGHTENMENT, RIGHTS AND REVOLUTION
Essays in Legal and Social Philosophy
edited by Neil MacCormick and Zenon Bankowski

REVOLUTION AND ENLIGHTENMENT IN EUROPE
edited by T O'Hagan

ISSUES OF SELF-DETERMINATION
edited by W Twining

SHAPING REVOLUTION
edited by E Attwooll

WOMEN'S RIGHTS AND THE RIGHTS OF MAN
edited by A-J Arnaud and E Kingdom

LAW AND ENLIGHTENMENT IN BRITAIN
edited by Tom Campbell

REVOLUTIONS IN LAW AND LEGAL THOUGHT

edited by
Zenon Bankowski

Series Editors: Neil MacCormick, Zenon Bankowski

ABERDEEN UNIVERSITY PRESS
Member of Maxwell Macmillan Pergamon Publishing Corporation

First Published 1991
Aberdeen University Press
© Aberdeen University Press for the collected works 1991

British Library Cataloguing in Publication Data

Revolutions in law and legal thought—(Enlightenment, rights and revolution series)
1. Law
I. Bankowski, Zenon *1946–*   II. Series
340

ISBN 0 08 040924 5

Typeset and printed by BPCC-AUP Aberdeen Ltd.

General Editors' Foreword

The Fourteenth World Congress of the International Association for Philosophy of Law and Social Philosophy (President: Professor Alice Erh-Soon Tay, University of Sydney, Australia) was held in August 1989. It was organised in Edinburgh, Scotland, in August 1989 on behalf of the UK Association for Legal and Social Philosophy (President: Professor Tom Campbell, University of Glasgow). There were over five hundred participants from some forty countries. It focused prophetically on the theme 'Enlightenment, Rights and Revolution'.

The sessions of the Congress produced a considerable number of papers discussing various aspects of the history of ideas and the theory of rights and of revolutions. Following on the volume of papers produced for the Congress's plenary sessions (*Enlightenment, Rights and Revolution*), it was decided to produce, under our general editorship, a series of volumes of selected papers from the Congress dealing in thematic form with some of the most pressing issues in legal and social philosophy and the history of ideas to emerge from the Congress. The present volume is the third of this series.

The Editorial Advisory Committee for these volumes comprises all those who presided over Plenary or Group Sessions of the Congress. Its Members are:

Aulis Aarnio, Helsinki; Robert Alexy, Kiel; André-Jean Arnaud, Oñati; Jose Faria, São Paulo; Åke Frändberg, Uppsala; Letizia Gianformaggio, Siena; Elena Gourko, Minsk; Eugene Kamenka, Canberra; Mikail Karlsson, Reykjavik; Roberta Kevelson, Reading, Pa.; Kalmán Kulcsár, Budapest; Nicola Lacey, Oxford; Jacques Lenoble, Louvain-la-Neuve; Adam Łopatka, Warsaw; Nicolás López Calera, Granada; Burns Machobane, Maseru; Rex Martin, Lawrence, Kans.; Alan Milne, Durham; Karl Mollnau, Berlin; Enrico Pattaro, Bologna; Hubert Rottleuthner, Berlin; Setsuko Sato, Yokohama; Roger Shiner, Edmonton; Ton-Kak Suh, Seoul; Raymond Wacks, Hong Kong; Ota Weinberger, Graz; Carl Wellman, St Louis, Mo.; Elizabeth Wolgast, Hayward, Cal.; Mitsukuni Yasaki, Seijo; Marek Zirk-Sadowski, Łòdz.

All of them gave us, immediately after the Congress, their impressions of papers presented in the various sessions, some indeed giving extremely thorough appraisals and comments. This was of great value, both to the general editors of the series and to the individual editors of particular volumes. We record our warm gratitude to them all, and to other colleagues who helped in the editorial process. Anne Bankowska was an extremely thorough assistant editor. Sheila Macmillan as Congress Secretary, and Elizabeth Mackenzie, who succeeded her as our secretary in the Centre for Criminology and the Social and Philosophical Study of Law, both gave very great help. The series editors (and their helpers) acted with an unfailing promptness and efficiency and kept to a demanding schedule which enabled us to achieve the ambition of having all the texts ready for publication within a year of the Congress itself.

Finally we record particularly warm thanks to Colin Maclean, who has recently retired from his post as Managing Director of Aberdeen University Press. From the earliest stages of Congress planning and preparation he gave us wise advice and kind support. Without his enthusiasm and shrewdness, it would have been impossible to get so much of the proceedings of the Congress so speedily into print.

Zenon Bankowski
Neil MacCormick

The Volumes in the present series are:

1 *Enlightenment, Rights and Revolution*, edited by Neil MacCormick and Zenon Bankowski
2 *Women's Rights and the Rights of Man*, edited by André-Jean Arnaud and Elizabeth Kingdom
3 *Revolutions in Law and Legal Thought*, edited by Zenon Bankowski
4 *Issues of Self-Determination*, edited by William Twining
5 *Shaping Revolution*, edited by Elspeth Attwooll
6 *Revolution and Enlightenment in Europe*, edited by Timothy O'Hagan
7 *Law and Enlightenment in Britain*, edited by Tom Campbell

A further two volumes of Congress Proceedings, on themes concerning human rights, are being published as *Beihefte* of the *Archiv für Rechts- und Sozialphilosophie* for 1990 under the editorship of Werner Maihofer and Gerhard Sprenger.

Erratum in volumes 2 and 7 of this series:
We apologise most sincerely for the fact that certain names are missing from the editorial committee as listed in the Foreword and blurb in the above volumes. The full, and correct, list is as shown in volumes 3, 4, 5 and 6.

Contents

List of Contributors

KAZIMIERZ OPAŁEK, University of Cracow

MATTI SINTONEN, Department of Philosophy, University of Helsinki

JES BJARUP, Institut for Retslaere, University of Aarhus

YOSHIHARU MATSUURA, University of Osaka

GRAŻYNA SKĄPSKA, Institute of State and Law, Polish Academy of Sciences, Warsaw

EUGENE KAMENKA, Australian National University, Canberra

FRIEDRICH LACHMAYER, University of Innsbruck

ANDREAS GÄNGEL, Academy of Sciences, German Democratic Republic

MARIA BORUCKA-ARCTOWA, University of Cracow

ADAM CZARNOTA, University of Torun,

MARTIN KRYGIER, University of New South Wales

JYRKI UUSITALO, National Research Institute of Legal Policy, Helsinki

FRITZ DOLDER, Ingenieurschule Zürich

PIERLUIGI CHIASSONI, University of Genoa

DAVID JABBARI, University of Reading

THOMAS WILHELMSSON, University of Helsinki

MATS FLODIN, University of Östersund, Sweden

H PH VISSER'T HOOFT, University of Utrecht

Introduction

Zenon Bankowski

The essays in this book are a selection of papers on the theme of 'Revolution' delivered at the working groups of the World Congress in Legal and Social Philosophy which was held in Edinburgh in 1989. The general theme of the Congress was 'Enlightenment, Rights and Revolution'. It is appropriate that this be the case since '89 turns out to be a magic number for revolutionaries. In 1689 we had the Glorious Revolution in Britain, in 1789 the French Revolution and in 1989 we saw the beginning of revolutionary changes in the 'socialist bloc' countries of Central and Eastern Europe.

What happens when legal orders change? On one view of it, the question we are asking is one of identity. How can we tell, in times of rapid social and political change, if we are dealing with the same legal system? What are, indeed, the criteria for continuity in individuation of legal orders? There have been many and various answers to this question, using such parameters as constitution, leaders, geography etc. Though this gives us criteria for discerning what amounts to change from one legal system to a different and successor system, does it really get at what revolutions are about? In one sense it certainly does, for a change of legal and constitutional identity is seen as necessary for the state and the legal system to define itself as clearly distanced from what went before. In legal theory and in law the process of revolution is often discussed in these terms and many ex-colonies of imperial powers, on being granted their independence, go through what constitutional lawyers call autochthony; a symbolic local revolution, so to speak, so that their constitutions have an entirely local and popular root and cannot be traced back to the constitutional forms of the old imperial state. What is important is the severing of connections with the old system. It is this, then, that gives us some of the flavour of revolution. Where the transition is not from colonial status to independence, but one by way of radical political and social transformation in a single country, the need to lay down new constitutional roots may be scarcely less acutely felt.

xi

In his contribution, Kazimierz Opałek shows how social science and legal or juristic thinking, though different in their approach, can usefully combine. He distinguishes three levels in the way that political and social science look at revolutions. Firstly, they look at particular revolutions and describe their causes and their effects. Secondly, they try to locate them in the general process. Finally, they try to make historical generalisations. Legal science can here make a twofold contribution by exploring the legal aspects of these situations and also by giving a clearer definition of revolution than the vague social scientific one which talks of profound, rapid and violent change. For Opałek juristic definitions of revolution are able to give some fixed point for research in areas that would otherwise be far too vague; they demarcate an area for the social sciences to work upon. This area is not, of course, as clearly demarcated as might be hoped. Indeed another book in the present series of books emanating from the World Congress (*Shaping Revolutions*, ed Elspeth Attwooll) deals with the problems of the legal definition as well as the moral problems that occur for those taking part in the activity of revolution. On any view, revolution must involve change of a really profound kind.

The present book sets out to explore the vague notion of 'profundity'. What, aside from juristic definitions, constitutes a profound break in a legal and social order? When is a change so profound and deep that it can be called a revolutionary one? What consequences does that have?

One view of what constitutes a profound and therefore revolutionary change is when a *paradigm shift* occurs. This view uses a concept taken from Thomas Kuhn and claims that in this event our conceptual scheme is rearranged, which involves changes not only in empirical beliefs but in the language in which the world is described, in goals of inquiry, in epistemic values, and in the standards of rational thought and intelligible explanation. This in itself raises problems, for it could be argued that the notion of conceptual revolution is incoherent because no conceptual scheme adequate to the task of describing beliefs or wants can be radically alien to us.

Matti Sintonen explores some of these points in his paper. He tries to show what counts as conceptual change. Conceptual schemes change, he says, by way of metaphors and analogies, step by step, until one day we see that we have a different scheme of interpretation. Thus what appears to be an evolutionary change is in the end a revolutionary one and, contrariwise, what seems revolutionary can turn out not to be so. If we take, for example, Darwin's theory of evolution we find that, though it appears to be a revolutionary jump and Gestalt-switch, it was not accompanied by a conceptual revolution; the field was restructured but the methodological standards and the standards of intelligibility remained largely the same. Copernicus' discovery, on the other hand, was acompanied by a conceptual revolution in that it saw the gradual emerging of a new way of seeing motion, which culminated in Newton's laws of motion. Thus there evolved, step by step, a new conceptual scheme. Conceptual changes, then, are brought about by rational piecemeal innovations which change the boundary conditions for rational belief. In social and political revolutions also, small changes lead to unexpected results because the boundary conditions for rational action change. In this way, though we may not be able to predict the outcome of the revolution, each step will be rational.

Jes Bjarup takes up much the same theme and shows how social revolution and conceptual revolution can go together. For him intellectuals are important because they provide the concepts through which the activity makes sense. As R L Stevenson put it, 'Man is a creature who lives not by bread alone but principally by catchwords.' Concepts, and the words and sentences in which they appear, are thus important for constituting political beliefs and action. But we cannot understand words and sentences in the abstract; they are only intelligible if we look to the way people put them to use in history. It is only in their use in this way that they have a meaning. This is for Bjarup a characterisation of the methodology offered by Hart when he claims that his analysis of the concept of law is at the same time an essay in 'descriptive sociology'. In this way, Bjarup claims, we can understand the conceptual changes which also illuminate the social phenomena. Through this we can reconcile innovation and tradition, for we can see that there are many different and diverse strands within the western legal tradition, and it is at crisis points like revolutions that they are explicitly competed over.

But what about non-western legal traditions? Yoshiharu Matsuura gives an example of this kind of 'descriptive sociology' in relation to Japan. He argues that legal theory should not be seen as merely an abstract affair with universally applicable findings, but rather it should be considered as something formulated and operating in, consciously or unconsciously, particular cultural and legal contexts which limit and give life to theoretical arguments. In looking at the case of Japan he emphasises how bureaucracy is the key concept for understanding the system. He then goes on to show how this affects the understanding of key legal concepts and points to the similarities and differences they have with the concepts as used in western systems.

Grażyna Skąpska, looking at the intertwining of many competing strands in the western legal tradition, shows how one revolution (the French) had within it two models of organising society which have had a great influence on succeeding social forms. Firstly there was the conception characteristic of modern liberal society where institutional conceptions of law are paradigmatic. This might be called 'contractual' society, where the aim is to have a framework of law within which people can pursue their activities in liberty. The second conception is more instrumental and stress is put on the effective realisation of ends for the good of society. Here stress is put not on people pursuing their own ends but rather on the law providing for their *real* needs. This tends to produce authoritarian systems in that it concentrates power in those who claim to know people's real needs. We can see the legacy of this latter model, she says, in the old arrangements in countries of the old 'socialist bloc'.

Apart from the concept of paradigm and the Kuhnian idea of scientific revolution, a key concept used by many of the authors presented here is that of tradition. This is used to show how legal institutions and arrangements have a continuity deeper than at first appears. To say that something completely breaks with the old order then is rather difficult because at the same time as we are pointing to the discontinuities we can also point to the continuities. Eugene Kamenka claims that even the Jacobin-type revolutions which sought a complete break with the past developed and consummated trends in government, law and administration that had been there before. Thus one can see, through the legal and administrative history of Napoleonic France, Russia and China, striking continuities both in law and in legal philosophy. These continuities are in fact more surprising than the differences. Friedrich Lachmayer takes up the same theme in a novel way. For him too revolutions tend to reimpose patterns of dominion. Though they are dialectical processes one can see copying at work. Thus old patterns of dominion replicate themselves in strange ways in new patterns of dominion. In the French revolution, for example, Royal dominion is replaced by Imperial dominion.

Andreas Gängel also takes up the point of continuity. From the point of view of more orthodox communist theory he writes that the creation of a new socialist law must be understood as a process of coming to terms with the traditional legal order, which is not in total contradiction. The proletarian revolution is not to be understood as the incarnation of discontinuity. The development of socialist law is hardly possible without some reference to the inheritance and enduring traditions of bourgeois legal culture. It is this reference which maintains continuity on the way to a system which rests on completely unique, developed social foundations. Gängel was writing before the dramatic changes in the DDR of late 1989, followed by its effective collapse and its union with the Federal Republic in 1990. However his general thesis still stands, especially if seen in relation to Sintonen's idea of evolutionary revolutionary change.

Maria Borucka-Arctowa takes this theme further. She looks at the concepts of innovation and tradition and shows how they are indispensable elements in the formation and development of law. She looks at the relationship between innovation and tradition during periods of rapid change and comes to the conclusion that rapid political transformations do not have to be combined with the complete severance of ties with the institutional framework of the system. Thus, for example, the Polish system after the advent of communism still had a degree of continuity with the old tradition (based on the western legal tradition) while adapting to the changed social conditions. Again the revolutionary changes being introduced at present will still have to start from the basis of the old communist system. It remains to be seen how far the new social order will be severed from the old discredited one and what continuities will remain. As we have seen, *do novo* starts are very rare.

Martin Krygier and Adam Czarnota take up Arctowa's theme and look at change and continuity in its relation to tradition and revolution. Legal continuity goes well beyond mere identity of elements and indeed can occur in the absence of such identity. Legal traditions are both complex and layered. Some elements and layers are more easily changed and dispensed with than others but at the deepest layers of values and techniques in the system revolutionary change hardly occurs. Here we find elements in layers which go to accounting for the very meaning of the tradition at a hardly conscious level. When looking at revolutions, one must attend to important distinctions, especially those that flow from two types of relationship between state and society and the place and significance of law. Revolutionary change takes place within the context of these traditions and thus continuity is preserved through seeming revolutionary change.

Jyrki Uusitalo, from a modified Kuhnian perspective, agrees with this view of change. He asks how concepts of scientific revolution make sense and attempts theoretically to reconstruct legal dogmatics by using an adjusted Kuhnian model. He compares law as a paradigm with Ludwig Fleck's view of medicine as a paradigm. How could an evolutionary view, he asks, accommodate the actual workings of legal science seen in this Fleckian way? It has no criteria for rationally evaluating its success other than by the fact of persuading others to act and think according to its criteria. But how do we evaluate that? And, for a tradition to progress one needs some rational criteria of success. In law the evolutionary way cannot work because the assumptions we make about everything coming from the past cannot be strong enough to ground that. We thus proceed in an analogical way. The most important thing to note here is the conceptual and theoretical interaction that exists between received conceptions and new ones; while previously unfamiliar situations are fashioned as instances of the familiar, the familiar itself is seen in a new light. Thus we re-interpret the past in relation to the present and it is this dynamic interaction that is the motor of progress in traditions. Revolutionary research ideas stem from pragmatic motives and are solutions that have been made to work by scholars constructing the rational possibility of such normative solutions. One should note also the links with Sintonen's view.

But though this links up with the position of Czarnota and Krygier as to the motor of movement in tradition, they do not characterise these 'revolutionary jumps' as the profound conceptual changes that those influenced by Kuhn might do. Their view is that profound change comes at the level of tradition and not what jurally, or even politically, is called revolution. But profound change in legal tradition is on their view very difficult.

Fritz Dolder seems to confirm this thesis. An important element in legal tradition, says Czarnota and Krygier, is what Roscoe Pound called 'received techniques and ideals' which deal with ways of handling legal material and which determine, in the broadest way, the process of legal reasoning. We sometimes call these the 'style' of a particular tradition. In an empirical study of the reasoning of the Swiss federal court (1881–1980), Dolder concludes that there has been no change in the style of reasoning in that court. Thus, although major currents of legal thought were discussed within the professional legal community, the style of reasoning remains a highly conservative activity not much affected by social and cultural change.

Pierluigi Chiassoni puts forward the legal-economic approach to legal reasoning as one which can turn a not very rigorous legal science into one which will be able to devise legal policies, oriented to precisely defined goals and which is rationally testable. He shows how injecting economic concepts can transform the basic concepts of a given legal field. Does this amount to a revolutionary change? He claims that it does, in the sense that it is a sweeping technical improvement on old-style legal reasoning. However, if we go to the deeper layer of values then we cannot be so sure, for he sees the techniques as neutral in respect of values and in fact many lawyer-economists claim they are merely making the law's intrinsic reasoning clear. Thus they will not make an impact at the deepest cultural levels of the legal tradition.

Of all the recent movements in western legal thought, that which has most claimed to be revolutionary in style and impact has been the Critical Legal Studies movement in the USA. David Jabbari puts its claims to the test. In particular he examines its claims to translate legal criticism into a programme of radical social transformation, since it believes that the potential for this transformation lies within legal rules and doctrine. He deals mainly with the 'deviationist' doctrine of Unger which he sees as the positive side of deconstruction. In the present context 'deconstruction' means that theory which splits the text into a conceptual dualism where one pole is favoured at the expense of the other (for example, in contract individualist values are favoured at the expense of solidarity ones). The deviationist doctrine takes the unfavoured pole and emphasises it. He sees two problems with this which the CLS movement is not able to answer. First of all there is the implicit belief that change at the level of legal doctrine can bring about changes in wider social relationships, but there is no clear specification of how that can be so. Secondly, he asks whether favouring the disfavoured pole is in fact a profound social change; for one could say, turning CLS criticism around, that this merely represents as partial and biased a view of human association as did the view it attacks. Here again the changes are not seen as profound for, though there is indeed change, the tradition is not really affected since it already holds within it those conflicting values (compare the essays of Bjarup and Skąpska).

Jabbari does, however, adumbrate some ideas which point the way towards transformation, namely, through systems which provide for the most democratic determination of a legal dispute. Thomas Wilhelmsson takes up this point, agreeing with Jabbari that the possibility of profound change lies with European critical theories. He discusses two theories in the development of modern law which he claims are similar. These are (a) the theory of reflexive law put forward by Gunther Teubner and others in which self-regulation is the ideal and the theory is oriented towards procedure; and (b) the Finnish theory of need-rational argumentation which lays stress on the concrete and real needs of members of society. Can they contribute to a theory of critical legal dogmatics and, if they can, how revolutionary or profound a change is it? He sees both of these views as helping in producing new forms of democracy different from mere liberalism and self-determination. They are not, however, only concerned with form and the Finnish theory provides an explicit theory of content which the reflexive theory provides implicitly in terms of a 'reflexive logic' which stimulates reflexive processes. They thus provide both short-term change and the possibility of genuine long-term social transformation.

Mats Flodin also looks at the possibilities of change, but in a more normative and speculative way. In the full Kuhnian sense a legal paradigm does not exist because there is no agreement concerning fundamental values, world views and ideology. We can, however, use paradigm in a more colloquial sense and this enables us to discern local paradigms or, we might say, traditions such as common law, socialist law, civil law, etc. What norms and values, he asks, can we agree so that a full and mature paradigm can be established?

Universally agreed-upon norms might help show us the rationality of the world. Material conditions and technology will also force this change of thinking.

H Visser't Hooft, in the last paper in the book, takes this point up. The ecological impact of present-day technology, he says, forces us to look to our obligations to future generations and thus consider the grounds for intergenerational justice. The principles are not so very revolutionary but it is at the level of motives that we face a challenge. We have to overcome the 'moral distance' between the present and the long-term future. We have to make ourselves see, and treat as equal, people and a way of life which are beyond conjecture.

For me as editor, a particular pleasure in putting together this book arises from the juxtaposition of its themes with the rapidly changing social and political events of Central and Eastern Europe. The Congress itself saw the first stirrings of this with the appointment of the Mazowiecki government in Poland, the first non-communist government in Central and Eastern Europe since the Second World War, and the end in not yet in sight. I end my introduction then, with some reflections on these themes.

I start with the idea, considered at length by our authors, that continuity and change go hand in hand; though our social and political circumstances change, we are still in some respects related to what went before. This is a theme also taken up by Neil MacCormick in his essay, 'Is Nationalism Philosophically Credible?', which appears in another book in the present series arising from the World Congress (*Issues of Self-Determination* ed William Twining). MacCormick explores the philosophical and political credibility of nationalism, showing how the assertion of particularity and separateness does not thereby cut a nation off from recognition of its universality in humankind. In the present book this is expressed as the idea that change is not to be seen as something that cuts us off from our past, for continuity, though it may run at deep levels, can always be found. Often this has been seen as rather a conservative point which sees change as dangerous, as a blind alley which tries to break off from tradition but in the end always reverts back to it. On this view revolutions, past and present, are seen as trying but failing to get away from 'good old traditional values'. But we must not forget that the reversion to 'good old traditional values' can itself be seen as a revolutionary change, as for example, the events in Central and Eastern Europe. We must then look to the continuities between *that* revolutionary change and what went before, we cannot just forget it. Our tradition is not just an unalloyed good, it will have its bad aspects and we must come to terms with these as well. At these crisis points the tradition comes to an understanding of itself by confronting itself with its past and not by forgetting that past. In this way the crisis becomes a way of moving forward and not backward to the golden past.

This brings me to my second point. In the present book there is much discussion of metaphor and analogy as the way of going forward in tradition, especially at the conceptual level. In this as well, we can see how change and continuity go hand in hand. Metaphor and analogy can only operate within a tradition. For though they may effect quite creative and revolutionary changes, they depend for their effect on being able, so to speak, to span both sides of the change. Sintonen shows how this might gradually effect a conceptual change, but this need not go against the main thrust of Czarnota's and Krygier's views of traditions, if one insists, as they do, on their layered nature.

Analogy and associated methods, then, work by showing the future in the past and the past in the future. It is this futurity that I want now to stress. Tradition does not mean that we must merely look back, for it also implies that we should look forward. Where this will take us we might not necessarily know. If, however, we are, as our tradition understands us to be, active social subjects, then we must take the forward-looking part of our tradition seriously, and this implies intergenerational justice. We must take future active subjects seriously, for they are as much part of our identity in tradition as those living and those dead. This implies paying serious attention to ecological and green issues, for we must leave to those in the future a world in which they can be as active social subject as we are. The future, as much as the past, must really become part of our present.

CHAPTER 1

Law and Revolution

Kazimierz Opałek

I *Introduction*

Problems of revolution are investigated on the one hand by the social sciences, mainly history, sociology and politics and on the other by the legal sciences. These two groups of disciplines make use of different concepts of revolution with important consequences for the scope and approach to the problems under consideration. Consequently, in the social and legal sciences we are dealing with differing views on the relation between political revolution and legal change. I compare both approaches and their results. While not disregarding the contributions of the social sciences, I discuss the merits of the juristic point of view in looking at the legal aspect of political revolution and the influence of revolution on the subsequent changes of law.

II *The Concept of Revolution: Ordinary Language, Political Discourse and the Social Sciences*

Reconstructuring current linguistic institutions one can roughly say that 'revolution' is understood as: (a) profound, (b) rapid or occurring in a short time, and (c) violent change in some sphere. It is a change which is, mostly *ex post,* evaluated as one of some particular relevance. This concept is vague. It describes a certain kind of change on the base of quantitative and evaluative criteria. The word 'revolution', and similarly 'counter-revolution', is strongly loaded emotionally and this becomes particularly pronounced in political discourse. The champions of revolution ascribe to it a positive value because of the profoundness of the change (for the better), its speed and even because of its violent character, which in social and political revolutions they justify as 'acts of social justice'. The opponents of revolution ascribe to it a negative

1

value, as either accomplishing unnecessary and destructive changes, or introducing them too fast. Above all they condemn the violence as criminal acts of terror. The label 'counter-revolution' because of its pejorative tinge is not much in use among the advocates of the return to the old order, while revolutionaries condemn counter-revolution as the work of reactionaries, hampering 'progress'. The advocates of major changes who exclude the use of violence, or make a pretence of not resorting to it, call these changes 'clement revolution' (e.g., in Poland at the end of the eighteenth century), or 'peaceful revolution' (as did Salazar in Portugal), mainly in contrast to the patterns of the French Revolution in the first instance and the Russian Revolution in the second.

Social sciences adopt in substance the current meaning of the word 'revolution', while attempting its objectivisation on the basis of the analysis of concrete data, their classification, and by the introduction of additional concepts like 'revolutionary situation', 'revolutionary process', and so on. They also distinguish the sphere of revolutions. Thus one can distinguish scientific, scientific-technological, agrarian, industrial, commercial, cultural, social, and political revolutions and try to ascertain their specific traits. The uncertain quantitative and evaluative criteria of qualifying some change as 'revolution' grossly hamper such attempts. There are also difficulties connected with the complicated character of the data under research. A contemporary scholar dealing with problems of revolution writes:

> The historian of revolution works on material which is immensely heterogeneous and escapes classification. . . . When applying 'hard' criteria we inevitably violate the very historical matter we are dealing with, and when our criteria 'soften', we get a blurred picture which will not satisfy the adherents of solidly systematized knowledge.[1]

Finally we must observe that within the above disciplines we find revolution in the sense of activities with certain objectives being confused with revolution in the sense of the result of such activities (i.e. an accomplished or materialised change).

We shall not go into the problems of the relations and connections between revolutions of different kinds. In the examination of our problem I shall limit myself to the question of the relation of law to political revolution, although one could also investigate the connections of other kinds of revolutions with law, especially their influence on the processes of legal regulation.

The concept of 'political revolution' itself has quite a few problems associated with it. Firstly, those in connection with 'successful' and 'unsuccessful' political revolutions. The successful revolution is seen in terms of the result (the attained change). The unsuccessful revolution however, is seen in terms of kinds of activities. With respect to the result it is not a revolution because it is not a change, or at least not such a change as was intended to be accomplished through the activities in question. Secondly, do 'revolts' such as *coups d'état,* or palace upheavals, have to be included in the concept of political revolution? It is generally felt that they do not, the argument being that the revolt is not a 'profound' change. The criteria of 'profound-ness' of a change can however be variously understood, as we shall see below, when discussing the juristic concept of revolution. Thirdly, one can distinguish revolutions 'from below' and 'from above'. Sometimes changes achieved by acts violating the constitutional structure, performed by authorities, are understood in the later sense, but sometimes changes achieved by acts within the limits of legality, when the changes are of a radical and profound character are also so understood. Such revolution 'from above', however, cannot easily be distinguished from a (major) reform. This point will be discussed below. Fourthly, one speaks of revolution in the wide sense (as the 'revolutionary cycle'), and in the narrow sense (a 'singular' or 'concrete' revolution). The 'revolutionary cycle' is a theoretical construct consisting in isolating by con-vention certain changes occurring over a long period of time; here, 'singular' revolutions and reforms alternate. Fifthly revolution is rarely considered as 'simply a change'. Much more frequently the regularity of such change is assumed at least implicitly, treating revolutions as manifestations of the laws of social development. In fact we can find traces of this in the concept of the 'revolutionary cycle'. The following remark of Ginsberg is applicable here:

> People are sceptical of the possibility of establishing any general law of social change, yet cannot reconcile themselves to the view that in history there is no plot, rhythm or pattern, but only a series of emergencies, the play of the contingent and unforeseen. . . . Very few writers avoid using the conception of levels or periods of civilization, though the criteria for comparing different peoples or periods are rarely stated explicitly.[2]

When the view that revolution is a regularity of social development is adopted, then there is a danger of searching for revolutions everywhere by, for example, assuming universal regularities, by forcing insignificant facts into the suggestive patterns of 'classical' revolutions.

We now turn to consider how the relation between revolution and law, in the light of the concept of political revolution adopted by historians, sociologists and political scientists appears. One side of this concept includes the violent change of political power, this change being legally tantamount to abolishing the old and instituting new fundamental (constitutional) norms. The other side of the concept also includes, at least for some representatives of these disciplines, radical political changes accomplished legally 'from above'. Therefore, when political revolution can be both legal and illegal (from the point of view of hitherto existing constitutional order), then the element of law is not an essential component in the concept. We can see this by the fact that (successful) revolt, which is a violent change of political power constituting a new legality, is not prevailingly considered as political revolution. There can be, then, no revolution in spite of abolishing legality, and there can be revolution in spite of the preservation of legality. For the representatives of the above-mentioned disciplines the extra-legal characteristics of the change as 'profound', 'radical', and 'violent' are essential. The approach is empirical and realistic, though it is distorted many times by the vagueness of the criteria which are applied.

III *The Juristic Concept of Revolution*

The problems of revolution are dealt with in such legal disciplines as theory of state and law, legal history, constitutional law and public international law. After the fight against the formalism of legal positivism and analytical jurisprudence, many representatives of the above disciplines are influenced by the social sciences and this also finds expression in their views on the problems of revolution. Stress on the legal aspect of political revolution, or even treating this aspect as essential has, however, remained a specific trait of legal science. As a matter of fact, legal science employs a juristic concept of revolution which is different from the one discussed already. It can be somewhat blurred in the writings of authors adapting the views of the social sciences, but appears in a clear-cut and consistent way in normativism and contemporary analytical jurisprudence.

While not attempting a broad review of literature, I will present the representative standpoint of Kelsen, adding some remarks on the views of Hart. Revolution from the legal point of view is the change of fundamental norms of the political system (of the constitution in the wide sense), which comes into effect not legally, i.e. not in accordance with the constitution hitherto in force. Kelsen says that for revolution what is essential is, '. . . dass die geltende Verfassung auf eine Weise abgeändert order durch eine neue Verfassung gänzlich ersetzt wird, die nicht in der bisher geltenden Verfassung vorgeschrieben ist'.[3] According to Kelsen this amounts to the change of the basic norm:

> Mit dem Wirksamwerden der neuen Verfassung hat sich die Grundnorm, das heisst die Voraussetzung geändert, unter der verfassungsgebende Tatbestand und die gemäss der Verfassung gesetzten Tatbestande als Rechtsnorm-erzeugende und Rechtsnormanwendende Tatbestande gedeutet werden könne.[4]

H L A Hart employs practically the same juristic concept of revolution, but in a different way. The problem is investigated from the internal and external point of view. Revolution amounts to the change of the 'ultimate rule of recognition' from the one hitherto applied to the one now accepted and used. Hart analyses the intermediate and transitory situations ('half-way stages') between the hitherto existing and new constitutional structure and cases of 'suspension' of the question of which legal system exists; the old, or the new.[5] Kelsen deals only with the 'final' situation where there is effective change contrary to the previous constitution. Hart's analysis looks at the important and complicated legal questions which arise in transitory situations. These observations are not incompatible with Kelsen's conception. Kelsen's conception, however, leaves out of account the meanderings of the 'half-way stages', concentrating on the abstractly conceived 'mystical hour' of the revolution.

The juristic concept of revolution differs in relevant aspects from the concept of political revolution in history, sociology, and political science. Firstly, representatives of these disciplines speak of revolution both in the sense of actions aiming at producing change, and in the sense of the change that is the result of them; the juristic concept is restricted to this latter sense only. Consequently, it includes only successful revolution. Secondly, from the legal point of view, revolution is solely political change coming into effect not in accordance with the constitution hitherto in force. Change 'from above', even 'profound' change is not a revolution when performed in accordance with this constitution. Thirdly, unsuccessful revolution is not revolution, but 'crime', according to the legal system which has remained in force. Fourthly, a successful *coup d'état,* though it may lead up to a non 'profound' change of the ruling group, is revolution as it abolishes the previous legality and institutes a new one. Fifthly, from the legal point of view it is immaterial in which way the change has occurred and so will include ways of producing the change which will not be counted as revolutionary by the social sciences (e.g., effective occupation of the territory of another state), or ones which would be recognised as 'revolutionary' only with reservations (e.g. liberation from foreign rule).[6] Sixthly, the question of whether revolution is simply a change, or a regularity of social development, is quite immaterial from the legal point of view. It is left to the social sciences to ponder over such questions. Legal science is also unconcerned with methodological uncertainties revealed by the concepts of 'singular' revolution and the 'revolutionary cycle'. It is not interested in the antecedents, but only in the facts which directly produce the change.

Social sciences and legal science share a common ground only in so far as they deal with revolutions in the sense of the successful result of actions which have not conformed to the constitution hitherto in force (perhaps the 'singular', or 'concrete' revolution can also be included here). Social sciences consider as essential the change of the political power, while for legal science the change of the constitutional structure is essential. According to the normativistic identification of state and legal system we are here dealing only with two different formulations referring to the same thing, while according to social sciences both changes, though related, are of a different order. Other problems, investigated by social sciences under the heading 'revolution', are excluded from juristic considerations. Thus one might say that the juristic concept of revolution is much more precise.

IV *Law—Revolution and Reform*

Social sciences, since they treat broadly the problems of political revolution, do not limit themselves to the instances where the juridical concept of revolution applies. They are also concerned with 'revolutionary activities', the 'revolutionary cycle', 'unsuccessful revolution', and 'revolution from above in accordance with the constitution'. Each of these topics can have some legal aspects: revolutionary activities can tend, *inter alia* towards changes in law, the revolutionary cycle can include a series of such partial and radical changes, the revolution even if unsuccessful can sooner or later lead to concessions fixed in law, and changes from above in accordance with the constitution in force can also include changes in legal regulation. The connections will be generally present since the law is not only an important instrument of social control exerted by the state, but also the means of securing the interests of social groups, and the 'fight for the law' is an essential element of the political process.[7] These connections, however, are not necessary, but contingent. They may not occur at all (e.g., the unsuccessful revolution may bring about no concessions), or occur to a limited extent.

The existence of such connections is not denied by authors employing the juristic concept of revolution, but in accordance with this concept they do not consider them as belonging to the problem 'law and revolution'. They are interested only in the instance, in which the connection of revolution with law is necessary or essential. This is interpreted somewhat differently in the social sciences: revolution is considered as a successful change of political power contrary to the constitution hitherto in force. Although the first part of this definition lays stress on a political fact (the change of power), the second includes the legal aspect of the revolution. Here, then, at least implicitly, the connection between revolution and law is considered necessary.

What happens to the law in case of an accomplished revolution can be called a fundamental or a small change according to the point of view employed. One can consider the change as fundamental, firstly, in its formal aspect since the foundation of validity of the whole legal order changes. Secondly, it can be fundamental in content inasmuch as the constitution is changed or replaced by another one. The same applies to other politically important laws. On the other hand, one can consider the change as small inasmuch as the bulk of the law hitherto in force is retained, either explicitly, or tacitly. The explanation of this well-known fact in the history of revolution is simple: revolution is a rapid change, and changing law takes time.

We are now faced with problems of the relations between the accomplished revolution and subsequent changes in law. These relations again have the character of contingent and not necessary connections. Revolution consisting only in a change of the ruling group resulting from a *coup d'état,* may subsequently bring no change in the contents of law; the changes of law in the period after such revolutions can have quite different causes. On the other hand a revolution having the character of a profound change of political power must be assumed to be leading up to legislative activities aiming at major trans-formations in the law. The causes of such transformations, however, may be varied and it is particularly difficult to judge the extent of the influence of revolution on changes in the law taking place some time after the revolution, when the political, social, or economic situation has altered.

The new political power, in the case of a profound political revolution, is as a rule interested in bringing about changes in the law. Such changes, however, can only be accomplished over a long period of time and they successively affect various branches of law or their parts. That is why, in the period immediately after a revolution, temporary measures are resorted to. They consist in exerting various kinds of pressure on juristic personnel inherited from the former regime, in respect of the interpretation and application of the law that has been retained in force. The new political power also strives to fill juridicial posts with its own, new staff, counting on their devotion to the cause of revolution, or on their opportunism. The success of such endeavours is mostly a partial one and in many cases the new power is forced to tolerate an interpretation and application of law which is guided by the professional skills and ethos of juristic personnel.[8] Generally speaking, in the post-revolutionary situation, there is a disjunction between the rapidity of political change and the insurmountable slowness of the transformation of law, between the political demand of total 'renovation' of the juristic personnel and the scarcity of loyal professionals which force use to be made of the former personnel.

Coups d'état, resulting only in the change of ruling groups, do not, as a rule, aim at far-reaching changes of the law, and the changes in juridical personnel are in such instances limited to filling key-positions with persons close to the ruling group, regardless of their professional competence.

One has to distinguish two kinds of changes in the law. The first sort are revolutionary changes. They consist in an unconstitutional change of the constitution hitherto in force or of substituting it for another one, and in repealing other politically important laws while laying down others. In this way the constitutional structure of the state, and consequently the foundation of the validity of the whole legal system changes. The second sort are changes of law within legality when the constitution is not abolished. We have two kinds of such changes; firstly there are those that take place at the constitutional level—total or partial. Secondly there are those changes that take place at hierarchically lower levels, carried out legally. Changes of both sorts can come into effect under the influence of the revolution (e.g., a full new constitution replacing an incomplete act drawn up at the moment of formation of the new regime). They may also come about through other factors, or under the joint influence of revolution, as far as the general direction is concerned, and the concrete factors of the ever-changing political, social, and economic situation. Changes of law which take place in the 'normal' and 'peaceful' period and which have no connection with revolution belong here also. One may see this as the distinction between revolution and reform.

As we have already seen, in the social sciences there is a tendency to consider as revolutionary changes within legality 'from above', when these changes are sufficiently 'profound'. The criterion of distinguishing revolutionary from non-revolutionary changes is a question of convention, but the criterion of a greater or lesser 'profoundness' of the changes has a low operational value. It is hardly possible to measure the degrees of profoundness of the changes. Whether a given change is sufficiently profound to be considered as revolutionary will be a subjective question. The border between revolution and reform becomes blurred. That is why we adopt the criterion of legality: revolution creates a new legality in a way which is illegal from the point of view of the previous legality, and reform brings about changes, of law *inter alia,* within legality.

The reform of law then, as change within legality, is that change which is carried into effect by a competent organ of the state (and so change 'from above'), fulfilling formal requirements (of procedure) and material ones (of what actual things are permitted by a particular normative act). Particular legal institutions serve the purpose of eliminating normative acts which do not fulfil these requirements. Further, the reform of law is an intentional change. Legal science does not consider changes of particular rules as reforms of law, limiting this concept to changes in the legal regulation of whole branches of law or legal institutions. There is also a tendency, particularly distinct in statutory law countries, to limit the concept of legal reform to the changes in law by legislation.

Apart from legal reform we may look at reforms of other kinds, such as economic, agrarian, or educational reform. An element of change in legal regulation is here present also. One can only say that legal reform focuses its interest on law, whilst not disregarding the extra-legal implications. Reforms in other domains have as an immediate objective the change of these domains, whilst law is one of the necessary means of carrying these changes into effect.

We return now to the concept of revolution in social sciences as that of a profound, rapid, and violent change. Quite frequently reform as a partial (moderate), slow (gradual) and clement change is opposed to this. Thus Marxism characterises and criticises the programme and activities of the Social-Democratic movement as 'reformist' as opposed to 'revolutionary'. The above remarks do not fix a clear difference between revolution and reform. One can thus distinguish profound reforms from non-profound ones (for example the profound reforms of Bismarck in the years 1866–71 and 1881). The reform can also be introduced rapidly (e.g., political reform in Poland in April 1989).[9] The reforms can also be accomplished in a violent way (e.g., agrarian reforms in Socialist countries).

The question of the profound or partial and moderate character of the reform of law can be considered firstly from the point of view of the scope of the new legal regulation, and secondly, from the point of view of the contents of the changes introduced. When looking at the scope of regulation one can qualify codifications as profound reforms because they pertain to whole branches of law; partial reforms would be those of merely particular legal institutions. When looking at the contents of the regulation, a partial and moderate reform would be one introducing slight changes, a profound reform one introducing far-reaching ones. Here one has to consider the strength of legal convictions in society and the ineffectiveness of changes disregarding them. That is why profound reforms in content run the risk of provoking friction, disobedience to law or its evasion, and other phenomena. Therefore, reforms in law are seldom governed by dogmatism but rather most frequently by a prudent moderation.

Turning now to the rapid or slow (gradual) character of legal reform, I would like to make the following remarks. The changes of law introduced by legislation are rapid ones in the sense that singular, concrete, reformatory acts abrogate regulations hitherto in force and substitute them for new ones which take effect in a fixed moment. Change of law occurs by one stroke of the legislator's pen, as the saying goes. What was the law yesterday is no longer the law today; from today we have another law. Preparing the reform can take a long time but that is another matter. The reform of law can be considered as a slow and gradual process only in a larger time-scale, when we examine the course of reformatory changes.[10]

When we look at the antinomy violent-clement, there is hardly a difference between reform and revolution. The reform of law, admittedly, is mostly of a clement character, but it may also have a cruel despotic character.

Although these qualifications are of a fluid and vague character, I have considered them as applied to legal reform, because they reflect the current way of distinguishing reform from revolution and are also rooted in the social sciences.

V *Final Remarks*

One can distinguish three levels in social scientific research on political revolutions. The first is the description of particular revolutions, of the social and political forces involved in them, of the course of revolutions, their antecedents and their after-effects. The second is the explanation of the causes of particular revolutions and of the role in the historical process. Such descriptive and explanatory tasks are mainly historical. On the third level are attempts at elaborating certain generalisations concerning the mechanisms of revolutionary processes and at classifying revolutions. These investigations are mainly sociological and political-science based.

The contributions of legal science to research on political revolutions are twofold. They consist, on the one hand, in exploring legal aspects of the revolutionary and transitory situations, mentioned above, as well as such topics as revolutionary programmes of the changes in law and the impact of revolution on legal reform. These problems belong to the limited area of legal specialisation. On the other hand, however, the juristic approach to the problems of political revolution makes it possible to eliminate some theoretical drawbacks in research on revolution. The concept of political revolution as counter-constitutional change of constitutional structure has a higher operational value than the vague concept of revolution as profound, rapid and violent change. The juristic concept clarifies some of the problems connected with revolution and gives a clear distinction between revolution and reform. These contributions are of general importance to research on revolutions.

NOTES

1   J Baszkiewicz, *Wolność, Własność. Rewolucje Burżuazyjne (Freedom, Equality, Property. The Bourgeois Revolutions)* (Warszawa, 1981) p 42.
2   M Ginsberg, *Essays in Sociology and Social Philosophy*, vol II *Reason and Unreason in Society* (London, 1960) p 124.
3   H Kelsen, *Reine Rechtslehre*, II ed (Wien, 1960) p 213.
4   H Kelsen, op. cit. p 214. On the basic norm see also his *Allgemeine Theorie der Normen*, K Ringhofer and R Walter, eds (Wien, 1979) pp 203 ff.
5   H L A Hart, *The Concept of Law* (Oxford, 1961) pp 114 ff. See also note on p 248.
6   Compare H L A Hart, op. cit. p 115, 116 f, and J M Eekelaar, 'Principles of revolutionary legality'; J M Finnis, 'Revolutions and continuity of law', both in *Oxford Essays in Jurisprudence*, II series, A W B Simpson, ed (Oxford, 1973).
7   K Opałek, 'Law and politics in time and space', *Polititiikka* (Helsinki, 1977) pp 21 ff.
8   Compare J Stone, *Legal System and Lawyers' Reasonings* (London, 1964) pp 28 ff.
9   The evaluation of these reforms depends on what standpoint is taken. The change introduced in April 1989 together with subsequent ones is in the juristic sense a reform and not a revolution since it was a change in accordance with the constitution in force. One cannot, of course, rule out the possibility of a revolutionary change but the course of events so far makes it hardly probable. On the other hand, from the point of view of social sciences one would be inclined, especially after elections of June 1989 and formation of the Solidarity government, to recognise the changes in question, although accomplished without use of violence, as akin to revolution (the transition from an authoritarian to a democratic state).
10 Compare K Opałek, 'Rechtsnormen und sozialer Wandel', in *Theorie der Normen. Festgabe für Ota Weinberger zum 65. Geburtstag*, W Krawietz, H Schelsky, G Winkler and A Schramm, eds (Berlin, 1984) pp 62 ff.

CHAPTER 2

Scientific and Conceptual Revolutions

Matti Sintonen

I *Conceptual Schemes*

Scientific and conceptual revolutions are troublesome entities: we are hard put to define, in the abstract, what they are and to determine whether one is going on at a particular time. There is also the problem of identifying a conceptual scheme, and of specifying what counts as a transition from one scheme to another. As some writers have argued, scientific and conceptual revolutions involve not only changes in empirical beliefs but also in the language in which the world is described, in goals of inquiry, in epistemic values, and in standards of rational thought and intelligible explanation.

But if this is true, it becomes somewhat of a mystery how the empirical beliefs can be identified across different conceptual schemes. And indeed, as Donald Davidson has argued, for precisely this reason the very idea of a conceptual revolution or massive conceptual change should be given up as incoherent (Davidson, 1974). The principle of charity, Davidson writes, demands that in interpreting a fellow speaker most of what he or she holds true must come out as true in our conceptual scheme. No conceptual scheme adequate to the task of representing beliefs and wants can be radically alien to us. And as Davidson puts it, this principle is not a contingent constraint but rather *a priori* and forced on us. It follows that the dualism of conceptual scheme and experience is unintelligible.

The distinction, as drawn by Davidson, is probably incoherent. But this way of solving, or dissolving, the question of the identity of conceptual schemes puts us in an awkward position. There clearly have been changes in concepts and systems of concepts that count as revolutionary, and some less demanding notion of a conceptual scheme is needed. I shall proceed on the assumption that such a notion not only makes sense but is needed, and focus on some recent attempts to elucidate scientific and conceptual revolutions.

11

One specific question I shall address arises from difficulties in attempts to locate revolutionary changes in time, and to ascribe them to identifiable individuals. Some scientific revolutions take a long time to complete, while others are sudden and can be perceived as revolutionary by contemporaries. But as several philosophers and historians of science have noted, what may appear to contemporaries as revolutions in a conceptual scheme may turn out to be mere empirical changes. Whether a new idea counts as a revolution (or a spark of a revolution) can sometimes only be determined with the benefit of hindsight.

Another specific question concerns rationality and intelligibility: if each conceptual scheme incorporates a notion of rationality and a preferred mode of intelligible explanation, and if there can be changes in these, we face a major interpretative problem: how can a change from one scheme to another be exhibited as rational and intelligible and by whose lights?

To tackle these questions I shall first discuss some examples and then suggest a quasi-Tolstoyan view of history. According to that idea big scientific revolutions that perhaps span several centuries are accompanied by conceptual changes, and the totality of these changes is not something individual persons (or even groups of persons) plan (jointly plan). Rather, the totality emerges as an unforeseen outcome of a sequence of more limited shifts: the sequence, though not the individual steps, is something that happens to spectators who survey the passing scene, to use Davidson's apt phrase. Paradoxically, such upheavals are gradual and should be likened to evolutions.[1] Small revolutions which can be located at particular times and attached to particular individuals are milestones in saltatorial evolutionary development. As far as rationality and intelligibility are concerned, these saltations can be directly perceived as rational, and the *longue durée* of history as indirectly rational, as a joint outcome of rational choices and evolving standards of rationality and intelligibility.

II *Revolutionary Change*

Let us first take a look at a recent elucidation of revolutionary scientific change. According to Thomas Kuhn, such change contrasts with normal-scientific change in that it is no mere 'growth, accretion, cumulative addition to what was known before' (Kuhn, 1987, p 7). He sorts out three features in such upheavals. First, revolutions are somehow holistic and cannot be likened to cumulative piecemeal change, such as the expansion of knowledge through, say, Boyle's law. Such holistic change, says Kuhn, is also perceived as a Gestalt switch: although revolutions leave 'much piecemeal mopping up to do, the central change cannot be experienced piecemeal, one step at a time'. Secondly there is a change in the way words and phrases attach to nature. Normal science also alters the way terms attach to nature, but in revolutions the very criteria by which terms attach to nature undergo a change. There is rearrangement in 'the set of objects or situations to which those terms attach'. For instance in the transition from Aristotle to Newton 'a natural family ceased to be natural; its members were redistributed among pre-existing sets; and only one of them continued to bear the old name' (Kuhn, 1987 p 19). Thirdly, all of Kuhn's examples have involved a central change of model, metaphor, or analogy—'a change in one's sense of what is similar to what, and of what is different'.

What these features amount to is a characterisation of scientific revolutions in which change in knowledge about nature is accompanied by change in the language which is used to describe the world. To the extent that there are shifts in several taxonomic categories we can say that the prerequisites of scientific description and generalisation change. Since these taxonomic categories are used to give scientific and everyday descriptions and generalisations they are prior to these descriptions and generalisations. And since they come in interrelated clusters, it is natural to say that crucial elements in the conceptual scheme change.

Revolutionary change as a holistic *Gestalt* switch is an early theme in Kuhn, but as his recent remarks make it clear, this idea, imported from perceptual psychology, is accompanied by a particular view of scientific acculturation and language acquisition. Roughly, Kuhn seems to think that scientists are introduced to a discipline through textbook examples of models and exemplary problem solutions, and through attempts to extend and apply these to novel areas. During this process would-be members of a scientific community learn a number of fundamental laws and associated linguistically and mathematically formulated generalisation. However, what the basic terms refer to and how they are to be understood cannot be made explicit in a rule-book of applications. For this reason there always is leeway of judgement and even idiosyncratic interpretation (Kuhn, 1977, 1983b). To put it somewhat metaphorically, the linguistic lore passed on in the form of symbolic generalisations is brought down to earth through models and descriptions of exemplary solutions—but like lore in general, scientific lore is amenable to conflicting interpretations. There are different and possibly to some extent idiosyncratic ways of picking out referents for terms: 'Two people may, moreover, speak the same language and nevertheless use different criteria in picking out the referents of its terms' (Kuhn, 1983a, p 681).

The way the conceptual apparatus is brought to bear on reality shows that expansion to new areas always involves non-trivial interpretation—indeed, so much that the partitioning of knowledge into knowledge of the world and knowledge of language only crystallises in retrospect.[2] This is why, according to Kuhn, the historian of science is less of a translator than an interpreter. A translator knows two languages and can put one story in both. It is crucial that the language into which a translation is being made is known in advance: it is already there. Furthermore, in translation words and phrases are replaced by others, without glosses and translators' prefaces. These features are not true of interpretation: an interpreter initially only knows one language. Kuhn's idea is that understanding earlier (or later) theories is more like interpretation in that the interpretor acquires a new language, and an ontology to go with it.

Such interpretation may involve a new way of structuring the world, in accordance with terms that do not have counterparts in the language already known.

Kuhn thinks that this is true of phlogiston and the central terms of many eighteenth- and nineteenth-century theories. It may appear at first sight that phlogiston language translates to modern English in an unproblematic way, but there were some troublesome key terms, such as the phrase 'chemical principle'. When the term disappeared from usage, more was lost than two words, namely a perspective that structured phlogiston thinking, the generalisation that qualities like colour and elasticity provide direct evidence of chemical composition. Now historians of science are interpreters in the sense that they must learn the language-cum-ontology involved in phlogiston talk and phlogiston theory.

> Only after they have been thus acquired can one recognize eighteenth-century chemistry for what it was, a discipline that differed from its twentieth-century successor not simply in what it had to say about individual substances and processes but in the way it structured and parceled out a large part of the chemical world. (Kuhn, 1983a, p 676.)

III *The Big Man Theory and Timing Problems*

Let us now turn to an example, the so-called Copernican Revolution. Popular views have it that Copernicus overthrew Ptolemaic planetary astronomy by putting the sun at the centre and letting the earth revolve around it. But as Herbert Butterfield and Thomas Kuhn have argued, Copernicus was not the first representative of a new world view but the last one of the old. His picture of the universe was not the modern one, and some of his argument smacked of outmoded Aristoteleanism, that is, old fashioned from the point of view of modern cosmology.[3] It took a long development to yield the modern view, and it was not until Newton gave a sound physical basis for heavenly motions that the revolution was finished. New elements and new observational techniques were necessary to the completion of the revolution, but there is more than this. It was also necessary that post-Copernicans learned to see the world in a new way. Perhaps the most important change occurred in ideas of motion, in what is natural motion.

Let us take another example of a revolution, the discovery of the theory of evolution through natural selection, made independently by Charles Darwin and A R Wallace. In his book *On the Origin of Species By Natural Selection* Darwin argued, first, for the reality (*vera causa* nature) of natural selection, and secondly, for the sufficiency of this principle to explain the emergence of new species, as well as a host of other phenomena, such as geographical distributions of, and systematic affinities between, various kinds of organisms, morphological similarities, embryological facts, and the like. Here we can identify at least two of Kuhn's three criteria of a scientific revolution. Both

Darwin and Wallace described the holistic transition and the effect of seeing the familiar phenomena in a new light. I shall quote, at length, Wallace's account of the impetus he received from Malthus's ideas on population checks and balances:

> It then occurred to me that these causes or their equivalents are continually acting in the case of animals also; and as animals usually breed much more rapidly than does mankind, the destruction every year from these causes must be enormous in order to keep down the numbers of each species, since they evidently do not increase regularly from year to year, as otherwise the world could long ago have been densely crowded with those that breed most quickly. Vaguely thinking over the enormous and constant destruction which this implied, it occurred to me to ask the question, Why do some die and some live? And the answer was clearly, that on the whole the best fitted live. From the effects of disease the most healthy escaped; from enemies, the strongest, the swiftest, or the most cunning; from famine, the best hunters or those with the best digestion; and so on. *Then it suddenly flashed upon me* that this self-acting process would necessarily improve the race, because in every generation the inferior would inevitably be killed off and the superior would remain—that is, the fittest would survive. *Then at once I seemed to see the whole effect of this,* that when changes of land and sea, or of climate, or of food-supply, or enemies occurred—and we know that such changes have always been taken place—and considering the amount of individual variation that my experience as a collector had shown me to exist, then it followed that all the changes necessary for the adaptation of the species to the changing conditions would be brought about . . . The more I thought over it the more I became convinced that I had at length found the long-sought-for law of nature that solved the problem of origin of species . . . (Wallace, 1905, pp 361-3. Italics added).

Clearly, although both Wallace and Darwin went through a long process of deliberation, the fundamental idea came as a sudden insight.

Secondly, changes in models, metaphors, and analogies were instrumental in the transition. Darwin (but not Wallace) resorted to the analogy between artificial selection, and in both paths the struggle for existence analogy, borrowed from Malthus, was instrumental. The new analogies also helped to see so-far unperceived similarities between human and wild populations, between breeders' results and changes in nature. How about Kuhn's third criterion, changes in the ways key terms attach to nature? This does not appear to be the case. True, Darwin noted with satisfaction how new observations on organisms supported his budding theory-to-work with. But regroupings also occur in normal science, and it is not evident that there was changes in the criteria by which terms attached to nature.[4]

Thus there was, it seems, no radical change in the language which was used to describe and give generalisations. As Philip Kitcher writes, Darwin did introduce a new method of fixing the referent of 'homology', and acceptance of his theory brought about alterations in the traditional criteria for identifying species (Kitcher, 1985, p 145). But by and large Darwinians and non-Darwinians could agree on the proper description of a phenomenon, and indeed Darwin based his work on the descriptions of others.

This difference between two revolutions brings me to the main claim of my paper. A new way to see natural motion was necessary for the completion of the Copernican Revolution. But as several historians of science have argued, although the old Aristotelean view of motion began to erode in the fourteenth century, in the work of Buridan, or even earlier, it was not embedded in a satisfactory explanatory view until Newton. There were a great many philosophers and scientists who contributed to the cause of the so-called Copernican Revolution, but there was no one who did it. Indeed, the revolution was not perceived to be a revolution at all. As I Bernard Cohen writes,

> There is no historical evidence that either Copernicus or his contemporaries ever conceived that the set of ideas and principles that today we call 'Copernican' constituted a revolution (Cohen, 1987 p 25).

Darwin's idea was perceived differently, for it was thought to be a revolution both by him and his contemporaries. Actually, it can hardly be said that the revolution amounted to the acceptance of the principle of natural selection, still less the view that there is evolution, for the principle followed from facts already available, and evolution was a widely recognised fact. Nor did it amount to the introduction of radically new theoretical concepts: the claim of the theory could be made in sketchy qualitative terms, and its fate was not tied to this or that hereditary mechanism. Rather, the revolution consisted in the vistas opened by the claim that the principle indeed is sufficient to explain the various domains in the opening of a new set of questions to be tackled by help of the organising idea, and in the new focus on the population level.

What, then, was the difference between the two revolutions? I suggest that it can be located in Kuhn's second feature of revolutions, for it does not apply universally to what we call revolutions. The view I advocate here is that the Copernican Revolution was not just a scientific revolution, but one which was accompanied by a conceptual evolution, the gradual emergence of a new way of seeing motion, and the gradual emergence of new methodological standards and new standards of intelligibility, such as the rejection of uniform circular motion as 'natural' for heavenly bodies. In the Darwinian revolution there was restructuring of the field, but the methodological standards and standards of intelligibility remained largely the same. The former revolution satisfies Kuhn's second criterion, the latter does not. That is why the Copernican Revolution could not be seen as a revolution at the outset, while the latter could: the conceptual elements were all there.

Furthermore, the Copernical Revolution in its entirety was not a piecemeal realisation of someone's masterplan. If some one individual had plans, the outcome differed pretty much from that plan, and in unpredictable ways. In contrast to this, the outlines of the Darwinian revolution were already there in the *Origin* and earlier, and some twenty years after it was made public, a revolution along precisely these lines had succeeded. The reason why the Copernican Revolution was not perceived to be a revolution is, I suggest, that it was not something done by an individual but something that happened: no one could foresee the results that the introduction of smaller contributions, ideas or technical innovations, would have on the way later workers saw the world. But development such as this is evolution not revolution.

This gives me occasion to speculate on the nature of heroic deeds in general, and I shall do so by distinguishing, following Sir Isaiah Berlin (Berlin, 1969), between personal and impersonal theories of history. Personal theories hold that there are exceptional individuals with a decisive influence on matters, while impersonalists hold that what happens does not occur as a result of the wishes and purposes of identifiable individuals, but of those of large numbers of unspecified persons. Impersonalists thus eliminate individual responsibility and propose an alternative mode of explanation in terms of the operation and evolution of unidentifiable forces other than free human will and free choices.

This view of history can be seen in Hegel and Marx, and in an extreme form in Tolstoy. The former two paint a picture of agents who pursue their daily affairs

> with touching hope and simplicity . . . trusting in the permanence of their particular way of life, their own economic, social, and political order, treating their own values as if they were eternal standards, living, working, fighting, without any awareness of the cosmic processes of which their lives are but passing stages. (Berlin, 1969, p 61).

Tolstoy went further still, and turned heroes into pathetic pawns in the hand of history: thus Napoleon viewed himself as the master theorist who acted on the assumption that he understood and controlled the course of events through his superior intellect. But as Berlin interprets Tolstoy, Napoleon was under an illusion, and the real actors were the people who went about their ordinary business. As to the course of history, 'only unconscious activity bears fruit, and the individual who plays a part in historical events never understands their significance' (Berlin, 1979, pp 34–5).

Applying this idea to history of science has some initial appeal, for normal science is characteristically conducted with touching adherence to a paradigm: normal scientists are gathering new facts to fit an already existing edifice, and they take their particular scientific way of life, including its values, for granted. However, taking this view literally only gives a caricature—scientists are not mere spectators of a passing scene, and great minds are needed to put pieces together.[5] But there is a lesson to be drawn, for a quasi-Tolstoyan perspective is needed to balance an excessively voluntaristic reading of history of science. Note that even in the impersonalist picture everyday activities are rational, and so is normal scientific puzzle-solving in a quasi-Tolstoyan view. However, it might still be the case that unconscious activity bears fruit in history of science, and that individuals who harvest a particular yield are not aware of the type of fruit to be picked in years to come. Underneath cumulative and rational puzzle-solving activity, whether practical or theoretical, there are imperceptible shifts in the horizon of possibilities, metaphors, analogues, and scientific values, in short, in boundaries of rational action and piecemeal theory choice.

Occasionally these changes amount to ways of seeing new possibilities and hence localising revolutions. And some of these changes can be pooled into paths that culminate in wholesale rearrangements recognised, in retrospect, as global revolutions. The point remains, nevertheless, that the paths traversed in the latter are not mapped in advance by any single individual.

IV *Rationality and Incommensurability*

Let me next show how the quasi-Tolstoyan angle into history of science throws light on a recent debate over rationality and incommensurability. Larry Laudan (Laudan, 1984) has criticised Kuhn for making theory choice irrational and subjective. What Laudan objects to, in particular, is Kuhn's holism. According to Kuhn paradigms are holistic packages which include a specification of ontology (characteristically in terms of heuristic and meta-physical models), problem areas and exemplars, fundamental laws (given in the form of symbolic generalisation), and also cognitive values, such as simplicity, accuracy, scope and fruitfulness. Holism seems to involve holistic change in which one all-encompassing package is swapped into another. But since everything is changed in one fell swoop, the transition from one paradigm to another indeed looks irrational.

What Laudan wishes to do is dissect this holistic picture into smaller changes, all of which are rational:

> The point, of course, is that a sequence of belief changes which, described at the microlevel, appears to be a perfectly reasonable and rational sequence of events may appear, when represented in broad brushstrokes that drastically compress the temporal dimension, as a fundamental and unintelligible change of world view. This kind of tunnel vision, in which a sequence of gradual shifts is telescoped into one abrupt and mighty transformation, is a folly which every historian is taught to avoid. Yet knowing that one should avoid it and actually doing so are two different things. Once we recognize this fallacy for what it is, we should probably hesitate to accept too quickly the models of the holists and big-picture builders. For, if our fairy story has anything of the truth about it (that is, if change is, or more weakly even if it could be, more piecemeal than the holistic accounts imply), there may yet be room for incorporating changes of methods and of cognitive values into a rational account of scientific activity (Laudan, 1984, p 78).

Laudan argues for what he calls a reticulational model of scientific change in which there are rational ways to amend not just factual theories but also methodological standards and cognitive aims. The model has much to it, and I do not wish to play down its merits. But I think it misses a few important insights in Kuhn's account.[6] First, Laudan makes too much of the notion of incommensurability. As Kuhn has recently made clear, the notion was incorporated from mathematics and only applies locally. In particular, it does not involve the idea that two incommensurable theories are incomparable.

Kuhn has said, from his book *The Structure of Scientific Revolutions* on, that he does not think that choice between two paradigms is irrational, for there are good reasons and arguments for both. But he does think that there are no knock-down arguments for a new paradigmatic theory, largely because new interpretation involves changes that are perceived as natural and which demand explanation.

But secondly, both long-standing and localisable scientific revolutions involve new ways of seeing, sometimes in the light of new theoretical principles, sometimes using principles already available. Here the theme touched above becomes relevant. Scientists do not approach the world with a blank mind but rather with expectations provided by the linguistic lore and the exemplary solutions. Now we have seen that imperceptible shifts in the analogies, models and metaphors colour the way linguistic lore and exemplars are applied to the concrete chunks of reality to be explored. There is no unique way this can be done, and although the minor shifts in interpretation can all be construed as rational and even piecemeal, they may cumulate into a situation in which a more wholesale rearrangement suddenly becomes and option. Both minor and major rearrangements may take place in accordance with the perceptual paradigm, and hence involve an element of perceptual taking which is in part beyond cognitive control.

The reason, I think, is that Kuhn thinks that underlying rational arguments there are changing standards of intelligibility and changing ontology. These changes are literally unpredictable. To resort to the parallel already drawn, just as in social and political revolutions small changes lead to unanticipated results because boundary conditions for rational action change, so in scientific and conceptual revolutions rational piecemeal innovations bring about changes in boundary conditions for rational belief. However, where Kuhn and Laudan seem to disagree is over the way standards of intelligibility change. Laudan is a rationalist and voluntarist with respect to the aims and standards of science, whereas in Kuhn we can detect traces of impersonalism, though no full-blooded Tolstoyan frame of mind. Rationality can be discerned at the level of individual theory choices, but where the boundaries of rational thought and action gradually evolve, we have revolutions that we do not make but revolutions which make us. This explains why conceptual revolutions are hard to pin down. When a novel idea sparks a would-be revolution, no one knows if it is aborted at an early stage, because the tools are not adequate to the task; or what precise ramifications its introduction will have on the career of the programme. Similarly, an idea that at first sight might look like a minor modification of a conceptual scheme may prove to be impetus for a major change.

REFERENCES

Isaiah Berlin, 'Historical inevitability', in *Four Essays on Liberty* (London, Oxford, New York, Oxford University Press, 1969).

Isaiah Berlin, 'The hedgehog and the fox', in *Russian Thinkers* (London, The Hogarth Press, 1979).

Herbert Butterfield, *The Origin of Modern Science* (London, G Bell and Sons, 1968).

Bernard Cohen, 'Scientific revolutions, revolutions in science, and a probabilistic revolution 1800–1930', in *The Probabilistic Revolution*, Lorenz Krüger, Lorraine J Daston and Michael Heidelberger, eds (Cambridge, London, The MIT Press, 1987).

Charles Darwin, *The Life and Letters of Charles Darwin*, vol I, F Darwin, ed (New York, Appleton & Co, 1903).

Donald Davidson, 'On the very idea of a conceptual scheme', in *Proceedings and Addresses of the American Philosophical Association*, vol XLVIII (New York, The American Philosophical Association, 1974).

Philip Kitcher, 'Darwin's achievement', in *Reason and Rationality in Natural Science* Nicholas Rescher, ed (Lanham, Maryland, University Press of America, 1985).

Thomas Kuhn, *The Copernican Revolution* (Cambridge, Massachusetts and London, Harvard University Press, 1957).

Thomas Kuhn, 'Objectivity, value judgment, and theory choice', in Thomas Kuhn, *The Essential Tension* (Chicago, University of Chicago Press, 1977).

Thomas Kuhn, 1983a, 'Commensurability, comparability, communicability', in *PSA 1982*, vol 2 (East Lansing, Michigan, The Philosophy of Science Association, 1983).

Thomas Kuhn, 1983b, 'Rationability and theory choice', *The Journal of Philosophy*, vol 80 (1983) pp 563–70.

Thomas Kuhn, 'What are scientific revolutions', in *The Probabilistic Revolution*, Lorenz Krüger, Lorraine J Daston and Michael Heidelberger, eds (Cambridge, London, The MIT Press, 1987).

Larry Laudan, *Science and Values. The Aims of Science and Their Role in Scientific Debate* (Berkeley, Los Angeles, London, University of California Press, 1984).

Matti Sintonen, 'Selectivity and theory choice', in *PSA 1986*, vol 1 (East Lansing, Michigan, The Philosophy of Science Association, 1986).

A R Wallace, *My Life, A Record of Events and Opinions*, vol 1 (London, 1905).

NOTES

1 See Cohen (1987), 'A three-hundred-year period of development in modern science might be too long to be a revolution and hence more properly an evolution'.

2 See Kuhn (1987), p 21: 'The metaphorlike juxtapositions that change at times of scientific revolution are thus central to the process by which scientific and other language is acquired . . . In much of language learning these two sorts of knowledge—knowledge of words and knowledge of nature—are acquired together, not really two sorts of knowledge at all, but two faces of a single coinage that a language provides'.

3   Copernicus was as much as his predecessors imbued with the idea that the universe is spherical 'either because that figure is the most perfect, as not being articulated but whole and complete in itself; or because it is the most capacious and therefore best suited for that which is to contain and preserve all things . . .' Similarly, he thought that uniform circular motion is natural for celestial bodies, and that the mind abhors irregularities and departures from such motions. *De Revolutionibus,* Book I, 4. Quoted from Thomas Kuhn (1957) pp 145–7. See also Herbert Butterfield (1968) p 32.

4   Thus he wrote, in a letter to Lyell prior to reading Malthus: 'I have lately been badly tempted to idle—that is, as far as geology is concerned—by the delightful number of new views which have been coming in thickly and steadily,—on the classification and affinities and instincts of animals—bearing on the question of species. Notebook after notebook has been filled with facts which begin to group themselves clearly under "sublaws"' (Letter to Lyell, 13 September 1938, Darwin, (1983) p 268).

5   Compare Berlin (1969) p 44: 'Who or what was or is (or will be or could be) responsible for a war, a revolution, an economic collapse, a renaissance of arts and letters, discovery or invention, or a spiritual transformation altering the lives of men?'

6   For a discussion of some other aspects, see Sintonen (1986).

CHAPTER 3

The Concept of Revolution

Jes Bjarup

1 *Introduction*

When the news arrived at Versailles of the fall of the Bastille in 1789, the French King Louis XVI asked: 'Is it a revolt?' The Duc de la Rochefoucauld-Liancourt answered: 'No, Sire, it is a revolution.'[1]

Since 1789 the concept of revolution has become fashionable to denote a major political change in the structure of government. As Thomas Paine put it: 'As revolutions have begun . . . it is natural to expect that other revolutions will follow. . . . They are become subjects of universal conversation, and may be considered the order of the day.'[2] Later events have shown the truth of Paine's statement. Revolutions have indeed become subjects of universal conversation, and not only within the political area which was Paine's concern but within any area of human activity. Thus we have witnessed the industrial, scientific, and philosophical revolutions. Today we face the genetic revolution within biotechnology which may change human nature beyond recognition, as well as the computer revolution which may have the same effect. There are the urban, agricultural and population revolutions, not to mention the revolutions taking place within art and fashion. Thus revolutions are the order of the day. The concept is also the subject of my paper. In section 2 I shall try to present the historical background of the use of the concept in order better to understand its present use.

In section 3 I shall try to present the role of intellectuals based upon the thesis that in circumstances of great social and politcal upheavals intellectuals tend to have great influence.

2 *The historical background*

In former times the concept of revolution was connected with return and restoration. Today it is used to denote radical novelty, which some people may deplore, and others applaud. Concepts are used to express beliefs which in turn are connected with actions. Hence the importance of language for political activity, which to a large extent is carried out in and through the use of concepts to solve present practical problems. Hence also the importance of the study of political language in order to understand the society in which we live. Understanding the modern concept of revolution implies understanding social and political activity. This modern use has, however, a historical background which makes it worthwhile to consider the vicissitudes of its application to different phenomena. The historical use of the concept in the past may illuminate its present application, and thus provide a better understanding of society and social phenomena.

The concept, which implies change and movement which returns to its starting point, is first applied within astronomy as can be witnessed in the title of Nicolas Copernicus' *Concerning the Revolutions of the Heavenly Spheres* (*De Revolutionibus Orbium Coelestium Libri* IV) published in 1543. In this book Copernicus argues that it is the sun, and not the earth, which is at rest in the centre of the universe. It is the earth and the other planets which move orbitally around the sun. Consequently the sun must be taken as the centre of the heavens. Copernicus' hypothesis, that is to say his fundamental principle that all motions of heavenly planets are circular and that every such motion is uniform around the sun, offers the truth concerning the unity of natural regularities among the planets. This in turn implies that they can be described in mathematical language. It must be noticed in passing that Copernicus' way of thinking is tantamount to a rejection of the physical ideas of the Middle Ages relying on Ptolemy as well as contrary to Scripture. Copernicus was considered, by Luther, as 'an upstart astrologer', and his thinking rejected in a remark conveying a rather anti-intellectual message: 'This fool wishes to reverse the entire science of astronomy, but sacred Scripture tells us that Joshua commanded the sun to stand still, and not the earth.'[3]

The importance of astronomy must be seen in relation to astrology which was considered to be a science capable of informing people of their personal fate. In order to cast a true horoscope it is necessary to have exact knowledge of the planetary movements, presented in a system of astronomy mapping them correctly. I cannot pursue the relationship between astronomy and astrology, but the idea that there is a causal relationship between the universe and man or that the movements of the heavens directly influence a man's course of action was widely accepted among the Italian Renaissance Humanists.[4]

It is also among these writers that the concept of revolution is introduced to describe social and political events.[5] Perhaps Copernicus' use of the term has played a role. In any case the meaning of 'revolution', implying a change of cyclical character, fits with the idea of the humanist view of history as cyclical, that is to say that the course of human events can be shown to proceed in a series of recurring cycles.

This idea is a revival of the Aristotelian and Roman view, put forward by Polybius and Cicero, that there is a cycle of constitutions involving growth and decay.[6] It is, perhaps, of some interest to notice that whereas Copernicus rejects the Aristotelian view of the universe, the Renaissance Humanists endorse the Aristotelian view concerning the cyclical change of constitutions.

Although the Humanists are committed to the idea of men's creative powers, there still lingers the idea of 'the powers of the stars', that is to say men are still under the sway of fortune or fate. The human power is counter-balanced with superhuman forces which interfere in human affairs and which cannot be opposed by human effort.

From the turbulent life in the Italian city states the term is adopted in other parts of Europe. In England the political events of the seventeenth century were called a revolution in their own day, for example by Thomas Hobbes, to denote 'a circular motion of the sovereign power through two usurpers'.[7] By contrast, the Humanists use the term to refer to the effect of fortune on men's political activity, and the inevitability of the decay of government due to corruption. This is rejected by Hobbes as well as the idea that God interferes directly in human affairs. Although Hobbes continues to use the term, he appropriates it to account for his own view that men, by using reason, can establish a well-ordered state safe from any revolution.[8]

Turning to France, the philosophers used the meaning of the concept revolution in political discourse to signify 'a considerable change that has occurred in the government of a state'.[9] It is taken for granted that revolutions inevitably appear in any state, and this fits with the acceptance of the cyclical theory of historical change. Perhaps what the Duc de la Rochefoucauld had in mind, in the remark quoted above, is the meaning of 'revolution' as an irresistible force of nature, determining human activity, and beyond human control. Cohen presents as the frontispiece to his book a contemporary display which supports the view held by the Humanists that the revolution of the heavenly spheres determines the revolutions on earth.[10]

It may, however, also be the case that there is a change in the use of the concept 'revolution', away from the idea of the cyclical character of political change of government towards the idea of its non-cyclical character. This may be dubbed the modern sense of the word. Stemming from the events in France in 1789, this use of the concept implies a radical change of political institutions and their administration, and this change has a definite direction of progress. Thus, according to Marquis de Condorcet, the aim of a revolution is freedom:

> From revolution we have derived revolutionary and the general meaning of this word expresses everything which appertains to a revolution. But we have made it our own, in that one of the states, which was oppressed for a long time by despotism, has made in a few years the only republic where liberty has been based entirely on equal rights. Thus the word revolutionary can only be applied to revolutions which have liberty as their object.[11]

Condorcet also claims that the French Revolution is not only a political revolution, involving a change in government, but also a social revolution, involving a new social order and a new stage in world history.

The political and social events in 1848 in France, Germany, Austria and Italy, as well as the publication of the Manifesto of the Communist Party made an impact on the use of the concept of revolution. Marx and Engels accept the idea that it implies a change and a transformation in all spheres of life. As Marx writes, 'Any revolution breaks up the old society; to that extent it is social. Any revolution overthrows the old ruling power; to that extent it is political.'[12] And Engels concurs, 'Every real revolution is a social one, in that it brings a new class to power and allows it to remodel society in its own image.'[13]

It is also the case that it is entrusted to the proletariat to bring about the revolution against the bourgeoisie by changing the modes of production in order to establish a new society. The Russian Revolution in 1917, finally, is meant to exemplify this idea. Since then the concept of revolution has become part of the political vocabulary, used by political actors as well as political theorists to denote the breakdown of the ruling power which is replaced with a new class, dedicated to change all forms of social life, if necessary by force, in order to establish a new society in a new era. From a historical point of view this is significant. The former use of the concept was rather restricted, and when used the concept implied a circular movement where men's efforts were of little avail. This use was based upon a belief in a heaven-determined cyclical order of the universe determining men's activity. The modern use departs from this belief, since it is possible for men to break the cycle of nature and establish society according to men's planning. Thus the modern use of the concept implies a radical break with the past and a unilateral movement forward towards a better society. In the past the use of the concept was based upon the view of the world as a single frame of meaning where everything had a determinate direction of development. The modern use departs from this view and the use of the concept is rather based upon the view of the world as multiple varieties of meaning within linear developments of men's active pursuit of various ends. For Marx, this end is the establishment of the classless society, based upon the final revolution which signifies the violent transformation of the existing capitalist state progressing towards the communist society. Thus Marx stresses the linear development of history, but it is significant that this development will lead to the stage in history where there is no class conflict. So there is a return to the idea of the view of the world as a single frame of meaning, a society of freedom and the restoration of man as a truly human being.

3 *The role of intellectuals*

This brings me to consider the role of intellectuals, based upon the thesis that it is men's ideas, expressed in concepts and propositions, rather than men's conditions of material existence, which are important for ruling the activity of men. This thesis may be challenged by an adherernt of Marxism, claiming in support of Marx's dictum that

> the mode of production of material life determines the general character of the social, political and spiritual processes of life. It is not the consciousness of men that determines their being, but, on the contrary, their social being determines their consciousness. [14]

Or he may refer to Engels' speech at Marx's graveside where it is claimed that Marx discovered the law of development of human history. That is to say the simple fact that mankind must first of all eat, drink, have shelter and clothing, before it can pursue politics, science, art, religion, etc.

My answer to this challenge is that it is, indeed, a simple fact that men must eat, and produce food, in order to stay alive and engage in intellectual activities. From this fact it does not follow, however, that production of food is prior to thinking, since thinking is vital in order to stay alive. Further, the fact that men cannot pursue politics, science, art and religion unless they are alive is undeniable. Again, it does not follow that every man therefore adheres to historical materialism as expounded by Marx and Engels, although Marx and Engels most certainly would welcome this. Marx's and Engels' claim is based upon the assumption that men's social conditions determine their way of thinking. To be sure, there is a connection between men's social situation and their beliefs and actions. But it is an open question whether it is the material conditions of life alone which determine men's way of thinking. Marx and Engels seem to hold the position that the human being becomes like what he perceives. This is untenable since there is no reason why a man should become disorderly merely as a result of perceiving the disorderly, or become orderly merely as a result of perceiving the orderly. Perhaps what Marx and Engels have in mind is that the service produced by intellectuals is not just a passive reflection of basic social processes. On the contrary intellectuals and their concepts matter. Intellectuals have the ability to present a correct analysis of the existing social conditions within society, provided, of course, that they use the proper concepts. Thus Marx presents a historical analysis using economic terms to explain the rise and fall of capitalism due to its crises and struggle between the classes. What matters for Marx is only the factor of economic exploitation which will disappear by the revolution by the proletariat smashing the capitalists. Thus it seems to me that even an adherent of Marxism must admit that the intellectuals have an important role to play within society, and especially during great social upheavals. This is at any rate a key element in Lenin's thinking where the indispensability of an intellectual class for instructing and guiding the proletarian class is stressed. [15] This in turn implies that the use of language is important for constituting political belief and actions, and this makes the study of such language an essential task for understanding what happens within society.

The influence of intellectuals is also paramount in the French Revolution, according to Alexis de Tocqueville. The political programme offered by 'the men of letters keenly interested in all that concerned the government of nations' is based upon the single idea 'that what was wanted was to replace the complex of traditional customs governing the social order of the day by simple, elementary rules deriving from the exercise of the human reason and natural law'.[16] The question is how to explain the impact of the intellectuals? Tocqueville's answer is that in France, being 'the most literary-minded of all nations and quickest in uptake',[17] the intellectuals had ample opportunity to present their doctrines arguing for the abolition of all existing French laws and customs in the hope that this radical transformation could be effected almost painlessly, under the auspices of reason and by its efficacy alone.

According to Tocqueville the result was disastrous. The revolution ended in terror. What the French Revolution did accomplish was, however, to put the notion of revolution on the political agenda. The concept is now used by political actors as well as political theorists. The former may apply the concept as a call for radical changes in the political system. The latter may use the concept to identify characteristics of social activity. This raises the question concerning the definition of its meaning. In this respect, the change of the constitution is an essential element. The change must also be brought about by illegal means. The question is whether the use of force or violence also should be included as an essential element? The answer is, using the French Revolution as a sort of precedent, that violence is a defining characteristic. It follows that to speak of a non-violent revolution is a contradiction in terms. I would like to question this. It seems to me that to include violence as a defining characteristic is to rule out the possibility of a non-violent change of the constitution which nevertheless may be important since this implies a transfer of political power. This was the case in Denmark in 1849. The Lex Regia of 1665 (which also was a case of transfer of power involving no violence but establishing the King as a Hobbesian sovereign) was peacefully abolished and the Constitution of 5 July 1849 adopted, reducing the power of the King in favour of the elected parliament. If the need for violence or force is incorporated in the definition, it is on the other hand easily overlooked that the concept of law by definition includes force. This is so because any government must have the power to enforce the law. What is significant, however, is that there are constitutional limits to the exercise of force. This is not the case in revolutions. I am not denying that violence may accompany revolutions, but I am suggesting that to include violence as a defining characteristic in the concept may be a hindrance for understanding political and social phenomena. What matters in political revolutions is the change of the constitution of a state by illegal means, that is to say the definition is in terms of the illegal change of the constitution

The concept of a constitution is another legacy of the French Revolution, leading to the distinction between public and private law, and the importance of the separation of powers, as can be seen from Article 16 in the Declaration of the Rights of Man and the Citizen of 1789. This declaration presents a catalogue of fundamental rights regarded as inhering in all men in virtue of their humanity alone, which again is an illustration of the importance of intellectuals putting their ideas into words and thereby creating a conceptual framework which structures political and social activity.

The French Declaration of Natural Rights evoked Jeremy Bentham's scathing reply: 'Nonsense upon stilts.'[18] For Bentham the only effectual antidote against the fascination of political enthusiasm advocated by the French intellectuals is a sober and accurate conceptual analysis of the import of fundamental concepts. It is important to notice that Bentham is as much a political intellectual as the French philosophers. Bentham shares their aim of championing reason against passion, extirpating prejudice and superstition in favour of happiness or utility based upon law. Law as a means of establishing happiness must be based upon reason. This in turn implies for Bentham that there is a need for clear and distinct concepts. The legislator must use the language of reason and plain sense in contrast to the 'terrorist language' used by invoking natural rights. In order to improve the language of the law and as a corollary help to bring about a better world there is need for a conceptual analysis called 'the method of paraphrasis' by Bentham.[19]

According to Bentham the process of analysis of an idea is different from the process of describing its historical origin. This approach is tantamount to treating the meaning of ideas, expressed in words and sentences, as having an eternal and independent meaning to be accurately stated in a dictionary. This is again an idea of The Enlightenment that the recipe for perfection is to create a perfect language to be used by the legislator to control human actions. Bentham shares this view and is concerned 'to frame a Dictionary of moral terms; a dictionary in which clear ideas shall stand annexed to each expression'.[20] Bentham's assumption is that 'until . . . the nomenclature and language of the law shall be improved, the great end of good government cannot be fully attained'. This is Bentham's vision concerning 'a complete code, new in point of substance as well as form'. But, I submit, the meaning of words in sentences cannot possibly be independent of man. A word is a man-made contrivance, and its meaning can only be what some man means by it. If we follow Bentham's advice, and instead of looking at the individual words associated with ideas, we look at sentences, the question is not 'What does this sentence mean?', but rather, and more accurately, 'What do (or did) certain persons use this sentence to mean?' All meaning of ideas, expressed in words and sentences, is meaning by or for some living being. Thus to write a dictionary as Bentham envisaged, is to take into consideration not only Bentham as the definer using the method of paraphrases, and the hearer to whom the proper meaning of a word is being explained by this method, but also the people whose usage of the word gives it the meaning it has. To take the latter persons into consideration is to take the historical use of the term into consideration. Bentham, it seems to me, underrates the importance of the historical context of the use of sentences in his analysis. Or perhaps it is rather the case that Bentham is aware of the traditional associations of words, and his vision of designing a new code is precisely to create fresh associations and in this manner to mould people's minds and their conduct. This is rule by intellectuals, overruling tradition in favour of reason which called forward Tocqueville's criticism of the philosophers for upsetting justice. 'When the State tampers with the course of justice, the effect is to unsettle men's minds and make them at once servile and revolutionary.'[21] The result of this, as Edmund Burke already had noticed in his criticism of 'the moral politicians', is that 'kings will be tyrants from policy when subjects are rebels from principle'.[22] Thus a political revolution may lead to a centralisation of power, which easily can be turned into a regime of terror.

I suggest that one remedy is 'a sober and accurate apprehension of the import of fundamental words', as Bentham suggests, but also taking the historical context into consideration. This element is underrated, or set apart by most writers within the school of legal positivism, as can be seen by the characterisation of conceptual analysis offered by Hart. To be sure, Hart himself claims that his 'essay in analytical jurisprudence' is at the same time also 'an essay in descriptive sociology'.[23] If this is the case, then an analysis of legal language and discourse about it cannot be pursued without an investigation of the historical background and its development, in order to understand the conceptual changes which also illuminate the social phenomena.

4 *Conclusion*

Within the legal area, Harold J Berman claims that Western legal tradition was born of the Papal Revolution in the twelfth century and later transformed by other revolutions.[24] Berman also claims that 'we are in the midst of an unprecedented crisis of legal values and of legal thought, in which our entire legal tradition is being challenged'. This is not exactly right, since the French Revolution also presented a crisis of legal values. So did the Russian Revolution of 1917, aiming at, according to E B Pashukanis, abolishing bourgeois law.[25] Now the term 'crisis' is used to denote the turning point in a development, which is decisive of better or worse. What Berman has in mind, is, no doubt, that a decisive change for the worse is imminent. I would suggest that the crisis also can make us aware of the need for a proper remedy: a conceptual analysis which will further the understanding of the value of Western legal tradition by adopting a historical point of view. This, I suggest, will show that there are many strands within the Western legal tradition which compete for rulership. This battle is not to be deplored. On the contrary, as Machiavelli remarks, 'All the laws made in favour of liberty result from the discord between two opposed factions.'[26] Conflict and crisis are not the solvent but the cement of a living tradition and values which hold people together in society.

NOTES

1　Cited from *The Concise Oxford Dictionary of Quotations* (Oxford, 1964) p 175.
2　Thomas Paine, *Rights of Man*, G J Hoyoake, ed (London, 1915) p 153 (Part II, Introduction).

3 Luther, Table Talk 1539, quoted from Daniel J Boorstin, *The Discovers* (New York, 1983) p 302.
4 Cf. Quintin Skinner, *The Foundations of Modern Political Thought* (Cambridge, 1978) vol 1, p 95 f, cf. vol 2, pp 278, 292 on the concept of fortune.
5 Cf. Arthjur Hatto, '"Revolution": an inquiry in the use of a historical term', *Mind* 58 (1949) pp 494 ff at p 502.
6 Cf. Quintin Skinner, *Foundations*, vol 1, p 109 f and p 187 for Machiavelli.
7 Thomas Hobbes, *Behemont*, F Tönnies, ed, second edn (London, 1969) p 204. Cited from Mark Hartman, Hobbes's Concept of Political Revolution, *Journal of the History of Ideas* 47 (1986) pp 487 ff.
8 Cf. Thomas Hobbes, *Leviathan*, C B MacPherson, ed (Penguin Books, 1974) ch 29.
9 See Denis Diderot's definition in his article 'Revolution' in the Éncyclopédie, here quoted from I B Cohen, *Revolution in Science* (London, 1985) p 205. It should be noticed that Diderot's article also covers revolutions in the non-political area of geometry, astronomy and geology.
10 See I B Cohen, *Revolution in Science*.
11 Marquis de Condorcet, *Sur le Sens du Mot Révolutionnaire, Oeuvres* (1847) vol XII, p 516, Sarah Lutman, trans, quoted from *Revolution*, Krishan Kumar, ed (London, 1971) p 93.
12 Karl Marx, *Critical Notes on "The King of Prussia and Social Reform"* in *Writings on the Young Marx on Philosophy and Society*, L D Easton and K H Guddat, eds and trans (New York, 1967) p 356, quoted from *Revolution*, Kumar, ed, p 96.
13 Friedrich Engels, 'On social relations in Russia', in Marx-Engels, *Selected Works* (Moscow, 1962) vol 2, p 53.
14 Karl Marx, 'Preface to contribution of political economy', in Marx-Engels, *Selected Works*, vol 1 (Moscow, 1962) p 363.
15 See V I Lenin, 'What is to be done?' (1902), in Marx-Engels, *Selected Works*, vol 1, pp 148 ff.
16 Alexis de Tocqueville, *The Ancien Régime & the French Revolution*, Stuart Gilbert, trans, Hugh Brogan, ed (Fontana Books, 1966) p 161.
17 Tocqueville, op. cit. p 167.
18 Jeremy Bentham, 'Anarchical fallacies', in *Nonsense upon Stilts*, Jeremy Waldron, ed (London, 1987) p 53, cf. p 64 for Bentham's criticism of Article 16 as 'self-conceit inflamed to insanity'.
19 Jeremy Bentham, *Of Laws in General*, H L A Hart, ed (London, 1970), p 245. Cf. H L A Hart, *Essays on Bentham* (Oxford, 1982) pp 109 ff. and Ross Harrison, *Bentham* (London, 1983) p 58 f.
20 Harrison, *Bentham*, p 13. Also here the following quotation from Bentham's *Nomography*.
21 Tocqueville, *The Ancien Régime*, p 83.
22 Edmund Burke, *Reflections on the Revolution in France*, Conor Cruise O'Brien, ed (Penguin Books, 1968) p 172.
23 Hart, *The Concept of Law* (Oxford, 1961) p 253, cf. Preface, p VII. Cf. Tocqueville, 'The study of the connexion between the history of language and history proper would certainly be revealing'. A study of the English word 'gentleman' is 'the history of democracy itself', *The Ancien Régime*, p 109.
24 Harold J Berman, *Law and Revolution. The Formation of the Legal Western Tradition* (London, 1983). The quotation in the text is at p 33.
25 E B Pashukanis, *Allgemeine Rechtslehre und Marxismus*, 1929.
26 Niccolo Machiavelli, *Discourses on the First Decade of Titus Livius*, Book I, ch 4, quoted from *Maciavelli*, A H Gilbert, trans, John Plamenatz, ed (Fontana Books, 1972) p 152.

CHAPTER 4

General Jurisprudence and the Elucidation of Its Assumptions

Yoshiharu Matsuura

1 *Jurisprudence and the aspiration for universality*

When we study law, we never think it superfluous to know how a nation is organised, the relation of the judiciary to other state branches (the legislature and the executive in particular), the hierarchy of courts, the structure of the legal profession, the influence of the academic and the religious institutions upon the state organs and so forth.[1] But a striking fact about jurisprudence is that writers rarely refer to these aspects of particular legal systems when they discuss such topics as legal reasoning, justice and right, law and morals, and law and state. We do not learn much from legal theorists about their own legal systems. Instead, it is usually the case that we find in their works legal theories of general and abstract nature.[2]

This may be explained in terms of the aspiration of legal theorists to formulate theories which transcend the limits of time and space and are thus universally applicable. John Austin, for example, expressed this aspiration by claiming that 'the various principles common to maturer systems . . . , are the subject of an extensive science: which science . . . has been named General (or comparative) Jurisprudence, or the philosophy . . . of positive law'.[3] The aspiration of a similar sort seems to have been shared by legal theorists like Kelsen[4], Hart[5], MacCormick[6] and Dworkin.[7]

Indeed, legal theorists would not deny the importance for their jurisprudential reflections of the knowledge concerning the characteristic aspects of particular legal systems.[8] They might even concede that their theories are formulated through careful observations of their own societies and legal systems. This concession will amount to the recognition that legal theory begins from certain basic assumptions about the society where it originates. What we should be careful about these assumptions is, however, that in spite

31

of their critical importance to legal theory, they are likely to remain implicit, because they are, for the theorists, too obvious and elementary to mention. As a result, a legal theory takes on universal form separated from its native soil. Its background details and its organic relationship to a particular legal culture tend to disappear. But this general outlook of a legal theory is, it seems to me, a sign of its weakness rather than its strength. Because this generality blinds us to the cash value of a legal theory. Without the sound knowledge of particular circumstances under which a theory is meant to operate, it is impossible to appreciate its real strength and potential.

Some attempts have been made to bring some of these 'taken-for-granted' assumptions out of the darkness and to integrate them into a general theory so as to create a more satisfactory approach to jurisprudential topics. For example, Professors Atiyah and Summers collaborated to explicate legal theory and legal reasoning in terms of legal institutions.[9] According to them, 'The American and the English legal systems, for all their superficial similarities, differ profoundly' (Atiyah and Summers, 1987, p 1). For instance, legal reasoning in the United States is highly substantive and flexible, while in England it is surprisingly formal and rigid. Their whole book is regarded as a bold attempt to elucidate why this is so in terms of courts, the competence of the bureaucracy, the law making process, jury, legal education, academic lawyers and their impact upon legal practice, the structure of the legal profession and so on. I believe their view is basically sound and that their book has succeeded in adding a new aspect to jurisprudential analysis. Therefore, I entirely concur with them, when they claim,

> We do not deny that it may be possible to devise theories at a sufficiently high level of abstraction to accommodate all the variations between the differing conceptions of law used in particular legal systems. But it seems to us much more promising for the theorist to work at the level of conceptions as well as the level of concepts, and this requires a degree of understanding of the nature of valid law in a particular society or societies ... In our view, then, the primary subject matter of jurisprudence is not single universal subject matter, abstracted from the various phenomena of law in all societies. It should, rather, consist of the relevant features of the phenomena of law in one or more particular societies (Atiyah and Summers, 1987, pp 417–18).

If this perspective is proper, then, what we should do is to descend from the level of theoretical generality to the identification of the implicit and taken-for-granted assumptions of each legal theory. This move will enable us to promote deeper understanding of legal theory and to find some theoretical questions which have thus far remained unnoticed.

In this paper I shall describe some aspects of contemporary Japanese legal system[10] and identify certain implicit, though fundamental, assumptions when the concept of law, legal reasoning and the mechanisms of dispute resolution are discusses in the Japanese context. In turn, I shall argue, these assumptions will make a clear contrast to those of Anglo-American legal systems, which may invite reconsideration and further critical analyses of the taken-for-granted assumptions of the Anglo-American and other Western legal theories.

2 The taken-for-granted assumptions of Japanese legal theory

The Western legal theories introduced into Japan in the late nineteenth century have, ever since, been making a profound and lasting impact on the shape of Japanese society as well as her legal system.[11] Basic notions and distinctions commonly used in the Japanese legal discourse are familiar ones to the Western legal mind. In this sense, the vocabulary of Japanese law is predominantly that of the West.

In spite of this abundance of Western legal vocabulary, some writers, both Japanese and foreign observers of Japan, used to depict Japan as essentially different from Western societies. According to them, Japan is a peaceful community with a homogeneous and conforming population and hence litigation is the exception rather than the rule.[12] Legal theory of Western origin is, it is said, a mere decorative finish of Japanese society and it is something very indigenous which really governs it. Though this view contains some truth, I believe that it is not tenable any more.[13] Instead of mystifying or romanticising Japan, we now need to clarify in more rational terms the causes of the Japanese reluctance to invoke litigation. This effort will also lead us to better grasp of fundamental assumptions of Japanese legal theories.

I mentioned earlier that assumptions of critical importance to legal theory are likely to be ones that are taken for granted by legal theorists and thus easily escape conscious examination. When I reflect on Japanese law from this persepective, the first obvious assumption is the widely-shared perception concerning how the nation is organised. Compared with England and the United States, Japan is far more centralised. Though the nation is divided into forty-seven local districts and further sub-divided into many cities and towns, even the largest units called *To-dou-fu-ken* (prefectures) do not enjoy the same degree of autonomy from the central government as the states of the US or English local governments.[14] It is the national government, including the legislature and the executive, that monopolises the major decision-making processes. Even local matters of some importance cannot be well disposed of without careful negotiations with and the endorsement of the national government.[15]

The second obvious assumption is the dominance of the national bureaucracy. It is often pointed out that the Japanese political process is dominated and controlled by the Liberal Democratic Party, leaders of large businesses and elite bureaucrats of ministries.[16] The bureaucracy has been responsible for the preparation of long-term policies, the creation of national 'consensus', the implementation of policies and the adjustment of policies and laws to changing social situations.[17] The bureaucracy is doubtlessly an integral part of Japanese social management. Unlike the United States, public officials including those in the higher echelons are not political appointees and thus they will not be affected by the result of elections. Compared with politicians and judges, they tend to stay longer in a particular field of administration and accumulate more expertise. National ministries such as the Ministry of Finance and the Ministry of International Trade and Industry[18] attract the very best graduates of the elite universities. Though the bureaucracy is frequently criticised, nobody disputes the competence of ministerial bureaucracies in implementing policies or frustrating proposals they find unwise.

The third well-known assumption is the bureaucratic involvement in the legal process. Though article 41 of the Japanese Constitution provides that 'the Diet shall be the highest organ of state power, and shall be the sole law-making organ of the State', the majority of bills are prepared by the hands of the bureaucracy and submitted by the Cabinet to the Diet. Without the assistance of the bureaucracy, politicians of either House could not draft a bill of high quality. In preparing a bill the bureaucracy communicates with business as well as political leaders to secure basic endorsement of a future enactment. The bureaucracy here works as a midwife to the law-making process. Just before the Cabinet's decision to submit a bill to the Diet, the bill must go through the review process of the Cabinet Legislative Bureau, whose staff are recruited from the experienced bureaucrats of various ministries. Thus, the bureaucrats are deeply involved in law-making and law-management, though most of them have never attended the Legal Training and Research Institute of the Supreme Court, which is the one and only school for vocational training of future lawyers.

On the passage of a bill through the Diet, the ministry which has been in charge of the bill will issue an administrative guidance that explains the policy of the bill and adds comments concerning its implementation. In addition, if the bill is of primary importance in fields such as tax, road construction, zoning, pension, pollution control etc., very detailed manuals specifying guidelines on how to interpret and apply the law will be published by the relevant ministry (or semi-public body closely related to the ministry) for the use of people in business and well as public officials. When questions and doubts arise concerning the law, they are referred to the ministry which prepared and promoted the bill and, in turn, ministerial answers will be returned in a written form, when the ministry finds it proper to do so. These questions and answers are accumulated and in due course printed as a book which is widely circulated and regularly relied upon in daily administration. When the law is outdated or needs to be amended, the bureaucracy rather than the Diet responds first. In this way, the bureaucracy is a major figure in the legal process.

The fourth obvious assumption is the process of recruitment and promotion of judges.[19] Like the bureaucracy, the Japanese judiciary is highly centralised. It is a unitary system where there is a Supreme Court, eight High Courts, fifty District Courts[20] and about five hundred Summary Courts. In England and the United States experience of practice as a barrister or attorney is a prerequisite to a judicial appointment. But judgeship and private practice are two different careers in Japan. Except for the appointment to the Supreme Court, it is very rare for lawyers in private practice to be appointed judges. Those who wish to become judges apply for assistant judgeships at the end of their vocational education at the Legal Training and Research Institute of the Supreme Court. They pursue judgeship and will gradually climb up the judicial hierarchy. There is a strong expectation on the part of judges that those who are appointed in the same year will be promoted more or less in a similar way.[21] Judges are frequently (on average, every three years) transferred from one jurisdiction to another, which is also linked to promotion. Promotion and transfer are said to be in the hands of the General Secretariat of the Supreme Court. Therefore, it is obvious that promotion and transfer easily become powerful tools to influence the judicial behaviour of judges and that Japanese judges enjoy much less independence than American and English ones.

Given these assumptions, Professor Upham's claim that 'many characteristics of Japanese law thought to be traditional are in fact the consequence of recent and conscious'[22] choice of the national government sounds very persuasive. According to him,

> The bureaucracy does retain a surprising degree of control over the pace and course, if not the substance, of social change in Japan, and one of its major instruments for such control is the manipulation of the legal framework within which social change and its harbinger, social conflict, occur.[23]

In short, the Japanese legal system is designed and has been consciously manipulated to turn major social issues from the judiciary to other channels, to the bureaucracy in particular.

This manipulation becomes possible, given the very narrow range of judicial review[24] and the effective use of mediation or arbitration schemes. For example, when widespread environmental pollution triggered a series of litigation in the 1960s and 70s, the bureaucracy quickly introduced the law which successfully diverted disputes from courts to a mediation scheme that is to operate under the bureaucratic initiative.[25]

The traditional approach of the Japanese government to encouraging and promoting the use of informal dispute resolution schemes had created the deep-rooted perception and expectation among the people that the government is *primarily* responsible for almost all social evils and that the government is under a moral obligation to provide remedies. Therefore, if something goes wrong, people will go, at first, to the administrators of national and local levels. Thus, Upham reports this perception as

> . . . it is the government that has been the major player. The defendants may be private companies and their doctrines private law, but the object of the struggle is official policy and attitudes. Even among activist lawyers with their strong antigovernment bias, there is the general expectation that the ultimate actor in any protest movement must be the government.[26]

Under this moralistic atmosphere, even the litigation process itself tends to be interpreted by the people in terms of morals. How a journalist narrated the internal attitudes of plaintiffs in a major pollution case vividly represents a common perception of the people toward litigation and law. He reports:

... it wasn't money, just compensation. It was to make the presidents of the companies that had inflicted this illness on them say just one word, 'I am sorry'. The advocacy system pretty completely shattered this hope. At the very instant that the plaintiffs' lawyers were denouncing the defendants' crimes, at the very instant that the patients were making their embittered appeal, 'Mr President' was sitting in his nice, deep office sofa, not in court![27]

These are some illustrations of the taken-for-granted assumptions when Japanese writers address themselves to the problems of jurisprudential theory. In the next section I shall make a comparison of Japanese assumptions with those of Anglo-American legal theory and discuss some implications of this comparison for legal theory.

3 A critical comparison of implicit assumptions

The purpose of this section is not to identify every implicit assumption of Anglo-American legal theory, but, given certain assumptions of Japanese legal theorists, to invite inquiries as to what implicit assumptions make Anglo-American legal theory what it is.

The first notion to be carefully assessed is the concept of law itself. In the Anglo-American legal tradition, the concept of law seems to be inseparably connected with the notion of law-courts. That the law is a system of rules administered *by the judiciary* is a familiar image held by students of Anglo-American law.[28] The central importance of the judiciary does not seem to be questioned at all. In contrast, it should be clear from the observation in the previous section that Japanese legal theorists regard the very limited role of the judiciary as a matter of course. If the important issues that could have been decided by the judiciary are consciously diverted to bureaucratic mediation, and if the interpretations of law given by the bureaucracy are relied upon in the daily practice of the law-business, then what will prevent us from including the function of the bureaucracy in the discussion of the concept of law? We can safely say that the centrality of the judiciary in the Anglo-American sense does not hold in Japan. I must confess that the court-centred model of law appeared to me an absolute truism for quite a long time. But now it seems that the critical questions are what makes the judiciary so important in Anglo-American legal theory and what assumptions make it plausible to think of the judiciary as a major actor.

The second point of theoretical interest is the theory of legal reasoning. The expertise in legal reasoning is regarded as one of the most important skills of lawyers. The uniqueness of legal reasoning is not disputed in Japan. The assumption that legal reasoning is different in some important ways from practical reasoning in informal processes of dispute resolution such as mediation seems never to have been doubted both in Japan and in England and the United States. Thus, it is natural that Professors MacCormick and Dworkin should choose the process of legal reasoning as the main theme of their works. Dworkin's characterisation of legal reasoning and interpretation of law may be of particular interest to the observers of Japan, for what he maintains marks a significant move away from traditional assumptions about legal reasoning.

Dworkin advocates a kind of coherence theory of legal reasoning and interpretation. He claims 'that integrity rather than some superstition of elegance is the life of law as we know it . . . It [the principle of integrity in adjudication] asks those responsible for deciding what the law is to see and enforce it as coherent in that way.'[29] He does not limit the word 'law' to the explicit written texts and openly recognises moral and political theories as valuable resources for sound legal reasoning. The ideal judge, Dworkin urges, should attempt to make his decision in such a way that his decision has the best fit with the institutional history, texts of the constitution, statutes, precedents, moral and political theories. Though he rejects what he calls 'arguments of policy' at the crucial moment of reasoning, his position will accept almost any sort of reason as legitimate in interpretation of law. Hence the distinction between law and morals fades away in his legal theory.[30]

One prominent feature of mediation is lack of clear standards and specific procedural rules for decision-making. It is often reported that in Japanese mediation parties prefer informality, that is to say, parties feel more comfortable by departing from the formal litigation model.[31] As a result, arguments integrating a wide range of standards drawn from the spirit of the constitution, laws, ethical norms, moral 'common sense' and so forth compete with each other to justify particular decisions. This practical reasoning in the mediation process shows some family resemblances to Dworkin's model of legal decision-making. For Dworkin's 'integrity' does not mean rigid consistency that cuts through a series of cases but rather the inclusion in a coherent way, into the seamless web of law, of a judgement in a particular disputed case. In both cases reasoning is a dynamic process where reasons and grounds of diverse origin are invoked in a complex way.

Also we have to notice another remarkable aspect of legal reasoning in the Anglo-American legal tradition. Lawyers of common law are noted for their aversion to abstract theory. Their reasoning is said to start always from the concrete facts of the case and common law lawyers 'muddle through' to achieve the minimum level or reasonableness in their conclusions.[32] Their efforts, in effect, purport to do tailored justice to the case before them. If this is a proper way of interpreting the minds of common law lawyers, then the distance between legal reasoning and the practical reasoning of mediation seems to become much narrower.

Some may wonder how practical reasoning and legal reasoning differ in the Japanese context. Japanese lawyers think of litigation in terms of orthodox legal positivism. There is, indeed, a widely-held impression that legal reasoning in the formal legal process and informal practical reasoning in mediation are radically different. In practice, however, it is frankly recognised, that balancing of interests is an integral part of legal reasoning and interpretation of law.[33] It is admitted that to conduct balancing of interests we have to take various 'extra-legal' standards into consideration. Though Japanese courts prefer to use highly formal language in writing judgements, legal reasoning and practical reasoning have surprisingly so much in common.

So far I have stressed the similarities of legal and practical reasoning. Of course, I do not forget that there are many significant differences between legal and practical reasoning. But it is more important to remember that legal and practical reasoning in Japan and legal reasoning in England and the United States operate on wholly different assumptions. In Japan courts are not the cutting edge of social reform, given the bureaucratic dominance mentioned in the previous section. The formalistic style of reasoning of the courts as well as the practical reasoning of parties to mediation may be read as taking note of this fact very seriously. In other words, it is very likely that courts exploit formalistic reasoning to divert major issues to the bureaucracy and, on the other hand, parties to mediation make use of moralistic reasoning to invite the paternalistic intervention of the bureaucratic state. Though some crucial assumptions of Anglo-American legal theory have been elucidated by Atiyah and Summers, it is still necessary to conduct further research, for example, on the interaction of the judiciary and the executive in Engalnd and the United States. In this way, the theory of legal reasoning will become more accessible to outside observers.

The third topic is the theory of rights. Nobody doubts the fact that 'rights' is the key notion in the Western legal discourse.[34] The notion of right is related to the concept of freedom in the sense that rights offer a protected domain to each individual and in that domain one can do whatever he thinks right to do. Here I limit my focus to the notion of right as 'protected' domain. Since the Meiji Restoration in 1868, the notion of right has continued to be a source of deep puzzlement for Japanese. That so many academics devoted themselves to explication of the notion of right is a sure sign of it.[35]

Since the Meiji Restoration, the people have become accustomed to a political climate in which the government, assisted by a competent bureaucracy, runs the nation. The major social disputes are almost always channelled to mediation or similar schemes where the leading notion is the compromise and delicate balancing of relevant interests. Under this circumstance it would be far off the point to argue the case by the notion of right. There is no such thing as a protected domain. To think of it as such is wholly unrealistic. The experience the people feel to be correct is that the content of right is the end product, all things considered. It seems to me, therefore, that the interpretation of right as an amorphous concept[36] sounds more appropriate in the Japanese context. We may be able to say that this amorphous and elastic attitude is carried over to the formal process of litigation in Japan. As Upham reports, plaintiffs of major pollution cases and discrimination cases incline to construct their argument in moralistic terms.[37]

Then, the question will be why Anglo-American legal theory could articulate the theory of right in a way that appears very unreal to the Japanese. This becomes even more puzzling when we accept Dworkin's description of practice of law. If the content of right is filled by the result of the argument that invokes a wide range of standards, there will be no room for a clearly demarcated domain. It is of great interest to know what assumptions make the people of England or the United States believe in the notion of right.

4 *Conclusion*

Jurisprudence has been striving for general theories and universal truths. Of course generalisations and universalisation are an indispensable and valuable aspect of the growth of knowledge. But we must be properly warned against the danger of over-simplification. Elucidation of implicit assumptions will work as a reliable measure to keep the general theory of law at a proper level of abstraction. The jurisprudential study has been largely the study of the skeletons of various theories. It seems to me that further development of jurisprudence will go hand in hand with clarification of the taken-for-granted assumptions of each legal theory. Outside observers of legal theory surely benefit from such analyses.

With this move, Western legal theories will lose some of their mysterious authority to demand universal respect. But in return we will benefit far more from a profoundly enlightened understanding of jurisprudence.

NOTES

1 Needless to say, the knowledge of the history, culture, and social institutions of a particular society are indispensable to a deeper understanding of a particular legal system.
2 I do not deny the importance of generalisation. If we should stick to particular facts and reject any move beyond that, there would be no prospect for theory and the growth of knowledge. As to the status of theory, see for example, K R Popper, 'Science: conjectures and refutations' in K R Popper, *Conjectures and Refutations: The Growth of Scientific Knowledge* (4th ed, London, Routledge and Kegan Paul, 1972).
3 J Austin, 'The uses of the study of jurisprudence' (1863) in *The Province of Jurisprudence Determined,* H L A Hart, ed (London, Weidenfeld and Nicolson, 1955), pp 365 at 365. Of course, Austin does not conceive these 'common' principles in a mechanical way. He is careful enough to express his reservation that '[i]t is not meant to be affirmed that these principles and distinctions are conceived with equal exactness and adequacy in every particular system', idem at p 366.
4 H Kelsen, *The Pure Theory of Law,* M Knight, trans (Berkeley, University of California Press, 1970).
5 H L A Hart, *The Concept of Law* (Oxford, Oxford University Press, 1961).
6 N MacCormick, *Legal Reasoning and Legal Theory* (Oxford, Oxford University Press, 1978).
7 R Dworkin, *Law's Empire* (London, Fontana Press, 1986).

8   Austin himself says that jurisprudence becomes particular or national when we limit our study to a particular legal system. But his main interest is consistently in general jurisprudence. Austin, *supra* note 3 at p 365.

9   P S Atiyah and R S Summers, *Form and Substance in Anglo-American Law: A Comparative Study of Legal Reasoning, Legal Theory, and Legal Institutions* (Oxford, Oxford University Press, 1987).

10 For a general and reliable description of the Japanese legal system and its history, see *The Japanese Legal System: Introductory Cases and Materials,* H Tanaka, ed (Tokyo, University of Tokyo Press, 1976).

11 See generally, Tanaka, idem ch 3.

12 The recent and penetrating critique of this traditional view is F Upham, *Law and Social Change in Postwar Japan* (Cambridge, Harvard University Press, 1987). See also J O Haley, 'The myth of the reluctant litigant', *J. Japanese Studies* 4 (1978) p 359.

13 See my review essay on Upham's *Law and Social Change in Postwar Japan.* Y Matsuura, 'Law and bureaucracy in modern Japan', *Stanford L. Rev.* 41 (1989) p 1627.

14 Tanaka describes Japanese local government in the following way. 'It should be noted, however, that Japan is definitely a unitary state, and the status of prefectures [the largest unit of the local government] in Japan is not comparable to the states of the USA, either constitutionally, legally or politically. Most of the important items of local government are regulated by national statutes' (Tanaka, 1976) *supra* note 10 at p 44.

    In the United Kingdom, England, Scotland, and Northern Ireland respectively enjoy a considerable degree of independence. Or, at least, the word 'United' carries much significance with it. However, it is utterly impossible to find in Japan counterparts of England, Scotland and Northern Ireland.

15 See generally *Public Administration in Japan,* K Tsuji, ed (Tokyo, University of Tokyo Press, 1984).

16 See D F Henderson, *Foreign Enterprise in Japan* (Tokyo, Charles Tuttle, 1975); M Muramatsu and E S Krauss, 'Bureaucrats and politicians in policymaking: the case of Japan', *Am. Political Science Rev.* 78 (1984) p 126.

17 Widely publicised 'administrative guidance' of Japanese ministries is one of the means at the disposal of the bureaucracy. See generally M Young, 'Administrative guidance in the courts: a case study in doctrinal adaptation', *Law in Japan,* 17 (1984) p 120; R R Lury, 'Japanese administrative practice: the discretionary role of the Japanese government official', *The Business Lawyer,* 31 (1976) p 2109.

18 As to the Ministry of International Trade and Industry, Johnson's book offers useful information and analysis in English. C Johnson, *MITI and the Japanese Miracle: The Growth of Industrial Policy, 1925–75* (Stanford, Stanford University Press, 1982).

19 As of 1982, the providers of legal services in Japan are 2,700 judges, 1,200 public prosecutors, 12,200 practising attorneys, 14,600 judicial scriveners, 30,100 administrative scriveners, 2,600 patent attorneys, 105,600 tax attorneys and others. The population of Japan is, as of December 1981, 118 million. Practising attorneys are called 'Bengoshi' in Japanese and may be regarded as barristers in the English classification. See M Young, 'Foreign lawyers in Japan: a case study in transnational dispute resolution and marginal reform', *Law in Japan* 21, pp 84, 116 Appendix 1 (1988).

20 There are also fifty Family Courts which are ranked on the same level as District Courts.

21   As to this expectation, see C Nakane, *Japanese Society* (Penguin, 1973).

22   Upham, *supra* note 12 at p 218.

23   Upham, idem at p 17.

24   For brief comment on this, see S Matusi, 'A comment upon the role of the judiciary in Japan', in *Kyoto American Studies Seminar, Specialists Conference, 1987*, T Kamata ed (Kyoto, 1987).

25   As to the pollution litigation in the 1960s and 70s, see generally, J Gresser, K Fujikura and A Morishima, *Environmental Law in Japan* (Cambridge, MIT Press, 1981). See also Upham, *supra* note 12 ch 2.

26   Upham, *supra* note 12 at p 217.

27   Upham, idem at p 47.

28   See for example, Hart, *supra* note 5 ch 5–6. Dworkin's theory is also based upon the fact that the judiciary is the major actor in law. See Dworkin, 'Hard cases' in Dworkin, *Taking Rights Seriously* (Bristol, Butterworth, 1977), ch 4.

29   Dworkin, *supra* note 7 at p 167.

30   Hart persuasively advocates this distinction. See his 'Positivism and the separation of law and morals' (1958) in H L A Hart, *Essays in Jurisprudence and Philosophy* (1983) p 49. For the criticism of Hart's position, see Dworkin, *supra* note 28 (Bristol, Butterworth, 1977), chs 1–2.

31   See for example, *Chotei to Ho: Daitaiteki Funsou Kaiketsu (ADR) no Kanousei* [*Mediation and Law: Possibility of Alternative Dispute Resolution*] T Kojima ed (Yokyo, Chuo University Press, 1989) p 211.

32   P S Atiyah, *Pragmatism and Theory in English Law* 4 (London, Stevens, 1987). See also G Calabresi, *Ideals, Beliefs, Attitudes and the Law*, introduction (Syracuse, Syracuse University Press, 1985).

33   The leading advocates of this approach are Professors Ichiro Kato and Eiichi Hoshino, both of whom are Professors Emeritus at the University of Tokyo. For their views see generally I Kato, 'Ho-Kaishakugaku ni okeru Ronri to Riekikoryo' (1967) [Logic and balancing of interests in legal hermeneutics] in Kato, *Minpo ni okeru Ronri to Riekikoryo* [*Logic and Balancing of Interests in Civil Law*] (Tokyo, Yuhikaku Press, 1974) p 65; E Hoshino, 'Minpo Kaishakuron Josetsu' (1967) ['An introduction to hermeneutics of civil law'] in Hoshino, *Minpo Ronshu* [*Selected Writings on Civil Law*] (Tokyo, Yuhikaku Press, 1970) p 1.

34   Scheingold uses the expression 'the myth of rights' to refer to this aspect of the American legal culture. S A Scheingold, *The Politics of Rights* (New Haven, Yale University Press, 1974) p 1.

35   It is Professor Takeyoshi Kawashima who pursued extensive analysis of the Japanese legal consciousness in terms of notion of right. See for example, T Kawashima, 'The legal consciousness of contract in Japan' *Law in Japan: An Annual* (C Stevens trans, 1974) p 1.

36   Certainly I concede that the notion of right carries a normative significance. The notion of protected domain might have been indispensable for the establishment of liberalism and its ideological effect to convince people that they are entitled to some fundamental liberties is of great value. It is not doubted at all. But the notion of right as a protected domain always becomes puzzling, when we approach it with intensive theoretical analysis.

37   Upham, *supra* note 12 chs 2–3.

CHAPTER 5

Law and Social Activity: the Legacy of the French Revolution

Grażyna Skąpska

The concept of an active society so characteristic of the social sciences of the last decades, the interest in the history of social movements, in the sources and results of revolutions and, above all, in the concept of human agency—the rational and active, self-determined, and creative social subject—lead to a change in analyses of law. It opens up a view of law as an object and goal of social activity as well as an instrument of social reform. It opens up the possibility of viewing the law from the perspective of human rationality and creativity.

It should be stressed that linking the concept of human agency with that of creativity leads to an understanding of agency which encompass both actions and reflection. The former can be described as human efforts directed towards transformation of society and the latter as the understanding of how the *status quo* has come into being, conceptions of man and his environment, and ideas as to what should be understood as the good, the happiness and the interests of human beings.

Concepts of human agency, critical reflexivity and creativity, models of an active social subject as well as concepts of law as the institutional core of an active society, are not free from evaluative premises and hidden, general, philosophical assumptions.

Our discourse concerning these the most general problems then is never completely innocent and its practical consequences, in the form of existing law are embedded in general philosophical assumptions, ideas and ideals.

According to Isaiah Berlin one should not overlook the impact of philosophical ideas on practical solutions. The search for the transcendental conditions of the formation and existence of society and its institutions, of the nature of man and the social order, also has an influence on the practical arrangements of our life.[1]

Methodological observations as well give us this starting point. Here, the old problem of the intermingling of philosophy, theory and practice in the domain of law must be stressed.[2] Thus, the whole set of assumptions about the nature of both the phenomena and the statements dealing with law, the nature of man as legal subject and with legal order are still important and such terms as 'vision', 'pre-scientific image' or 'philosophical model' can be applied to them.

Secondly, we may say that axiological premises which make up an important part of such a 'vision', together with assumptions about the nature of the reality under study, make up its partial, fragmentary ontology and axiology.[3] They, together with the prominent philosophical ideas which influence legal-philosophical discourse and have an impact on practical solutions, determine the concept of the active legal subject and of the legal order of the active society. In such a way then, they also determine the concept of modern law.

In the history of human efforts to transform societies and of self-liberating activities based on critical reflexivity, the French Revolution marks the most important milestone. This is usually explained by examples of the development of the rationalistic, critical thought of the Enlightenment as well as the development of social institutions created as a result of revolutionary ideals and efforts—social arrangements on the micro- and macro-scale promoting further development and self-determination of social subjects and their creative self-realisation.

In the law that heritage finds its practical realisation in the form of civil rights, freedoms and liberties. Yet, the history of the French Revolution, and still more the history of those inheritors of its rationalistic and critical thought and the radicalism of its revolutionary creativity as the Bolshevik Revolution in 1917, point to the all too well-known truth that revolutionary efforts undertaken in the name of rational reflexivity and creativity too often end in stagnation, misery and oppression.

We should, therefore, ask ourselves which part of the ideas of the French Revolution, and their practical realisation, can still lead to further development and self-reflexivity, creativity and social activity, and which pose a danger to the development of a society and its institutions understood in this way.

I will not be able to answer fully in this paper. My aim here will be to point out the problems involved in attempting an answer and to develop the outline of such an answer.

Such problems are naturally of greatest practical importance for those societies which find themselves in the process of the 'Great Change' and which realise that their future depends on steps taken now, on the possibilities given within the framework of the institutions that have been created. It seems that the success of the measures undertaken relates to the freedom of conceptions, decisions and projects, the possibilities of self-reflection and self-determination guaranteed to social subjects. The success of change, then, relates to guaranteed freedoms and liberties.

However, it is also important to look at social activity and human agency from a different angle. Here we must take into consideration problems of the legal order which stem from seeing it as being the necessary premise of mutual social action. The law is understood as the agreed-upon and stable basis of mutually undertaken actions, giving them a relatively stable basis. These are problems of the predictability of actions and results therefrom and of the guarantees and protection given to the projects and decisions that have been agreed. So, these are problems of the law looked upon as a measure of secure social planning and as a set of institutions constituting the normative structure of social relations and interactions, thus enabling people to predict their mutual actions as well as their rights and obligations.

The conception of law as the normative structure of actions determining the mutual rights and obligations of legal subjects poses a good starting point for further considerations. It enables the analysis of the possibilities of creative actions within the framework of rights and obligations, which demarcate the area of actions and the place of the legal subject within it.

One can differentiate between at least two possibilities of defining an active society and human agency. They refer to two different conceptions, and two different sets of ideas concerning the active subject and legal order of an active society.

The first of these possibilities can be explored within the framework of the conceptions characteristic of the liberal model of society. For such a model institutional conceptions of law seem to be paradigmatic. In the second the instrumental conceptions of law are paradigmatic. Here stress is put on the effective realisation of some ends (here also of the projects for an ideal society characteristic of the evolutionary and naturalistic models of society).

My claim is that both perspectives find their foundations in the legacy of the Enlightenment in general, and in the legacy of the French Revolution in particular. They differ in the concept of the rational legal subject embedded in the ideas, philosophical models and images of rationality preached by the great men of the Enlightenment. As a consequence of this difference one can point out differences in concepts of social order. If we take into account time-space dimensions[4] of legal order and assume that power relations are the important part of the legally- determined structure of social relations, then the liberal and the naturalistic model of society (and in consequence the institutional and instrumental conceptions of law) can be differentiated according to these criteria as well as the concept of the rational legal subject.

According to the broadly understood institutional conceptions, every member of society takes an active part in the functioning of the system, fulfilling in their action the institutionalised patterns of behaviour but by the same token changing them during the process of interpretation conflict-resolution and decision-making.[5] The aims of active social subjects are here the institutionalisation of social relations and the guarantee of equal chances in the process of the realisation of their goals as well as having institutionalised conditions adequate to the specific needs, interests and values of every participant in the social process. Moreover, the characteristic feature of the institutional, liberal conceptions is the joining of law, thought of as the basis of human activity and creativity, and law, thought of as the basis of the relative stability of the social order.

So the law (legal institutions) is understood in terms of the 'conceptual framework within which particular arrangements can be set up by particular person or persons . . .'[6]

However, such a conceptual framework of interests and activities of legal subjects is itself a product of social activity. The intertwinement of the concept of law as the product of social efforts and the law as the structure of social actions has its basis in the conception of the rational legal subject and the liberal model of society as the set of contracts (arrangements) concluded by rationally acting legal subjects.

Within the framework of liberal conceptions it is an axiomatic assumption that rationality is an attribute of every legal subject. In consequence people are able to pursue their own affairs, recognising the constraints imposed both by their projects and by the law.[7] The law can thus be perceived as above all a system of active rights, in shaping one's own relations with others, in choosing goals and the means of obtaining them and last of all, in taking an active part in the processes of formation of political organisation. Here belong the indisputable achievements of the age of bourgeois revolutions: the concept of citizen and his rights and liberties and the concept of political authority and the state which rests on the foundations of law which have been agreed upon within the framwork of a democratic constitution.

The organisational framework of social activity both on the micro- and macro-level is given by contract and the term 'contractual society' is a good description. More specifically, social activity on the micro-level is organised in the form of dispositive norms, based on the principle of *pacta sunt servanda,* guaranteeing the freedom of contracts for every social subject. That specific principle is the basis of the reliability of social organisation in everyday encounters and is decisive for the relative stability of social order.

On the macro-level the contract functions in the form of the delegation of power by citizens to authority, execution of power within the agreed framework of competence and control of that power by parliament and public opinion.

One could describe liberal law as transparent to the actions of legal subjects, their interests, goals and values. The transparency of legal norms to social actions, even when they exist in the form of dispositive norms, can, however, be strongly limited by the connection of law to its past, i.e. institutionalised previous contracts, which according to the principle *pacta sunt servanda* cannot be changed at will. Such contracts which incorporate the interests, goals and values of the contracting parties make 'the body of the law' claim a relative autonomy and independence from actual politics and its social role. They also impose limits on social activity by protecting specific, agreed rights. Thus, with the logic of *pacta sunt servanda* as a point of departure, the law could be perceived as the semi-autonomous component of the social system with close connections to its cultural development. Cultural development here being understood as the accumulation of social experience and the incorporation of social goals and values.[8]

We can now look at further problems concerning social action and the problems of its special and temporal decisions. We may start here with the proposition that the legal institutions forming the conceptual framework of particular social arrangements enable people to create more facts in the social world than there exist physical facts.[9] In consequence, the mere existence of legal institutions (being themselves products of social actions) leads to overcoming the scarcity of natural facts and to broadening the possibilities of actions. In this respect, the concept of law comes to be similar to the concept of culture. The possibilities of human creativity provided by legal institutions depend of course on their formal characteristics—the more general and transparent they are, the greater the scope and range of the possibilities given to legal subjects. Moreover, the existence of legal institutions and institutional facts makes possible a substantial change of ends. It makes possible the re-definition of goals which can now be expressed in terms of rights and not exclusively in terms of goods. The struggle for rights, being the deciding characteristic of the French Revolution, was greatly appreciated by Hegel who, in a letter to Schelling, praised the revolutionary fight of the humiliated to appropriate not goods, but rights.[10] Needless to say, it is the rights of self-determination in the shape of freedoms and liberties of citizens and economic subjects (i.e., the rights making possible further independent and creative actions and arrangements) that were of primary importance.

We can also see how, in contractual society, the liberal model of law as institution creates the further possibility of overcoming the natural barriers and natural determinants of social, and above all, political relations of power. Firstly, there is the possibility of overcoming such natural determinants of the power relation caused by natural, physical facts such as sheer strength. The institutionalisation of rights derived from the assumption of the rationality of every legal subject, and more specifically expressed in the principle of equal chances, made possible the arrangement and control of power relations on the basis of rights of participation and control by every citizen instead of the actual strength of some of them.

The term 'natural' has, however, in social sciences as well as in general discourse, a double meaning. 'Natural' facts can be interpreted not only as physical ones but also as ones which are not questioned, which are taken for granted as being rooted in history, embedded in tradition, in the sometimes mythical past of society. They are ones related to the most sacred values of the society. Paradoxically then, the term 'natural' becomes synonymous with the term 'cultural'.

The revolutionary efforts undertaken against the natural determinants of power relations were directed towards both types of 'natural' facts; physical facts such as sheer strength and cultural facts such as those related to the feudal traditions of society. The overcoming of those traditions was seen as the decisive step towards freedom.

The problem of the temporal dimensions of social actions played an important part in these efforts. For the protagonists of the new, liberal model of society realised that ruling over time is necessary for the rationalisation of social arrangements. It was thus the desacralisation of time and in consequence the desacralisation of traditional relations of power that was one of the fruits of the French Revolution. For traditional power relations were closely related to the traditional visions of time, one of the social functions of such being to legitimise power relations and social structure as stable (i.e. sanctified by tradition and 'time honoured') and eternal, as the everlasting order of things.[11]

Power relations in feudal societies found their particular support in the genealogical conception of time. 'In the Middle Ages—the powerful, eminent and influential man is one who is supported by generations of ancestors. This is the epitome of genealogical time which is also the time of history.'[12] To such a vision of time corresponded the vision of law, rooted in ancient customs and sanctified by tradition. The monarch, being the personification of tradition and the source of change interpreted ancient customs as well as proclaimed new laws, in that way ruling over time through imposed changes.

The French Revolution was thus also a revolution against such an intertwinement of time, authority and traditional social order,

> . . . for the Enlightenment philosophers did not remain at the level of interpretation of the past, but questioned the very principle of tradition itself, the authority which the past exercised over the present.[13]

Within the framework of the liberal model, social time re-defined as legal time, as time subordinated to the activities of legal subjects trying to arrange their interests in a rational way, took the shape of conventionally settled or stipulated periods. Thus terms of payment, of limitation, terms known as *vacation legis,* terms for bringing the law into force and for its disuetude. Institutional, legal time, within the framework of the liberal model of social order, has a conventional and dispositive character. However, according to the premises of the institutional theory of law, this has certain limits which are fixed by previously concluded contracts. According to the principle of *pacta sunt servanda,* they maintain their validity unless changed in accordance with valid, legal procedures.

Institutional time within the liberal model of contractual society is then synonymous with legal time. It is detached from natural events and subordinated to the interests and will of rational legal subjects and that in turn fixes the conventionality and dispositiveness of the social order.

We may conclude then that this model creates possibilities of broadening institutional space, actions and relations. Since it is general and transparent to the interests, needs and goals of legal subjects, the law enables the creation of institutional space according to the arrangements undertaken by legal subjects. Such arrangements are based on institutional facts which in turn make possible the creation of further institutional facts. However, these possibilities are not unlimited. Here the most important achievement of the French Revolution should be stressed: the re-definition of needs and interests into rights, thus into the form of institutional facts. The most fundamental of them, the rights derived from an axiomatic assumption of rationality of every legal subject such as the rights of self-determination, pose the 'hard core' and the 'orientation points' on the map of possible actions and arrangements, in this way organising the institutional space of action. Similarly, the possibilities of time management contained in the conception of conventional legal time also have their limits. The outlines and borders of the dispositiveness of time are given here by the general principle of the contractual society's order, that *pacta sunt servanda*. That principle fixes the relative continuity of the concluded arrangements, the predictability of the mutual actions as well as the possibility of such social reforms within which the future could be altered by small steps of a 'piece-meal' strategy. The above-mentioned features prompt us to look for *sui generis* laws generating human actions related to institutional space and conventional time and which generate the dimensions of the social order of liberal society.

Looking at the Revolution from another perspective could direct the discussion on its legacy to totally different problems and provoke the formulation of completely different conclusions as to the conception of the active social subject, the law and the shape of social order. The history of the Revolution is a starting point here. We can start with the case of the civil war in France, 1773, and especially that of the Vendée uprising. One can interpret the initial incentives to civil war as the break by the new Constitutional Assembly with the culture and tradition incorporated in the already existing, traditional law. Acting in the name of the values of freedom, equality and fraternity and also in the name of individual rights of citizens liberated from the traditional bonds, the Constitutional Assembly violated the older, pre-existing contracts, i.e., the old agreements made between the kings of France and their provinces. As the most significant instance of this, one can use here the announcement in March 1773 of the decree on conscription, according to which the whole country had to supply the army with 300,000 recruits. This decree violated two traditionally existing domains of law at the same time. Firstly, it violated the laws giving the citizen of France particular rights, as the agreement between King François I and the Province of Brittany, of 1532. That agreement (The Act of Unification of Brittany with the Kingdom of France) proclaimed that no inhabitant of Brittany could be recruited to army service outside his province without his own permission. Secondly, in order to dissolve such types of agreements and to rationalise the governing of the country, the Constitutional Assembly had already divided France in 1770 into eighty-three departments, thus violating the traditional structure of the provinces of France and dissolving specific laws connected with that territorial structure.

The decree on conscription was only the beginning of a long process. From the perspective of legislation that process resulted in a range of legal acts investing with the majesty of law the radical means which aimed at a radical reform of society. From the perspective of social activity and the rationalisation of law as a means of obtaining goals, it could be seen as the growing violence, massacre of civil populations (by for example, drowning ships loaded with people—*Quel torrent revolutionaire que la Loire*), in the breaking of such 'contracts' as the conditions of capitulation and in the killing of all 'civil' war prisoners.[14] All this was done in the name of revolutionary social reform, i.e., in the name of reason as well as Equality, Fraternity and Freedom—the fundamental principles of the future society.

The concept of reason has here two connotations: the first relates to the philosophical assumptions relating to the conception of social order, the second to the philosophical model of human rationality.

According to the above-mentioned intellectual paradigm of the Enlightenment and its naturalistic and evolutionistic vision of the social world, there is a *ratio* in social order contained in general, objective laws, which determine social organisation, institutional structure and social change. The assumption of determinism is closely connected with the concept of causality, as the general principle determining the occurrence of social phenomena. Consequently, the concept of rationality is primarily cognitive. It relates to the abilities of the human mind to discover the content of the objective laws of historical development and with this knowledge to realise social interests and fulfil social needs in the process of the growing reflexivity of progressive social forces. One of the consequences of seeing rationality as related to the deterministic and evolutionistic model of progressive social development is the relativisation of that concept. Rationality becomes understood not as the axiomatic property of every human being, but as the property and skill of some. Rationality is the property of those who are able to recognise the objective laws of social development and at the same time make use of them. Firstly, by the augmentation of the hidden, creative forces of society, in this way accelerating the progress of civilisation and secondly, by the use of means leading to the best fulfilment of human needs.

Such a conception of rationality brings about the possibility of an authoritarian imposition on people of what their needs should be and also the forceful imposition of particular views of the rational, progressive society. This then produces the problem that the most active social subjects, those who have enough intellectual abilities to recognise other people's needs and whose concepts of progress are in fact realised, have the power to impose their concept of progress and rational system. Thus we are also dealing with the instrumentality of reason. Rational means not only enlightened or possessing knowledge, but can be understood as a definite skill and competence in arranging human affairs and exploiting the environment according to the knowledge of the objective rules of social organisation and development. Thus to this conception belongs the idea of human activity understood as instrumental activity, as activity directed to the appropriation of nature. Indeed, it is claimed, that in the age of industrialism such an instrumental conception of rationality permeated the whole of society. [15] However, it should be added, that according to the further assumptions and beliefs of the Enlightenment, history progresses in accordance with some definite plan and instrumental reason should fulfil its destination: the achievement of ever higher levels of social development. What counts as a 'higher level' is the province of those who possess knowledge of the objective laws as well as the vision of the future, more rational and just stages of social development. In the name of such a vision they are able to activate and control human efforts.

Bearing in mind the double content of the term 'natural', we can see that the instrumental appropriation of nature also means control over social and cultural institutions, values and beliefs as well as traditional rights (especially those which are 'irrational', i.e., which are seen as not subordinated to the objective laws of social development and which do not fit into the vision of social progress).

It may quite plausibly be claimed that the model of social evolution and rational institutional organisation based on the cognition of objective laws of social development, combined with the conviction of the necessity of social progress, is especially characteristic of our century. Hence it is this century which has been witnessing the rise and fall of a quite consciously undertaken experiment. Its goal was to bring to pass beliefs in social progress and to construct a rational social order based on scientific knowledge, i.e., a social order enabling social subjects to make use of their knowledge about the objective laws of history.

Bearing in mind our previous comments about the uneven distribution of cognitive ability, here the rational social order means the promotion of those who best understand the existing stage of things and so are best able to realise the necessary future. It means in short the institutionalisation of uneven power relations. Such a vision of revolutionary social reform conducted in the name of reason found its most prominent materialisation in the idea of dictatorship of progressive social forces.

Such conceptions of the rational social order are strictly connected with the concept of law. Two modes of thinking can be differentiated. According to the first, characteristic of classical, critical Marxist thought, law is seen as the institutionalisation of class and power relations changing with the changing rules of historical development.

The second which is characteristic of our times has a strong conviction that the law can be used as the means of control of social processes as well as the realisation of social progress.

So, the main function of law is the implementation of ideas of rational 'scientific' social order and of progress in social and political practice. Such instrumental law gives those who are powerful enough to make use of it control over social space and social time, thus control over the dimensions of social activity. The space for activity is not determined any more by created institutions understood as conceptual frameworks for human actions and arrangements which enable people to make new arrangements and to create new institutions. Rather it assumes a quasi-natural character, as being subordinated to cognitive abilities and skills in the process of controlling natural and social events.

The organisation of the space for social activity, within the framework of the naturalistic and progressive model of social order, no longer depends on rights derived from the axiomatic assumption of human rationality and the fundamental assumption of self-determination. It is here subordinated to the standards of cognitive and technical rationality, and, at the same time, to the idea that the realisation of progress is in the hands of those who themselves claim to be the representatives of social development.

The paradigmatic functions of law become then its organisational, innovative and educational function. Being in the hands of the most progressive and powerful forces of society, the goals of law are fulfilled. These goals can be seen as the rationalisation of social structure, its subordination to the objective laws of social development and its progressive transformation.

As has been observed, the idea of law as a means of social engineering won particular popularity in communistic states. The political systems of such states attributed a decisive role to mechanisms of planned steering of social and economic processes and to the law as a technique of influencing social relations.[15] So the great significance of those functions is stressed especially in works analysing the concept and properties of so-called 'socialistic law', i.e., the properties of the legal system characteristic of societies realising the Marxist model of development.[16] In such works as well as in the policies of ruling elites, stress has also been put on the educational function of law, where education has been understood as the transformation of action and motivations in the whole society. The aim was to make people identify themselves with the particular vision of social progress and to internalise the law as an instrument of its realisation.[17] Such a model of social order also had assumptions concerning the possibilities of control over future stages of development and their subordination to the visions of progress. In such a way control over social time was effectuated.

As the transformation of society towards a better future is more easily done when the society has no normative models, it is cut off from its own tradition and thus cut off from its own identity. We can therefore note a strong *pro futuro* orientation in instrumental law. This is also based on the conviction that the future can be shaped by law according to visions of progress. A good example of the practical realisation of such a vision can be seen in the so-called plan norms, which are social, economic and technical development plans having binding legal force and based on a prognosis for and a vision of a desired future.

The legacy of the French Revolution can lead us then to the formulation of two different conceptions of law and social order: the liberal one presented in the form of 'contractual society' and the 'progressive one' presented as the 'progressive society'. Within the framework of both of these, stress is put on the links between the existing legal order and the activity of social subjects. But, as we have seen, each lead to different social results.

NOTES

1   Isaiah Berlin, *Four Essays on Liberty* (London, 1969) p 8.
2   Roger B M Cotterrell 'Law and sociology: notes on the constitution and confrontations of disciplines' *Journal of Law and Society* 1 (1986) p 16.
3   Stefan Nowak, 'Odmiany filozofii nauki', w *Wizje człowieka i społeczeństwa w badaniach naukowych* / 'Visions of philosophy of science' in *Images of Man and Society in the Theories and Scientific Research,* Stefan Nowak, ed (Warszawa, 1983) p 25.

4   Anthony Giddens, *Central Problems in Social Theory* (London and Basingstoke, 1979) pp 203–78.
5   Neil MacCormick, Ota Weinberger, 'Institutions, arrangement and practical information', *Ratio Iuris* 1 (1988) p 79.
6   Anthony Giddens, op. cit. p 49.
7   Spiros Simitis 'Die Loi le Chapelier: Bemerkungen zur Geschichte und möglichen Wiederentdeckung des Individuums', *Kritische Justiz* 2 (1989) pp 157–75.
8   Grażyna Skąpska, 'Problems of autonomy of law in the light of sociology of law', in *Studies in the Theory and Philosophy of Law,* forthcoming.
9   Neil MacCormick, Ota Weinberger, op. cit. p 85. John R Searle, *Speech Acts. An Essay in the Philosophy of Language* (London, 1977) pp 69–73.
10 Georg W F Hegel, A letter to Schelling in Joachim Ritter, *Hegel und die französische Revolution* (Frankfurt am Main, 1965) p 20.
11 Sławomir Kapralski 'Social time and legitimation of power' in *Culture and Legitimation,* Maria Luisa Maniscalco, ed (Rome 1989) pp 80–1.
12 Aron Guriewicz, *Kategorie kultury średniowiecznej* (Categories of Culture in the Middle Ages) (Warszawa, 1971) p 84.
13 Anthony Giddens, op. cit. p 201.
14 Paweł Jasienica *Wojna domowa we Francji* (Civil war in France) (Warszawa, 1989) pp 15–104.
15 Lech Morawski, *Argumentacje, racjonalność prawa i postępowanie dowodowe* (Argumentations, rationality of law and law of evidence) (Toruń, 1988) p 21
16 Winicjusz Narojek, *Społeczeństwo planujace* (*The Planning Society*) (Warszawa, 1973) p 15.
    Maria Borucka-Arctowa, *Świadomość prawna a planowe zmiany społeczne* (Legal Consciousness and the Planned Social Changes) (Warszawa, 1981) pp 92–114.
    Maria Borucka-Arctowa, 'Funkcje prawa socjalistycznego' *Prawo socjalistyczne* 'Functions of socialistic law' *Socialist Law,* Henryk Rot, ed (Warszawa, 1989) pp 191–261.
17 Andriej Siniawsij, *Der Traum vom neuen Menschen oder Die Sovjetzivilisation* (Frankfurt am Main, 1989) p 136.

CHAPTER 6

Law and Revolution:
What is 'Breaking with the Old Order'?

Eugene Kamenka

Revolution—a political revolution—has been defined as a sharp, sudden change in the social location of political power, expressing itself in the radical transformation of the process of government, of the official foundations of sovereignty or legitimacy and of the conception of the social order. Many see the revolution proper as a modern phenomenon, different from the successful revolts or rebellions of the pre-modern world. Legally, and often practically, such a revolution claims to constitute the Year 1 of a new world. It rests on the proclamation of legal and constitutional discontinuity: the changeover from subject to citizens, the location of sovereignty in the people, for instance, the pervasive abolition of formal inequality before the law. It proclaims its own legitimation and has done so increasingly in the name of reason and progress.

In this respect, the French the Russian and the Chinese Revolutions were more unequivocally revolutionary than the American Declaration of Independence and the formation of the United States of America, though the French did not become so until 1791 and though the American Revolution had a profoundly radical impact on its European contemporaries. That direct impact would have been greater if America had not been so far away. Neither 1770 nor 1776, however, constituted as radical a break, as new a start, in the political and legal life of the American colonists. They looked backward as much as forward; they rejected kings but not the traditions of parliamentary government or of the Common Law. They did not seek, at one blow, to transform the political revolution into a social revolution. By 1792 in France, by January 1918 in Russia and in 1911 and in 1949 in China, it was otherwise. The new order in each country claimed to be a totally new order.

Time has proved those claims false. Each of these radical Jacobin-type or Jacobin-led revolutions developed and consummated trends in government, law and administration that had been evident before the revolution. Each, to a surprising extent, adopted some of the style, methods and pretensions of the state it had overthrown while further developing its 'modernising' and centralising tendencies. Of course, there were changes—vast changes—but many of them rested on and expressed trends that existed independently of revolutionary pretensions and revolutionary realities. In the field of law, post-revolutionary developments clearly point to the fact that legal traditions, institutions and arrangements, legal problems and solutions, cannot be dealt with as mere handmaidens of ruling class or ruling power ideology. They display continuity as well as change even through social and political revolutionary breaks. They do so partly because law is confronted by and has to take account of social traditions and social facts independent of human will. One of these facts is the long-standing popular demand for justice and reciprocity in the relations between governor and governed; another is the demand and need for regularity, predictability, security. In tort, in contract, in criminal law, these continuities reassert themselves. More surprisingly, the same is true of legal philosophy, of the attempt to elevate, regularise and legitimise law and of the need to provide responses to public protests and demands, to the claims of interests and the assertion of rights. The study of law and revolution involves a rejection of the revolutionaries' claim that they can jump out of history and simply refashion their own society. It requires a subtle and differentiated appreciation of revolutionary aims and methods, of pertinent legal traditions and legal cultures and some understanding of the degree of cynicism and dishonesty of which revolutionary leaders and their followers are capable. It requires us also never to lose sight of what a social order means for the people who live in and under it—not the people as a metaphysical category but actual people whose lives can be enriched or destroyed, whose relations with others can be based on trust or on pervasive fear and suspicion. What is good and praiseworthy in relations between people is also good and praiseworthy in relations between people and their government; what is evil in the one case is evil in the other.

From his study of the Paris Commune, the October Revolution in Russia and the Civil War in Spain, Franz Borkenau derived his law of the two-fold development of revolutions. Every great revolution, he concluded, has destroyed the state apparatus which it found in a wave of anarchist sentiment; after vacillation and experimentation, it put another even more powerful bureaucratic apparatus in its place and suppressed all free mass movement, all spontaneity from below. There is a real sense in which Bertolt Brecht's jibe may be turned against the cause he supported: 'The people has lost the confidence of the government. The government has decided to dissolve the people and appoint another one.' The revolution militant may be the Paris of the Sections, Danton, the Kronstadt sailors, even Trotsky, the students of the May Four Movement in Peking in 1919; the revolution triumphant is Napoleon, Stalin and the new warlords who have just smashed the opposition in Tiananmen Square by rolling tanks over unarmed students and then lying about it.

A revolution, like all other great and complex social events, is part of many histories. Both its causes and its outcomes are as complex and differentiated as the event itself.[1] It is revolutionaries who seek to simplify. Students of revolutions and of revolutionaries must grapple with untold complexities. The tendency of violent 'total' revolutions to degenerate Bonapartism is well documented. For those of us who have passed middle age, it was the central event of our times. We watched the legal nihilism of the revolution militant give way, somewhat slowly and uncertainly, to an elevation of ever-increasingly bureaucratic-administrative conceptions of law and government as means of steering society in formalised, regularised, but still highly oppressive ways. We noted that concepts of socialist or other legality were elevated above the morally based concept of justice—a concept that had older and independent foundations and traditions, that was not dependent on definition from above. They were elevated just as firmly over notions of revolutionary spontaneity and grassroots democracy. Revolutions, in short, have turned out to be bitter unprincipled struggles for power, power unchallengeable and indivisible. The one thing revolutionaries cannot brook are equals who stand outside the fold.

Until recently, the history of revolutions and the history of Marxism itself was largely written by its more intelligent and critical practitioners as a story of the working out of internal logical imperatives and contradictions inherent in the struggle to reshape society. There was the tension between revolution as the vindication of democracy and revolution as the bitter and professional struggle for power. There was the tension between the future and the present, between shaping the people and listening to them. There was the tension, within Marxist thought itself, between an evolutionary, determinist elevation of productive forces and the revolutionary, activist elevation of class struggle as always primary, the tension between the dictatorship of the proletariat and the communist millennium, between planning and voluntary co-operation, etc. etc.

In the last twenty years, even this approach—with its echoes of classical Marxist revolutionary realism and historical science—fails to tell the whole story. In the West, 'The literature on Marxism', an able and lively student of Western Marxism has written,[2]

> threatens to drown both the theory and its students. To the cynical it confirms the obsolescence of Marxism: It has fled the streets and factories for the halls and offices of the university . . . A consumer's guide is required to stay abreast of the offerings and the recalls: structural Marxism, semiotic Marxism, feminist Marxism, hermeneutical Marxism. phenomenological Marxism, critical Marxism, and so on . . . Marxism does not escape the social conditions that it has always denounced as determinant.
>
> Everywhere Marxism has assumed characteristics of its specific environments. A single, homogeneous Marxism belongs to the past. Marxism takes on the color, and sometimes the content, of its conditions. Marxism devolves into Marxisms. This diversity is not benign. The world map of Marxism includes academics and political parties, entire states and cemeteries. There are Marxist revolutionaries and poets; there are also Marxist careerists, premiers and executioners. A common vocabulary, reality, and loyalty cease to exist. Boundaries between traditions and experiences rigidify.

Unrepentant Marxists seek to cope with all this by the law of uneven development, though they have been forced once more, as they were forced in the 1930s, to recognise the continuing and dangerous appeal, in times of social upheaval, of aggressive and xenophobic nationalism, religious fundamentalism and fear of freedom and progress in ways that are not reducible to simple economic interest and causes. Nevertheless, recent years have given the citizens of many Marxist-socialist societies grounds for hope that the most unpleasant features of the dictatorship of the proletariat, that the Bonapartist logic of revolutions, was itself but a phase in the development of socialism. Once the goal becomes more realistic, the means towards it could become less terrible: humanity no longer needed to be reshaped by an act of force and faith—i.e., by terror. If no one takes seriously any longer the belief in the withering away of law and state as the ultimate outcome of communist revolution, there is some hope among those who remain Marxists that the progress of industrialisation and economic sophistication in socialist societies does or will continue to undermine command politics (the party dictatorship) as it undermines the command economy. In the West, the development of a sophisticated industrial society drastically reduced the role of physical force in the allocation of goods and the exaction of services. Where Marxists used to denounce money as simply providing a different means of coercion, they now hope for similar developments in socialist societies.

But can the story of the very important but still precarious and uncertain 'liberalisation' of Marxist-socialist societies be written as part of the internal logic and history of socialist revolutions? Central to recent developments in communist-led societies has been the spread of world-wide communication, of economic interdependence and of the need for international co-operation. It is here that the American Revolution and a pluralistic, individualistic Western legal tradition that it elevated to a principle of law has suddenly proved itself as fruitful and as powerful as the revolutionary traditions that claimed to supersede it.[2] The analysis of law in Marxist-socialist societies is a matter to which many have been devoting increasingly complex and sophisticated attention, recognising rightly the struggle in those societies between quite different interests and attitudes concerned with 'promoting' law. But it is no longer possible to understand the aspirations of socialist citizens and their hopes for the future without recognising the growing strength in popular consciousness of basic aspects of Western legal and democratic traditions—the concept of rights, the notion of impartiality, the elevation of fair trials and due process, the concept of equality before the law, the independence of the judiciary, the principle *nullum crimen sine lege* and the belief that bad leaders and bad governments should be removable by popular vote, that governments, in short, should need to keep the confidence of their citizens. For Antonio Gramsci the pluralism of institutions in European society, the strength of civil society there, meant that the Leninist tactic of capturing state power and seeking to reshape society on that basis was neither possible nor appropriate in Europe—except, as he did not know, temporarily, by external military force. Gramsci's Euro-communist successors, with fifty more years of experience of communist revolutions, veered to the view that the socialist revolution required both the socialisation of the means of production, distribution and exchange and the acceptance and perfection of the democratic, political and social culture developed but not consummated by the bourgeoisie.

Today, both leaders and students of socialist societies are aware of ever-increasing complexity. It is no longer clear to them that modern economies function best under pervasive centralised planning and control. The call for modernisation of economies is a call in part for increasing decentralisation of authority and responsibility, in part a call for more direct relationships to market demands at home and abroad and in part a call for the freeing of economic enterprise from rigid political constraints. There are many within socialist societies who now believe that the four modernisations of agriculture, industry, science and defence require a fifth modernisation—that of political life, of government, administration and discussion.

It is, of course, no accident that these 'trends' have gone furthest and been most successful in those countries where independent institutions and independent traditions could confront the Party as living social ingredients— in Poland, in Hungary, in the Baltic states, in Armenia. But those—in the so-called Western camp—who assured us only twenty yers ago that the Chinese never had a conception of human rights or of democratic pluralism knew, as we can now see, nothing about China or about people.

NOTES

1   For a more extended discussion of revolutionary ideology and the impact of the French Revolution, see Eugene Kamenka, 'Revolutionary ideology and the great French Revolution of 1789–?', in *The Permanent Revolution: The French Revolution and Its Legacy 1789–1989,* Geoffrey Best ed (Fontana Press, London, 1988) pp 75–99.
2   R Jacoby, *Dialectic of Defeat: Contours of Western Marxism* (Cambridge, 1981) pp 1–2.

CHAPTER 7

Die Revolution als Erwachen vom kollektiven Traum

Friedrich Lachmayer

Abstract

Domination is realised in everyday life. However, it is founded in two realms which do not belong to the everyday, namely in the superconscious, as in law, and in the subconscious.

As far as the subconscious state of the dominated is concerned, they are in a dream-like state which is maintained by a kind of dream melody in the sense of a *creatio perpetua*.

Revolution can be characterised as the awakening from the collective dream, as a growing restlessness and a rude awakening. This does not always lead to a state of complete clarity.

It is more typical of revolutions that the new people in charge are interested in a new dream which stabilises their dominion, and thus they impose a new dream melody as soon as possible. The dominated sink into the new dream. So, for example, in the case of the French Revolution the royal dream melody was replaced by an imperial one, which led to the nightmare of war. An emperor took the place of a king.

Revolutions are dialectical processes. It is interesting to note the copying effects of the dialectic. The old patterns of domination, which are officially viewed as superseded, replicate themselves in a strange way in new patterns of domination. The dialectical negation is not complete; it transcends the old, but at the same time it represents it. The model of *tertium comparationis* can serve as a methodological approach to the elucidation of these processes of transformation.

1 *Der Schrei der demonstrierenden Massen*

Das Schlüsselerlebnis für diesen Beitrag ereignete sich vor etwa zwei Jahren: Damals fand in Wien eine Demonstration wegen einer in Aussicht genommenen Einschränkung staatlicher Leistungen statt. Es waren Angehörige vor allem der technischen Berufszweige, die gegen die Reduktion demonstrierten. Am Ziel des Marsches angelangt, stand eine große Menge beisammen und schrie. Je nachdem, wie treffend die Parolen des Sprechers waren, erhob sich ein lautes Schreien. Es war nicht mehr die Alltagssprache. Techniker sind Menschen, die ganz gut zu argumentieren vermögen, die zu rechnen und zu konstruieren gewohnt sind. Was sich da ereignete, lag aber unter dem Alltagsstandard der Kommunikation. Es war anders, als sich Techniker in ihrem Studium oder in ihrem Beruf auszudrücken pflegen.

Da wurde mir klar, daß das Argumentationsniveau unter anderem von der Anzahl der beteiligten Menschen abhängt. Desto größer die Menge der Menschen ist, desto geringer der Rationalitätsgrad der verwendeten Ausdrucksformen.

Der nächste Schritt war der, ob sich der Rationalitätsgrad nicht ins Irrationale wenden kann, daß also die Kommunikation keine bewußte sondern eine unbewußte wird.

Ein Zweiergespräch kann je nach den beteiligten Personen eine beachtliche rationale Argumentationsebene aufweisen. Sind mehrere Personen, etwa zehn beteiligt, so sind die Regeln der Gruppendynamik maßgeblich. Ist eine Masse da, so ist zur Erklärung die Massenpsychologie heranzuziehen.

Wendelt sich die Rationalität in die Irrationalität, dann stellt sich die Frage, ob nicht der Zustand der beherrschten Massen mit den Kategorien des Traumes beschrieben werden kann.

2 Der kollektive Traum

Herrschaft ist dann geglückt, wenn sich die beherrschte Masse in einem unbewußten Zustand befindet, wenn sie 'träumt'. Ein Traum ist keineswegs statisch. Es geschieht sehr viel darin, doch nach anderen Gesetzen als denen des Alltags.

Damit die Massen in dem kollektiven Traum verbleiben, bedarf es des Zutuns der Herrschenden. Es ist so etwas wie eine 'Traummelodie' notwendig, um den Zustand des kollektiven Traumes der Beherrschten herbeizuführen und zu erhalten. Im antiken Mythos wird von dem Thebanerkönig Amphion berichtet, der mit der Melodie seiner Leier die Steine zu Thebens Mauer zusammenfügte. Er hatte offenbar die Melodie gefunden, mit der er die Massen zur Gemeinschaft zusammenverband.

Die Traummelodie ist keineswegs die einzige Voraussetzung zur Herrschaft. Die Beherrschung realer Machtmittel gehört ebenso dazu wie der Zugang zum Norm- und Legitimationsmonopol des Rechtes. Der kollektive Traum ist eine unbewußte Komponente der Herrschaft so wie das Recht eine überbewußte ist. Damit wird möglich, daß sich die Beherrschten so etwas wie Herrschaft gefallen lassen. Es wird damit die Realität verzaubert, die Beherrschten gebunden. In dem Zustand des kollektiven Traumes kommt es dann zum Zwangskonsum des Rechtes.

Es kann nun sein, daß die ständige Erzeugung der Traummelodie gestört wird: Daß eine Seite reißt, daß eine andere konkurrenzierende Traummelodie ertönt und immer verlockender wird, daß die Realität immer enger wird, sodaß die Schläfer aus diesem Druck erwachen. Dann kommt es zur Revolution. Der revolutionäre Vorgang kann als Erwachen vom kollektiven Traum beschrieben werden.

Das Ziel der Revolution ist zunächst Rationalität, der Zustand des Wachseins.

Doch die neuen Herrschenden sind überhaupt nicht an diesem Zustand der Rationalität, der Argumentation, des Diskurses und damit der transparenten Verantwortung interessiert: Allzurasch wird eine neue Schallplatte aufgelegt und eine neue Traummelodie ertönt. Die Phasen basisdemokratischen revolutionären Diskurses sind kurz. Der Ausgang des Diskurses ist auch ungewiß, er könnte sich gegen die neuen Herrschenden, die zwischendurch an die Macht gekommen sind, richten. Die Stabilisierung der Herrschaft wird zum bestimmenden Ziel der neuen Herrschenden. Die neue Traummelodie ertönt—es kann auch die Alptraummelodie des Krieges sein—und allzurasch verfällt die Masse wieder in den kollektiven Schlaf, aus dem der Einzelne nur dann erwacht, wenn er unvermutet der Realität der Vernichtung gegenübersteht.

Daß oft eine Traummelodie nur durch eine andere ersetzt wird, zeigen viele historische Beispiele:

Bei der französischen Revolution wurde ein König getötet, um durch einen Kaiser ersetzt zu werden.

Die religiösen 'Revolutionen' der Gegenwart ersetzen ein mehr oder weniger ineffektiv gewordenes Herrschaftssystem durch ein religiös gefärbtes, mag dies in Europa oder außerhalb davon geschehen.

In all diesen Fällen kommt es—von einigen Zwischenphasen vielleicht abgesehen—nicht zur Rationalität des Massendiskurses, sondern ein Herrschaftssysstem ersetzt das andere.

In den Übergangsphasen kann es sich ereignen, daß die beiden ideologischen Optionen mit schrillen Mißtönen nebeneinander erklingen, wie zwei Orchester, die in einem Ballsaal konkurenzierend spielen, bis die einen Musiker den anderen das Feld überlassen und ihre Instrumente einpacken.

3 Der revolutionäre Kopie-Effekt

Oft werden die liegengelassenen Instrumente von den Kommenden benutzt und in das neue Orchester aufgenommen. Es tritt bei Revolutionen etwas auf, das man als 'revolutionären Kopie-Effekt' bezeichnen kann.

Die revolutionäre Negation ist keine vollständige. Die These, die es zu negieren gilt, kopiert sich strukturell auf die Antithese durch. Die dialektische Negation ist keine logische. Die Negation der Dialektik transformiert nur. Im Gegensatz dazu ist die logische Negation eine vollständige.

Durch die beschränkte Negationswirkung der Revolution wird der vorrevolutionäre Strukturmangel in modifizierter Weise auf den nachrevolutionären Zustand übertragen.

Haß fixiert mehr als Liebe und schafft innere, obsessive Gegenwart, auch wenn sich die Realität schon längst gewandelt hat. Herkules schleppte die Löwenhaut mit sich herum und verstarb am Kleid, das mit dem Blut des Nessus getränkt war. Der Horusfalke ist als sozialistische Friedenstaube neu erschienen. Die Semiotik der Herrschaft ist geeignet, die *translatio imperii* aufzuzeigen.

Der dialektische Kopie-Effekt ist ein gefährlicher Vorgang, weil er vor allem Haß-Muster überträgt. Die Träger der Masken sind zwar anders, zuweilen werden die Masken nur getauscht, aber die Masken sind die gleichen oder werden innerhalb des Typus nur gewandelt.

Es ist schwierig, aus diesem Vorgang des Maskenwechsels und der Maskentransformation herauszukommen. Darin ist auch die Tragik der neuen Machthaber begründet, die sich davon nicht zu emanzipieren vermögen. In ihrem Bestreben, die Macht zu festigen, werden die alten Motive neu instrumentiert. Durch den dialektischen Kopie-Effekt wird der alte Haß nicht negiert sondern neu maskiert. Wenn sich schon die Beherrschten nicht von der Herrschaft zu befreien vermögen, die Herrschenden vermögen es auch nicht, die alten, bloß übermalten Masken beiseite zu legen.

Jede Maske hat aber zwei Seiten: eine Außenmaske und eine Innenmaske. Beide wirken auf ihre Weise. Auch die Innenmaske. Das blutdurchtränkte Nessushemd war eine solche Innenmaske. Die Unterdrückung der Beherrschten ist ein Problem der Außenmaske, die Obsession der Herrschenden durch die überwunden geglaubten Schatten der Vergangenheit ein Problem der Innenmaske.

4 Das 'tertium comparationis'

Der direkte Vergleich zweier Traumsituationen erklärt nicht viel. Anders ist es schon, wenn man beide Traumsituationen auf den Typus, den Archetypus, zurückzuführen vermag und auf diesem Weg von einer zur anderen Traumsituation gelangt.

Die direkte Relation ist für das Feststellen einer Proportion nicht geeignet. Es bedarf dazu des Dritten, des Maßes. Das *tertium comparationis* spielt nicht nur eine Rolle bei juristischen Methoden, etwa bei der Analogie, wie Arthur Kaufmann aufzeigt, sondern ist auch geeignet, im unbewußten Bereich eine methodischen Brücke zu bilden, wo eine direkte Relation nicht möglich ist. Das Leibniz'sche Modell der prästabilierten Harmonie beruht ebenso auf dem *tertium comparationis* wie das platonische Höhlengleichnis.

Die Masken und ihr Wechsel und damit auch die Mechanismen des revolutionären Kopie-Effektes lassen sich nur dann erkennen, wenn man die direkten Relationen beiseite läßt und den Weg des *tertium comparationis* einschlägt. Manchmal ist eben erst über einen Spiegel, über die Reflexion sichtbar, was der direkten Ansicht verborgen bleibt.

Die revolutionären Vorgänge sind viel zu wichtige Ereignisse, die zahlreiche Menschen existentiell betreffen, als daß man die zu ihrer Erklärung möglicherweise geeigneten Methoden allzufrüh einschränken sollte.

5 *Krieg und Bürgerkrieg*

In Revolutionen werden Menschen von anderen Menschen getötet. Üblicherweise tötet man keine Menschen. Geschieht dies, so wird der Täter wegen 'Mordes' bestraft.

In Revolutionen ist dies anders. Die Menschen werden von den revolutionären Massen wie in Trance getötet. Es ist wie im Krieg, wo die einen auch nichts daran finden, wenn sie die anderen töten. Die kämpfenden Soldaten befinden sich in einer Art von Trance. Sie handeln darin auf eine Weise, wie sie außerhalb dieses Zusandes nicht handeln würden.

Krieg und Revolution sind einander sehr ähnlich. Früher war der Ausdruck 'Bürgerkrieg' gebräuchlich. Heute wird er vermieden. Vor allem wird er von jenen vermieden, die die Revolution anstreben. Krieg und Bürgerkrieg beeinflussen sich oft. Die Außenaggression wird nach innen hineingenommen, die Innenaggression nach außen exportiert. Kriegstechniken wie Plündern und Töten werden gegen Mitbürger eingesetzt. Beides geschieht in mörderischer Trance und ist von der angestrebten Rationalität weit entfernt.

Ilmar Tammelo hatte am IVR-Weltkongress in Mexiko einen Vortrag zum Thema 'Peace as a Dream and as More than a Dream' gehalten. Dieses Thema ist nach wie vor aktuell, wahrscheinlich ist es eng mit der *conditio humana* verbunden. Auch der Frieden ist ein Traum, so wie der Krieg ein Traum, ein Alptraum ist. Ebenso ist die Revolution in den meisten Fällen ebenfalls ein Alptraum und die Zahl der *lucida intervalla* im Sinne der erlangten kollektiven Rationalität und des herrschaftsfreien Diskurses sind kurz und instabil.

6 *Das Platonische Höhlengleichnis und das Träumen und Wachen der Herrschenden*

Im Nachhinein verklären die Herrschenden den Weg, der zur Macht geführt hat. Die Monumente mögen schön sein. Die Gebeine der Toten sind jedoch frei von Illusion, von kollektiver wie von individueller. Sie sind real da, nicht mehr und nicht weniger. Der Traum gibt nicht die Realität wieder, wenigstens nicht direkt. Diese Dissonanz von Traum und Realität ist es auch, was die Unruhe der Innenmaske der Macht ausmacht.

Die Wahrheit ist am ehesten in einem Herrschaftssystem dort angesiedelt, wo der kollektive Traum geschaffen wird und wo vielleicht noch das Wissen um die Realität vorhanden ist. An der Schwelle der Platonischen Höhle, wo sowohl die Schatten als auch die schattenwerfenden Gegenstände sichtbar sind. Bei den Kameras und bei den Schminktischen der Mediengesellschaft, wo die Schatten an den Fernsehschirmen ebenso wie die Schminke un erkennbar sind. Oder die ungeschminkte Realität.

Die Wahrheit ist in einem Herrschaftssystem aber auch dort zu Hause, wo die Menschen die Hoffnung verloren haben. Wo die kollektiven Illusionen nicht mehr Kleider der gemeinsamen Utopie sind, wo die Menschen das Es des Scheines nicht mehr ertragen sondern das Du ersehnen. Die fensterlosen Monaden werden auch durch die Wechsel des Gesellschaftskörpers nicht sehend.

Träumen die Herrschenden? Findet sich bei ihnen das Herrschaftswissen, das ihnen einerseits die Tiefe des Traumes der Massen und andererseits die Untiefen der Realität anzeigt?

Träumen die Herrschenden, so stellt sich die Frage, wer ihnen die Traummelodie spielt. Können sie auch daraus erwachen? Können die Herrschenden 'Revolution' machen?

Die Deutung der Träume der Herrschenden war stets ein Weg zur Macht. Träumem die Herrschenden nicht, so stellt sich die Frage 'Warum nicht?'. Stehen sie an der Schwelle der Platonischen Höhle und sehen sie Schatten wie Realität? Haben sie die Hoffnung verloren, wie die, die wach und illusionslos sind?

Unter welchen Bedingungen erfahren die Herrschenden ihr Herrschaftswissen? Odysseus hatte sich an den Mast binden lassen, um dem Gesang der Sirenen zu lauschen, den er den Matrosen nicht vergönnte. War es überhaupt ein Herrschaftswissen oder nicht vielmehr ein Metatraum, der ihm allein zuteil wurde?

7 *Revolution von oben*

Können die Herrschenden, sofern sie wach sind, überhaupt handeln? Können sie anders als durch die Änderung der Träume handeln? Läßt sich eine Revolution gewaltfrei durchführen? Kann eine Traummelodie von einer anderen abgelöst werden, ohne daß es zum Erwachen und ohne daß es zu Alpträumen kommt?

Dies ist ein Problem auch der Balance des Gesellschaftssystems. Eine Änderung läßt sich leichter durchführen, wenn es zu kontrollierten Verlagerungen kommt. Man geht mit zwei Füßen, indem man das Gewicht von einem Fuß auf den anderen verlagert.

In der französischen Revolution wurden neue Personifikationen geschaffen, nicht nur die verehrte 'Vernunft'. Auch 'Freiheit', 'Gleichheit' und 'Brüderlichkeit' sind solche kollektive Hypostasierungen, die die Außenseelen der Menschen in sich aufzunehmen und damit zu bannen vermögen. Auch heute werden die revolutionären Vorgänge, ob sie nun von oben oder von unten kommen, im Namen neuer Gottheiten durchgeführt, die den neuen Traummelodien ihren Namen geben.

Die kollektive Sinnproduktion ist eine dauernde Aufgabe, so wie das heilige Feuer zu hüten, das nicht erlöschen darf. Von Zeit zu Zeit müssen neue Statuen in das Pantheon aufgenommen werden, wenn der Herrschaftsbereich ausgeweitet oder stabilisiert wird. Die Verkörperungen, die hypostatischen Masken sind von Zeit zu Zeit zu erneuern, vor allem dann, wenn sie abgenutzt erscheinen.

Dennoch ist die Revolution von oben eine heikle Angelegenheit, vor allem weil die dialektischen Wirkungskräfte der Revolution viel zu wenig bekannt sind. Auch läßt sich mit Revolutionen nicht beliebig experimentieren, die Experimente sind nicht jederzeit wiederholbar.

8 Die kollektiven Alpträume

Kollektive Träume werden auch 'Prophetien', 'Utopien' und 'Visionen' genannt. Die 'Utopien' waren in den Sechzigerjahren modern, jetzt sind es die 'Visionen'. Ein guter Politiker, einer, der auf sich hält, hat 'Visionen'. Das gehört zum Berufsprofil hinzu. Das heißt, er soll kollektive Traummelodien vorgeben, spielen und mitspielen, 'Hüter der Träume' sein.

Ein anderes Kapitel sind die kollektiven Alpträume. Dazu gehören nicht nur die kollektiven Schreckensvisionen sondern auch die kleinen Alpträume, die Skandale.

Panem et circenses lautete eine römische Herrschaftsformel. Die Politikskandale von heute sind den Circusspielen von damals vergleichbar. Sie mobilisieren die kollektive Identifikation mit Gladiatoren, mit stellvertretenden Opfern, die—mehr oder weniger schuldlos—in ein widriges Schicksal verwickelt werden.

Das Schauspiel der Skandale und ihrer Aufdeckung gleicht der wirren Traumabfolge. Die Medienöffentlichkeit wird immer mehr zur Premierenbühne, wo in rascher Folge Erfolgsstücke, bei denen der Mißerfolg thematisiert wird, angesetzt werden. Die Masken und die Schauspieler sind großteils bekannt und wenn sie es nicht sind, so werden sie es ehestens. Stets neue Senatoren werden in den Circus gezerrt.

Die Skandale ändern den Stellenwert der Demokratie in Richtung Demagogie: Es geht nicht um die Kriminalität, die dort aufgedeckt wird, sondern um die geänderte Richtung der kollektiven Identifikation. Die Politiker, die noch nicht im Circus hingerichtet werden wollen, wissen das und richten ihr Verhalten danach aus und gerade dadurch entfernen sie sich von den realen Problemen.

Die realen Herausforderungen und die realen Lösungen treten zunehmend in den Hintergrund der kollektiven Anpassungsleistung. Man kann auch die Realität träumen und darin, dies zu vermitteln, läge ja die große Leistung der Herrschenden, eben die realen Traummelodien zu spielen: Wenn die geträumten Schatten der Wirklichkeit entsprechen, dann sind die Träume 'wahr'. Viel mehr läßt sich gar nicht erreichen, denn 'alles Vergängliche ist nur ein Gleichnis'.

Die Skandale hingegen führen zum Aggressions-Management, indem die kollektive Wut von den ungelösten realen Herausforderungen und den dafür Verantwortlichen auf Sündenböcke abgeleitet wird. Die Öffentlichkeit der vorgefundenen Kriminalität wird manipuliert. Den auf ihre Weise Schuldigen wird ein überproportionales Maß an öffentlicher Aufmerksamkeit zuteil. Der ganze Vorgang stabilisiert—vergleichbar den Witzen—zumindest vorübergehend das Herrschaftssystem, entspricht aber letztlich einem vorrevolutionären Stadium.

9 Der Traum im Traum

Es kommt zum 'Traum im Traum'. Die Realität tritt als bloß geträumte auf. In der Negation der Negation kommt die ursprüngliche These in gewandelter Gestalt wieder zum Vorschein. Die dialektische Negation hebt nicht völlig auf. Der dialektische Kopie-Effekt setzt sich durch. Es ereignet sich eine Umwälzung, eine 'Re-Volution'. Die tatsächliche Natur wird unter den verfremdeten Namen der 'Umwelt' (sprachlich mit 'Un-Welt' assoziiert) zum geträumten Traum von der Realität.

10 Schlüssel zur Selbsterkenntnis

Träume sind aber auch ein Weg zur Selbsterkenntnis. Ein besserer als die direkte Sicht der Dinge. Die Selbsterkenntnis ist über den Spiegel, über die Reflexion möglich. Die Träume maskieren die Realität und sind so ein Schlüssel zur Selbsterkenntnis, zur individuellen wie zur kollektiven. Die Erkenntnis ist beim Traum näher, als man fürs erste glaubt, nur durch die Maske getrennt. Es kommt darauf an, den Traum als Traum zu sehen und die Masken zu wenden. Auch dies ist dem Typus nach ein 'revolutionärer' Vorgang. Darin liegt eine Chance.

11 Die produzierten Träume

Keine Zeit verfügt über mehr Informationen als die jetzige. Die kollektiven Träume der heutigen Mediengesellschaft sind bereits Produkte. Sie sind Synthesen und Applikationen des Wissens um die Träume. Sie gleichen den Zeichentrickfilmen, die kompakter und damit prägender sind als andere Filme. Zeichentrickfilme sind nicht verbal kodifizierte Traditionsmärchen, sondern sie synthesieren und organisieren die Archetypen neu. In ihnen wird bereits das Wissen um die Träume genutzt.

Die Leier Amphions hat sich zum Bildschirm gewandelt, der ganze Vorgang ist rekonstruierbar und reproduzierbar.

Die religiösen Bereiche wurden zunächst beschworen, das Angesprochene war das Andere. Im Laufe der Entwicklung trat die Versuchung auf, das Angesprochene selbst zu produzieren. Im Zeichentrickfilm wird das Wunder reproduziert. Die Helden haben viele Leben und die Grenzen des Todes scheinen aufgehoben zu sein.

Zwei Fragen sind für die Produktion der Träume wichtig:

> Inwieweit entsprechen die kollektiven Träume den individuellen? Es ist dies die Frage nach der Demokratie, Zerbricht die Entsprechung, dann kommt es zur Revolution.

> Inwieweit stimmen die kollektiven Träume mit den realen Herausforderungen überein? Die Herrschenden repräsentieren nicht nur die Beherrschten sondern auch die zu lösenden Probleme.

12 Die Herrschaft der Schatten

An den Bildschirmen der Mediengesellschaft werden zunehmend die Verstorbenen auftreten, schon deshalb, weil der Anteil der alten Filme zunehmen wird. Die Medien werden so zu 'Medien' der Geisterbeschwörung. Die Toten unterhalten die Lebenden. Sie sind zwar nicht stumm, aber auch nicht ansprechbar. Die Zuseher merken nicht, daß sie von den Schatten der Toten unterhalten werden. Sie wissen meist gar nicht, ob der eine oder der andere im Medium Sichtbare bereits gestorben ist oder noch nicht. Sie träumen. Und solange sie nicht erwachen, gibt es auch keine Revolution.

CHAPTER 8

Rechtskontinuität oder diskontinuierliche Rechtsschöpfung in der proletarischen Revolution?

Andreas Gängel

Nein, wir sind keine Anarchisten, im Gegenteil, wir messen den Gesetzen eine große, zuweilen vielleicht eine übermäßige Bedeutung zu, aber nur den Gesetzen der neuen Gesellschaftsordnung, Und diese Gesetze entsprechen ebensoweit den alten Gesetzen, wie die neue Ordnung mit der gestürzten oder sterbenden Ordnung in Einklang gebracht werden kann (P I Stutschka).[1]

Abstract All revolutions break with existing law: social advancement goes hand in hand with a legal breach—but not necessarily with the end of law. Negation, modification and re-formation of the law are always the starting point for the production of the new. Hatred of the old and love of the new characterise the stormy process of advance and retreat at the beginning of every revolution. Continuity and discontinuity in the development of law thus necessarily dominate the transition from one type to another.
One of the common places of Marxist-Leninist theory is the postulate of the creation of a new socialist law when the bourgeois legal system is overcome in the proletarian revolution. This is seen as the essential consequence and specific expression of the most radical break to date with the property and power relations of the old order. But the socialist development of law must be understood as a process of interaction with the traditional legal order which is not in a total contradiction. The proletarian revolution is not to be understood as the incarnation of discontinuity, it is not an undifferentiated alternative to continuity in history. To put it more clearly: the development of socialist law is hardly possible without some link to the progressive inheritance, to enduring traditions, to a high bourgeois legal culture. The exploitation of the existing progressive potential of bourgeois law on the road to a socialist law which rests on its own social foundations thus defines the line of continuity in legal history.

Das Postulat der Schaffung eines neuen, sozialistischen Rechts und einer sozialistischen Gesetzlichkeit bei der Zerschlagung der bürgerlichen Gesetzlichkeit und des bürgerlichen Rechtssystems in der proletarischen Revolution gehört zu den Allgemeinplätzen der marxistisch-leninistischen Staats- und Rechtstheorie. Die Überwindung des bürgerlichen Rechts als essentielle Konsequenz und spezifischer Ausdruck des bisher radikalsten Bruchs mit den alten Eigentums- und Machtverhältnissen steht als Aufgabe für die Errichtung der Diktatur des Proletariats.[2] Hat von daher die gestellte Frage überhaupt eine Berechtigung, kann es eine Rechtsentwicklung im Sinne von Kontinuitäten in der historischen Phase eines bisher qualitativ nie dagewesenen Umbruchs von Formationen in einer Revolution[3] überhaupt geben?

Marx, Engels und Lenin haben nicht undifferenziert vom 'Zerbrechen des bürgerlichen Rechts' gesprochen, sondern davon, daß das Proletariat nach der Eroberung der politischen Macht, den alten Staatsapparat zu zerschlagen bzw. zu zerbrechen habe, die bürgerliche Gesetzlichkeit aufzuheben sei und es gelte, einen neuen sozialistischen Staatsapparat aufzubauen sowie ein eigenes Recht und eine eigene Gesetzlichkeit zu entwickeln. Wohl weniger als der alte Staatsapparat läßt sich das alte Recht mit einem Schlag beseitigen. Und dies nicht nur, weil schon eine sofortige und vollständige Außerkraftsetzung des alten Rechtssystems und seine Ersetzung durch ein neues in einem Zuge praktisch unmöglich ist, Revolution nicht mit oder nach der Fertigstellung neuer Gesetzbücher beginnen, sondern da das rechtliche Regelungsobjekt in der Revolution nicht von heute auf morgen ebensowenig ein völlig anderes wird, wie sich auch die Rechtssubjekte in dem erst beginnenden *Gesamtprozeß* der sozialen Umgestaltung allmählich verändern.

Jede Gesellschaft bringt bekanntlich ihr rechtliches Regelungsobjekt hervor, das sich mit der Entwicklung vor allem der materiellen gesellschaftlichen Verhältnisse qualitativ und quantitativ verändert. Gerät ein bestehendes Rechtssystem in einer Revolution unvermittelt unter ein neues politisches und in Folge unter ein anderes ökonomisches System, dann verändern sich der Kreis und das Niveau der rechtlichen Regelungsnotwendigkeiten weder sofort im Ganzen noch synchron. Es steht damit primär weniger die Frage nach Erweiterung oder Einengung des Regelungsobjekts zur Debatte als vielmehr die unmittelbare qualitative Neubestimmung, eine der neuen politischen Macht adäquaten Veränderung des bestehenden Regelungsgegenstandes entsprechend den politischen Grundsatzentscheidungen, seine unabdingbare Korrektur in wesentlichen i. S. von existentiellen Teilen des Rechtssystems. Dabei gibt es eine objektiv bestimmbare Hierarchie von Hauptregelungsnotwendigkeiten abgeleitet von einer Hierarchie der Hauptinteressen und dem Aspruch der neuen politischen Macht, den Lebensinteressen der Revolution.

Alle Revolutionen brechen das bestehende Recht: gesellschaftlicher Aufstieg geht mit Rechtsbruch—aber nicht mit dem Niedergang des Rechts— notwendig einher. Negation, Modifikation und Umbildung des alten Rechts sind stets der Ausgangspunkt einer orginär neuen Rechtsproduktion. Nihilismus gegenüber dem alten und Euphorismus hinsichtlich des Neuen kennzeichnen den stürmischen Prozeß von historisch-konkretem Vorwärts und Rückwärts am Beginn jeder Revolution. Kontinuität und Diskontinuität in der Rechtsentwicklung beherrschen zwangsläufig den Übergang von einem Rechtstyp zu einem anderen.[4] Auch die proletarische Revolution bedeutet nicht die radikale Verneinung des bisherigen Rechts, sie ist keine Inkarnation der Diskontinuität, keine undifferenzierte Alternative zur Kontinuität in der Geschichte. Ja, ohne ein Anknüpfen an das progressive Erbe, an bewahrenswerte Traditionen, an eine hohe bürgerliche Rechtskultur ist eine Entwicklung des sozialistischen Rechts überhaupt nicht möglich. Es ist daher stets historisch-konkret zu untersuchen, in welchen Bereichen und inwieweit das vorgefundene bürgerliche Recht über Fortschrittspotenzen verfügt, die auf dem Wege der Gestaltung eines sozialistischen Rechtssystems, das dann in seiner ausgeprägten Form vollständig auf eigenen, entwickelten sozialen Grundlagen beruht, nutzbar gemacht werden können.

Da das Niveau des Rechts bekanntlich nicht über dem der Ökonomie und damit letztlich über dem Kulturstand der Gesellschaft liegen kann, ist in der überaus schwierigen Phase der Schaffung des 'Fundaments einer wirklich sozialistischen Wirtschaft'[5] als der entscheidenden Basis für das sozialistische Recht das bürgerliche Recht, wie Lenin bezugnehmend auf Marx schreibt,

> nicht vollständig abgeschafft, sondern nur zum Teil, nur entsprechend der bereits erreichten ökonomischen Umwälzung, d. h. lediglich in bezug auf die Produktionsmittel. Das 'bürgerliche Recht' sieht in ihnen das Privateigentum einzelner Individuen. Der Sozialismus macht sie zum Gemeineigentum. Insofern—und nur insofern—fällt das 'bürgerliche Recht' fort.[6]

Die mit der Oktoberrevolution eingeleitete Epoche der proletarischen Revolution entwickelte sich als

> Zyklus von revolutionären Vorstößen, die demokratische und sozialistische Aufgaben in unterschiedlicher Phasenfolge und Kombination lösen und den Weg zum Sozialismus öffnen. Damit entsteht zugleich der für die Übergangsepoche vom Kapitalismus zum Sozialismus charakteristische Typ revolutionärer Prozesse, und damit zeigt sich deren progressives Maximum im Fortschreiten von der demokratischen zur sozialistischen Revolution bzw. in der Verknüpfung beider in einem einheitlichen revolutionären Prozeß mit unterschiedlichen Etappen und Zwischenlösungen.[7]

Zum zweijährigen Jubiläum der Sowjetmacht äußerte Lenin:

> Theoretisch unterliegt es keinem Zweifel, daß zwischen dem Kapitalismus und dem Kommunismus eine gewisse Übergangsperiode liegt, die unbedingt Merkmale oder Eigenschaften dieser beiden sozial-ökonomischen Formation in sich vereinen muß.[8]

Bezogen auf das Recht konstatierte er dazu an anderer Stelle:

In Wirklichkeit zeigt uns doch das Leben auf Schritt und Tritt, sowohl in der Natur als auch in der Gesellschaft, Überreste des Alten in Neuen. Und Marx hat nicht willkürlich ein Stückchen 'bürgerlichen' Rechts in den Kommunismus hineingebracht, sondern hat das genommen, was wirtschaftlich und politisch in einer *aus dem Schoß* des Kapitalismus hervorgehenden Gesellschaft unvermeidlich ist.[9]

Ergibt sich daraus eine 'gemischte Rechtsordnung'[10] bzw. das Nebeneinander-bestehen von zwei Rechtsordnungen oder geht es um absterbendes bürgerliches Recht[11] im Prozeß der Entwicklung von revolutionär proletarischem Recht, ein 'Sterbe- und Geburtsprozeß', der in differenzierter Weise den Rechtskörper betrifft?

Die Tatsache, daß die Menschen mit dem Erwerb neuer Produktivkräfte ihre sozialen Verhältnisse verändern und damit zwingend auch das Recht einem Wandel unterwerfen, gehört zu den Grundeinsichten des Marxismus-Leninismus. Von daher sind die rechtlichen Konsequenzen der politischen Umwälzung in der russischen Revolution letztlich nur über die ökonomische Lage, vor allem bezüglich des Standes der Wirtschaftsentwicklung, dem Niveau der Produktivkräfte und den Grad der Arbeitsproduktivität zu begreifen. Die Ideologen der II. Internationale hatten in dieser Frage Rußland objektiv fehlende ökonomische Voraussetzungen für den Übergang zum Sozialismus vorgeworfen, da insbesondere die Entwicklung der Produktivkräfte noch nicht die erforderliche Reife erreicht habe. In seiner letzten theoretischen Arbeit, dem Artikel 'Über unsere Revolution' (1923) erklärte Lenin die Rückständigkeit für unstrittig, entgegnete aber historisch optimistisch:

> Wenn zur Schaffung des Sozialismus ein bestimmtes Kulturniveau notwendig ist . . . warum sollten wir also nicht damit anfangen, auf revolutionärem Wege die Voraussetzungen für dieses bestimmte Niveau zu erringen, und dann schon, auf der Grundlage der Arbeiter-und Bauernmacht und der Sowjetordnung, vorwärtsschreiten und die anderen Völker einholen.[12]

Diese Umgestaltung der Produktionsweise nahm ihren Anfang in der zunächst politischen Veränderung der alten Eigentumsverhältnisse durch die formale Vergesellschaftung (Verstaatlichung) der Hauptproduktionsmittel, ihrer Besitzergreifung *im Namen* der ganzen Gesellschaft.[13] Dabei kann und konnte das Privateigentum nicht in einem einmaligen Akt abgeschafft werden, weil das neue gesellschaftliche Eigentum unvollkommen, entwicklungsbedürftig und -fähig auf die Welt kommen muß. Die vorherrschenden Eigentumsverhältnisse, als abstraktester Ausdruck der Produktionsverhält-nisse bestimmen zweifellos das Wesen von Staat und Recht im Sinne, um wessen Instrumente es sich handelt. Wie weit das Eigentum an den Produktionsmitteln real bestimmend für die Entwicklung der im Kern Produktions—und im weiteren gesamten sozialen Verhältnisse und damit auch für das Recht ist, hängt letztlich von seiner tatsächlichen Entfaltung ab, die in unmittelbarer Beziehung zum jeweiligen Entwicklungsstand der Produktivkräfte, insbesondere der Hauptproduktivkraft Mensch, steht.

Die besondere Schwierigkeit der russischen Revolution bestand im Vorfinden einer relativ rückständigen Gesellschaft und in dem Anspruch auf dieser Basis gegenüber einer am Entwicklungsstand der Produktivkräfte gemessen fortgeschritteneren Gesellschaft eine höhere gesellschaftliche Qualität in einem nicht nur friedlich verlaufenden Wettbewerb zu erreichen. Ein Anknüpfen an das alte nationale feudal-frühkapitalistische Rechtssystem war unter diesen Bedingungen wenig geeignet, das diskontinuierliche, revolutionäre Element in der Rechtsentwicklung mußte deutlich dominieren. Der Normenkörper des überlieferten Rechts und die vorrevolutionären richterlichen Entscheidungen gaben der neuen Entwicklung kaum Raum, der für eine sozialistische Rechtsgestaltung nutzbar gewesen wäre. Eine solche Kontinuität im Recht beim Übergang vom Kapitalismus zum Sozialismus ist erst dann besonders prägnant, wenn die Vorbereitung der alten auf die neue Gesellschaft durch ein hohes Entwicklungsniveau der Produktivkräfte und einen damit verbundenen hohen Vergesellschaftungsgrad erreicht worden ist. Denn folgt man Lenins These, daß der Sozialismus der *nächste* Schritt über das staatskapitalistische Monopol hinaus ist, oder, wie er sagt 'Sozialismus ist nichts anderes als staatskapitalistisches Monopol, das zum Nutzen des ganzen Volkes angewandt wird und dadurch aufgehört hat, kapitalistisches Monopol zu sein',[14] dann kann grundsätzlich auch das Recht diesen Schritt zum Nutzen des Volkes mitgehen.

Der überaus widersprüchliche Prozeß der Rechtsentwicklung in der Anfangsphase der Revolution, die Auseinandersetzung zwischen Altem und Neuem in Inhalt und Form des Rechts innerhalb und zwischen den schwer voneinander zu trennenden Rechtsbildungs- und Rechtsanwendungsorganen, vollzieht sich selbstredend nach keinem wissenschaftlichen Fahrplan. Er ist diskontinuierlich und illusionsbehaftet, von Fehlern, Irrtümern und Widersprüchen begleitet, aber es ist ein Prozeß, der in der Analyse— unabhängig von den konkret-nationalen Besonderheiten bei 'Überwindung und Erhalt', 'Diskontinuität und Kontinuität', 'Fortschritt und Tradition', 'revolutionärer Rechtsschöpfung' swoie 'Rechtsfortbildung'—eindeutige Zusammenhänge, eine Einheit in der Viefalt der Revolutionen als Ausdruck von Gesetzmäßigkeiten erkennen läßt. Da in allen Revolutionen der Kampf um die politische Macht geführt und entschieden wird, steht im Interesse des Sieges der Revolution zunächst die Forderung der Sicherung der politischen Macht durch die Zerschlagung sowohl des alten staatlichen Unterdrückungs- apparates wie auch der Außerkraftsetzung repressiven, diskriminierenden und inhumanen Normen des Rechts. Im Gegensatz zu allen vorausgegangenen Revolutionen hat die proletarische weder diesen Teil der Staatsmaschinerie noch jenen des Rechtssystems zu vervollkommnen.

Die ersten 'Schläge' gegen die bestehende Rechtsordnung in Sowjetrußland wurden gewissermaßen mit dem. 'Dekret über das Gericht' vom 22. November 1917 geführt und nicht durch radikale Rechtsaufhebungsdekrete.[15] Bekanntlich heißt es in Ziffer 5 dieses Dekretes, daß sich die Gerichte 'nur insofern von den Gesetzen der gestürzten Regierungen leiten zu lassen' haben, 'als diese nicht durch die Revolution aufgehoben wurden und nicht dem revolutionären Gewissen und dem revolutionären Rechtsbewußtsein widersprechen'. Im gleichen Sinne spricht sich das 'Dekret Nr. 2 über das Gericht' vom 15. Februar 1918 aus.[16] Durch Nichtanwendung starben auf diese Weise formal in Kraft gebliebene, Gesetze der Zarenzeit und Rechtsakte der Provisorischen Regierung zum Teil faktisch ab. Bis etwa zum Herbst 1918 wurde das vorrevolutionäre Recht bestenfalls als subsidäre Rechtsquelle angesehen.[17] Mit dem Dekret vom 30.10.1918 verbot man ein Jahr später die Anwendung früherer Gesetze generell. Im Jahre 1920 bestimmt das Dekret über das Volksgericht im § 22 folgendes:

> Bei der Entscheidung von Prozeßsachen hat das Volksgericht die Dekrete der Arbeiter- und Bauern-Regierung anzuwenden; falls ein zutreffendes Dekret fehlt, oder wenn ein solches Lücken aufweist, hat es das soziale Rechtsempfinden zur Richtschnur zu nehmen. Die Berufung auf die Gesetze der gestürzten Regierungen in Zivil- und Strafsachen ist verboten.

Damit wurde dem Gericht eine rechtsschöpferische Funktion ausdrücklich zugewiesen. Entsprechend schreibt Stutschka, der erste Volkskommissar für Justiz nach der Oktoberrevolution und spätere Präsident der Obersten Gerichts der RSFSR:

> Die proletarische Revolution verpflichtet zu schöpferischer Tätigkeit. Und darin besteht gerade die eigenartige Rolle der Gerichte in der proletarischen Revolution, daß sie die schöpferische Kraft beim Schaffen der neuen Rechtsordnung werden.[18]

Die große Rückständigkeit, der kleinbürgerliche Charakter Rußlands, erlaubten es der jungen Sowjetmacht kaum auf alten nationale Regelungen zurückzugreifen. Vorarbeiten und Erfahrungen fehlten fast völlig. Insofern finden wir für die Übergangsperiode in Sowjetrußland die Eigentümlichkeit einer weitgehenden Diskontinuität in der eigenen Rechtsentwicklung und ein Anknüpfen an das Recht in den fortgeschrittenen bürgerlichen Staaten durch 'Normenimport'. So sollen z. B. von den 435 Artikeln des ZGB der RSFR ca.400 Artikel nahezu wörtlich von bürgerlichen Zivilgesetzbüchern übernommen worden sein![19] Stutschka sah deshalb in dem Zivilgesetzbuch eine 'Rezeption des bürgerlichen Rechts des Westens in seiner reinen Form'.[20] Diesem Vorwurf hielt A G Goichbarg—Mitautor des ZGB—entgegen:

> Gleichlautende Artikel des sowjetischen und des bürgerlichen Zivilgesetzbuches sind unterschiedlicher Natur, weil sie zur Erreichung unterschiedlicher Klassenziele, in einer diametral unterschiedlichen sozialen Situation und von Gerichten angewandt werden, die prinzipiell unterschiedliche Positionen einnehmen.[21]

Paschukanis reflektierte die Entwicklung des ZGB mit folgenden Sätzen:

> Mit der neuen Wirtschaftspolitik kam die Notwendigkeit, ein sowjetisches Privatrecht aufzubauen. Das war eine der interessantesten Episoden in der Geschichte sowohl des Sowjetrechts wie auch der Geschichte der marxistischen

Rechtstheorie. Der erste Entwurf eines Zivilgesetzbuches wurde von einer Kommission der alten Juristen ausgearbeitet. Dieser Entwurf trug den Stempel einer Tendenz zur Wiederaufrichtung der kapitalistischen Rechtsordnung ... Dieser Entwurf wurde bei den weiteren Beratungen gar nicht mehr zugrundegelegt. In diesem neuen Entwurf finden wir einen unzweideutigen Hinweis auf die Unantastbarkeit der sozialistischen Eigentumsordnung (Nationalisierung des Grund und Bodens, der wichtigsten Produktions- und Transportmittel, das Außenhandelsstaatsmonopol usw.).[22]

Paschukanis sah das Sowjetrecht als grundverschieden vom bürgerlichen Rechtssystem an, vermerkte jedoch bzgl. der 'subjektiven Privatrechte', insbesondere zu Artikel 1 und 4 des ZGB der RSFSR:

> Merkwürdig ist, daß die theoretische Begründung dieser Bestimmungen aus dem Arsenal der westeuropäischen, bürgerlichen Juristen entnommen wurde, und zwar derjenigen bürgerlichen Juristen, die die sogenannte 'sozialwirtschaftliche Rechtsauffassung' vertraten.[23]

Die deutliche Anlehnung an fortgeschrittenen bürgerliche Zivilrechtssysteme geht nicht zuletzt auf den Politiker und Juristen Lenin zurück, hatte doch dieser im Vorfeld der Ausarbeitung des ZGB-Entwurfs in einem Brief Kurski diesen nachdrücklich aufgefordert 'alles, was es in der Literatur und Praxis der westeuropäischen Länder zum Schutz der Werktätigen gibt, unbedingt übernehmen.[24] Ganz im Gegensatz dazu stand scheinbar die Verabschiedung eines Strafgesetzbuches, das zu einer absoluten Neugestaltung auf diesem Rechtsgebiet führen sollte. Dazu vermerken ausdrücklich die 'Leitende(n) Grundsätzen des Strafrechts der RSFSR':

> Wie das Proletariat nicht in der Lage war, einfach die fertige bourgeoise Staatsmaschine seinen Zwecken anzupassen, sondern, weil es genötigt war, diese in Stücke zu schlagen und einen eigenen Staatsapparat zu schaffen, so konnte es für seine Zwecke auch die bourgeoisen Gesetzbücher der überlebten Epoche nicht anpassen, sondern es mußte sie dem Archiv der Geschichte übergeben.[25]

Dennoch sind selbst bei dieser Kodifikation Entwürfe des schwedischen StGB und Vorentwürfe des deutschen Strafgesetzbuches berücksichtigt worden. Aber auch die westeuropäische Jurisprudenz dürfte ihren Einfluß ausgeübt haben.

Grundsätzlich entscheidend für den Grad der Nutzbarmachung überlieferter rechtlicher Regelungssysteme im Verhältnis zur Neukodifizierung ist das Ausgangsniveau der betreffenden Gesellschafts- und Rechtsordnungen.

Begreift man den Kapitalismus als Vorbereitung auf sozialistische Gesellschaftsverhältnisse, dann ist ein Anknüpfen an das alte Rechtssystem verständlicherweise dort um so leichter, je weiter fortgeschritten sich die sozialen Verhältnisse (Kulturniveau) und damit das Rechtssystem darstellen.

Das Recht der sozialistischen Gesellschaft muß zweifelsfrei eine Eigenschöpfung dieser Gesellschaft sein, für die aber das Erbe des bürgerlichen

Rechts unter den beschriebenen Umständen in bestimmten Teilen nützlich bzw. unverzichtbar ist. E Buchholz und K A Mollnau schreiben daher in diesem Zusammenhang völlig zutreffend:

> Die Schaffung des sozialistischen Rechts in der DDR erfolgte auf dem Hintergrund tief eingefahrener bürgerlicher Rechtstraditionen, einer hochentwickelten Rechtskultur und eines differenzierten rechtswissenschaftlichen Erbes. Die kritische politische, ideologische und wissenschaftliche Auseinandersetzung mit diesen Gegebenheiten war eine Vorbedingung der Schaffung sozialistischen Rechts in der DDR sowie eine sie begleitende Aufgabenstellung, die bis heute nicht vollständig abgegolten ist.[26]

Da zwischen dem Zustand einer Gesellschaft und ihrer Rechtsbildung kausalgesetzmäßige Beziehungen existieren, kann das Recht in der Übergangsgesellschaft vom Kapitalismus zum Sozialismus nur ein Recht des Übergangs, ein frühsozialistisches Recht sein. Es ist in seinem Wesen, den Grundinhalten und seinen Zielstellungen nach sozialistisches Recht auf niedrigstem und keineswegs einheitlichem Niveau, das den Fundamentalinteressen der Arbeiterklasse und aller Werktätigen zu entsprechen hat. Dieses neue Rechtssystem ist ein embryonal sozialistisches, mit bürgerlichen Elementen behaftetes, das sich auf dem Wege zur Entwicklung seiner eigenen Homogenität befindet, um dann in einem langen Prozeß Klassizität auszuprägen. Es ist der Weg einer Emanzipation vom bürgerlichen Recht zur Ausprägung seiner ureigenen Identität. Die Muttermale der alten Gesellschaft, die auch das Rechtssystem zeichnen, verblassen allmählich, bis sie mit Abschluß der Schaffung der gesellschaftlichen Grundlagen des Sozialismus—nach der tatsächlichen Vergesellschaftung des Eigentums an den entscheidenden Produktionsmitteln im Anschluß an ihre Verstaatlichung—verschwinden. Die aus dem Kapitalismus stammenden Elemente des Rechts werden durch ihre Einordnung in den Gesamtrahmen der sozialistischen Gesellschaft und ihres Rechtssystems insoweit qualitativ umgestaltet und umfunktioniert, insoweit sie der gesellschaftlichen Entwicklung dienlich sein können. Dabei kommt der 'Politik des proletarischen Gerichts',[27] seiner korrektiven und innovativen Recht-Sprechung eine zentrale Bedeutung zu.

Die Ergebnisse der ersten zehn Jahre der sowjetrussischen Rechtsentwicklung reflektierte seinerzeit Heinrich Freund, der nichtkommunistische deutsche Rechtsanwalt und als Ostrechtsforscher profunder Kenner des Sowjetrechts, verbunden mit einer Hoffnung, die Ausdruck einer Haltung zur Sowjetunion war und damit zugleich eine Gegenströmung von Antikommunismus im Lager der bürgerlichen Politik, Wissenschaft und Wirtschaft repräsentierte, folgendermaßen:

> Aus der Erkenntnis der Mängel des Bestehenden erwächst eine bessere Zukunft. Möge das Bestreben der Sowjetregierung, auf dem Wege der revolutionären Gesetzlichkeit Tag für Tag bessernd fortzuschreiten, von Erfolg begleitet werden zum Heil des russischen Volkes.

Vieles, was unsere bürgerliche Welt der Menschheit an Rechtsgedanken gegeben hat, ist auch in das neue Sowjetrecht übergegangen. Einiges Neue, was drüben geschaffen worden ist, wird, daran ist nicht zu zweifeln, auch in der bürgerlichen Welt Beachtung und Verwendung finden.[28]

ANMERKUNGEN

1   P I Stutschka, 'Die proletarische Revolution und die Gerichte, in: *Die Internationale*, Heft 11/12 (1919) S. 238.
2   Vgl. *Marxist-leninistische allgemeine Theorie des Staates und des Rechts*, Bd. 4 (Berlin, 1976) S. 45 f.
3   Unter sozialer Revolution soll nachfolgend die Einheit von politischer Umwälzung (der Machtwechsel—Revolution im engeren Sinne) und sozial-ökonomischer Umwälzung (die vollständige Umgestaltung der Produktionsverhältnisse der Gesellschaft—Revolution im weiteren Sinne) verstanden werden. Vgl. E Kalbe, J Kuhlers, 'Methodologische Fragen der historischen Analyse des sozialistischen Revolutionszyklus', in: *Vergleichende Revolutionsgeschichte—Probleme der Theorie und Methode*, M Kossok, Hrsg (Berlin, 1988) S. 115.
4   'Ist doch die sozialistische Revolution per definitionem der radikale Bruch mit allen überlieferten Eigentumsverhältnissen und ihren Ideen. Aber es ist eben ein Mißverständnis, Revolution und Diskontinuität als Alternativen zu Kontinuität, Erbe und Tradition schlechthin auffassen zu wollen. Jede Revolution—auch die sozialistische—hat ihre materiellen und ideellen Voraussetzungen, die in sie und in ihre Zukunft hineinwirken' (K A Mollnau, 'Rechtsfortschritt und Rechtstradition', in: *Gesetzgebung und Rechtskultur*, H Schäffer, Hrsg (Wien, 1987) S. 40).
5   W I Lenin, 'Neue Zeiten, alte Fehler in neuer Gestalt', in *Werke*, Bd. 33 (Berlin, 1963) S. 9.
6   W I Lenin, 'Staat und Revolution', in *Werke*, Bd. 25 (Berlin, 1981) S. 481.
7   W Küttler, 'Bürgerliche Revolutionen in der Epoche des Imperialismus', in *Revolutionen der Neuzeit 1500–1917*, M Kossok, Hrsg (Berlin, 1982) S. 420. Paschukanis äußert in diesem Zusammenhang in seinem Beitrag 'Probleme des Sowjetrechts': 'Wir müssen dabei jedoch folgendes ins Auge fassen. Die Oktoberrevolution hat in mancher Beziehung Aufgaben gelöst, die eigentlich noch im Bereiche einer bürgerlich-demokratischen Revolution liegen.' In: *Das neue Rußland*, Heft 1/2 (1930) S. 38.
8   W I Lenin, 'Ökonomik und Politik in der Epoche der Diktatur des Proletariats', in *Werke*, Bd. 30 (Berlin, 1979) S. 91.
9   W I Lenin, 'Staat und Revolution', in *Werke*, Bd. 25 (Berlin, 1981) S. 486.
10   Vgl. z. B. A K Stalgewitsch, *Programm der allgemeinen Rechtstheorie* (Moskau, 1929) (russ.) sowie M A Reisner, *Recht, Unser Recht, Fremdes Recht, Allgemeines Recht* (Moskau, 1925) (russ.) S. 184.
11   So vor allem E B Paschukanis, der an eine nur kurze Übergangsperiode glaubte, in der das Recht als Übergangsrecht nur bürgerliches Recht sein könne. Vgl. ders., *Allgemeine Rechtslehre und Marxismus* (Wien/Berlin, 1929). Neuauflage Frankfurt/M. (1966) S. 16 und 142.
12   W I Lenin, 'Über unsere Revolution', in *Werke*, Bd. 33 (Berlin, 1963) S. 464 f.
13   So W I Lenin, 'Staat und Revolution', a.a.O., S. 409.

14   W I Lenin, 'Die drohende Katastrophe und wie man sie bekämpfen soll', in *Werke*, Bd. 25 (Berlin, 1981) S. 369.

15   Zu den Ausnahmen zählt z. B. das am 27 April 1918 erlassene Dekret 'Über die Aufhebung des Erbrechts'. Stutschka schrieb, daß die Sowjetmacht '. . . natürlich keinen Tag frühere Gesetze *voll* in Geltung belassen (konnte)'. (Unterstreichung der Verf.) P I Stutschka, *Die revolutionäre Rolle von Recht und Staat* (Frankfurt a. M., 1969) S. 137.

16   Darin heißt es in Ziffer 36: 'In Zivil- und Strafsachen hat das Gericht die jetzt geltenden Gesetze nur insoweit anzuwenden, als sie durch Dekrete des Zentralen Exekutivkomitees und des Rates der Volkskommissare nicht aufgehoben sind und mit dem sozialistischen Rechtsbewußtsein in Widerspruch stehen. Ohne sich auf das formale Gesetz zu beschränken und sich stets von Erwägungen der Gerechtigkeit leiten lassen . . .' Es existiert noch ein Dekret über das Gericht vom 13 Juli 1918, das die ersten beiden 'entwickelt und ergänzt', jedoch in Ziffer 3 weiterhin auf die Anwendung der Dekrete der Arbeiter- und Bauernregierung 'vom sozialistischen Gewissen geleitet', verweist.

17   So bestimmt z. B. Ziffer 8 des Dekretes vom 15.09.1918, daß im Zivil- und Strafprozessen das Verfahren nach der Gerichtsordnung von 1864 durchzuführen sei, soweit diese Regelungen nicht durch Dekrete aufgehoben sind bzw. dem Rechtsbewußtsein der revolutionären Masse widersprechen.

18   P I Stutschka, 'Die proletarische Revolution und die Gerichte', a.a.O., S. 238.

19   Vgl. die Berechnungen F I Wolfson, *Chosjaistwennoje prawo* (Moskau, 1927) S. 5. Lenin schrieb an Molotow in diesem Zusammenhang: 'Keine sklavische Nachahmung des kapitalistischen Zivilrechts, sondern eine Reihe von Beschränkungen im Geiste unserer Gesetze, ohne die wirtschaftliche Tätigkeit oder den Handel einzuengen', veröffentlicht in *Bolschewik* (1937) Nr. 2, S. 62.

20   P I Stutschka, *Kurs sowjetskowo grashdanskowo prawa* (Moskau, 1927) Bd. 1, S. 30.

21   A I Goichbarg, *Chosjaistwennoje prawo* (Moskau, 1924) S. 268.

22   E B Paschukanis, 'Probleme des Sowjetrechts', a.a.O., S. 39 f.

23   Ebenda, S. 40. Gemeint sind an dieser Stelle der französische Rechtswissenschaftler Dugnit und Hedemann in Deutschland.

24   W I Lenin, 'Brief an D I Kurski', in *Werke*, Bd. 33 (Berlin, 1963) S. 187.

25   Verordnung des Volkskommissariats für Justiz. Gesetzessammlung 1919, Nr. 66, Art. 590, abgedruckt bei H Freund, *Strafgesetzbuch, Gerichtsverfassungsgesetz und Strafprozeßordnung Sowjetrußlands* (Mannheim/Berlin/Leipzig, 1925) S. 89; A A Gerzenson, 'Aus der Geschichte der Schaffung des ersten sowjetischen Strafgesetzbuches', in: *Staat und Recht*, Heft 6 (1967) S. 974. ff.

26   E Bucholz/ K A Mollnau, 'Rechtssicherheit gehört zur Lebensqualität in unserer Gesellschaft' in: Neues Deutschland vom 18/19 Juni 1988 S. 11.

27   Vgl. dazu u. a. P A Lebedew, 'Grashdanski Kodex i gossudarstwennoje chosjaistwo' in: *Westnik Werchownowo Suda' SSSR*, Heft 2 (1927) S. 13, 16.

28   H Freund, 'Zehn Jahre Zivilrecht in der Sowjetunion', in *Das neue Rußland*, Heft 9/10 (1927) S. 62.

QUO VADIS 'RECHT'-(S)-'STAAT'?

Nachträgliches aus der DDR (Dezember 1989)

Die Geschichte steht nicht still.

Wenige Wochen nach dem Weltkongeß in Edinburg erlebt die DDR eine Revolution, die so vorauszusagen keiner wagte und von der heute niemand ihren Ausgang zu bestimmen vermag. Und wieder steht die Frage nach Kontinuität und Diskontinuität für die Gesellschaftsentwicklung im allgemeinen und für die Entwicklung des Rechts im speziellen in zugespitzer Weise auf der Tagesordnung. Die Geschichte ist offen, und es hängt vom Volk dieses Landes ab, welcher Weg eingeschlagen wird, ob ein demokratischer Sozialismus gestaltet werden soll oder ein bürgerlich-demokratischer Kapitalismus wiederentsteht. Es ist ein Prozeß im Gange, der aber nicht allein durch die Wahrnehmung des Selbstbestimmungsrechts in der DDR entschieden werden wird, sondern in starkem Maße durch Wirtschaftsund Bevölkerungsinteressen der BRD sowie darüber hinausgehende internationale Interessen (mit-?!) bestimmt ist. Welche Kontinuitätslinien in der weiteren Rechtsentwicklung gezogen werden, wo Brüche stattfinden, ist von der weiteren politischen Entwicklung abhängig.

Bei der Neugestaltung der Rechtsordnung innerhalb der nächsten Monate—uber vierzig Rechtsvorschriften befinden sich derzeit in der Über- bzw. Ausarbeitung—wird diese Frage sukzessive beantwortet werden. In diesem Erneuerungsprozeß der Justiz- und Rechtsordnung kommt der Verabschiedung einer neuen Verfassung naturgemäß die zentrale Bedeutung zu. Sie wird die Eckpfeiler für eine Gesellschafts- Rechtsentwicklung im Spannungsfeld von Kontinuität und Diskontinuität setzen. Ohne Zweifel verlangt die revolutionäre Veränderung der Gesellschaft auch eine entsprechende Dominanz der Diskontinuität in der Rechtsentwicklung. Doch diese kann im Abweichen von der bisherigen Kontinuitätslinie nach oben oder unten erfolgen, sie kann langfristig zu Rück-oder Fortschritt führen.

Die konkrete Ausgestaltung der Justiz- und Rechtsordnung in der DDR ist davon abhängig, welche Widersprüche unsere Gesellschaft heute produziert und morgen produzieren wird und welche Potenzen der Konfliktregulierung und -beilegung wirklich vorhanden sind. Der Zuschnitt des Rechtsstaates hängt insofern von der Entwicklung des gesellschaftlichen Körpers ab, von den sozialen Beziehungen, die ihn real gestalten, daß heißt ihn wachsen oder verkümmern lassen.

Genaue Voraussagen über die weitere 'Recht'-(s)-'Staat'-Entwicklung in der DDR gehören im Moment in das Reich der Spekulationen. Aber ganz gleich in welcher Richtung die Demokratisierung der Gesellschaft verläuft— eine deutliche Betonung der Kontinuität zur bürgerlich-demokratischer Rechtsstaatsentwicklung, ein Aufheben ihrer Errungenschaften wird unverzichtbar sein. Das bedeutet zugleich einen Bruch mit jeglichen rechtsnihilistischen Tendenzen in Theorie und Praxis. Inwieweit und an welche progressive Rechtsforderungen und Traditionen der nationalen und internationalen Arbeiterbewegung jedech angeknüpft werden kann, muß hingegen die Zukunft zeigen.

Noch ist das rechtliche Regelungsobjekt zu bewegt, sind vor allim die politischen Konturen zu unscharf, um ein klares Abbild als Grundlage für theoretische Verallgemeinerungen und Prognosen zu bekommen. Die Wissenschaft ist aufgerufen, durch eine kritische Bestandsaufnahme in Theorie und Praxis sowie mittels gezielter rechtssoziologischer Untersuchungen sowohl zum Fortschritt der eigenen Disziplin wie zur Entwicklung dieses Landes beizutragen. Dies ist eine Aufgabe für die nicht lediglich ein internationales Interesse bestehen dürfte, sondern die auch eine internationale Zusammenarbeit herausfordert.

CHAPTER 9

Innovation and Tradition Against the Background of Revolutionary Changes of Law—A Conceptual and Functional Analysis

Maria Borucka-Arctowa

Stability versus change is, by some authors, presented as one of the 'principal antinomies' in legal thinking (Friedmann, 1947, p 10). Is this a fully justified view when one considers that our concern is a notional and functional analysis of innovation and tradition? These phenomena are closely linked with change and stability in law and they are particularly important not only as regards their historical connection with the Great Revolutions of the seventeenth and eighteenth centuries but also in relation to modern times.

The aim of this paper is to show how innovation and tradition are indispensable elements of the process of formation and development of law. It attempts to depart from the extreme trends in the theory and philosophy of law which see the function of law exclusively as a stabilising factor, preserving existing relations and limiting the legislator's role to 'finding the law'. It is also a departure from the extreme instrumentalism that sees the law as a means of attaining current state goals and as a means of introducing new rules and institutions which differ from the 'cultural heritage' and values deeply rooted in society.

In order to continue our considerations we must provide a more precise definition of the concepts and the correponding phenomena, especially as their meaning is far from unequivocal. Innovation is a special kind of social change. The element of novelty is a constitutive feature of the notion of innovation whereas a change may mean a return to the solutions already applied; innovation must be introduced consciously and intentionally and it is often linked with directed and planned change whereas social change may have a spontaneous character. Innovation is linked with 'jumps forward' rather than evolution, hence its connection with rapid change.

The above characteristics of innovation distinguish it from reform which is also a consciously and intentionally introduced change. However, the Latin word *reformare* means to transform an already existing thing. Reformers do not intend to create anything new, although an accumulation of reforms might have an innovative effect. Reforming is a combination of decisions and actions to remove bad qualities and introduce some good ones according to the adopted scale of values (Lamentowicz, 1987, p 10). Unlike innovation, it is not an entry into a new field of social activity or the creation of new kinds of services, obligations and rights (Hall, Land, Parker, Webb, 1976, p 19). The concept of reform is associated with evolutionary changes which are introduced gradually, unlike revolutionary ones. Innovation, on the other hand, might be associated with revolution, but is not necessarily so.

The problem of innovation is at the centre of attention of contemporary social sciences. This concerns both studies related to some definite problems, especially those connected with technical progress, and to works showing greater theoretical ambitions. The theory of innovation, the process by which and the conditions under which men devise new additions to their culture, has, as R T La Pierre (1953, V) wrote, been neglected by social scientists. The problem of innovation diffusion and adoption is a subject of particular interest. Therefore studies should concern conditions which favour and obstruct innovation and persons who are ready to accept or reject new ideas, solutions and behaviour patterns.

The notion of innovation as such does not seem to arouse any serious doubts among the representatives of the social sciences. For example, E M Rogers (1962, p 13), defines innovation as '. . . an idea perceived as new by the individual'. H G Barnett (1953, p 7) determines it as follows: '. . . in defining an innovation that is qualitatively new, emphasis is placed upon re-organization rather than quantitative variations as the criterion of novelty'. The element of novelty is, consequently, a constitutive feature of all the proposed notions of innovation. Though novelty means something that was not existing before, no innovation is born in a cultural vacuum. Thus the notion of 'novelty' may present some difficulties which are not, it seems, fully perceived by authors who aim at building a theory of innovation.

The development of modern societies as well as legal systems demonstrates the growing importance of innovation. The innovation-through-the-law model draws on the concepts of innovation in social sciences. Likewise, while adding new elements to this concept, the model tries to adapt them to the investigation of the process of diffusion, acceptance or rejection of innovative law provisions (Borucka-Arctowa, 1973, pp 17 ff).

In this approach the process of forming innovation through law is viewed in terms of different social roles characteristic of the successive innovation stages. There are the roles of the persons acting in the capacity of initiators of innovation, the advocates of innovation (often called agents of innovation), and the receivers of innovation, i.e. its potential users and adopters. To the model of innovation through law we must add the role of official controllers and executors of innovation.

An innovation in law may consist of the introduction of a norm that regulates completely new behaviour within the culture of a society (e.g., regulations controlling the admissibility of live human organ transplants). Innovation may, however, represent a certain *novum* against the background of the legal system by granting the character of legal norms to norms functioning within other normative systems. Innovation may also consist in introducing a legal norm intended to suppress the hitherto existing customs, e.g., abolition of castes or polygamy.

Innovation may also create new organisations and institutions, the forms of action and organisational structure of which differ from those hitherto accepted in the given system of law. They may also significantly affect the course of proceedings and bring about a change in the citizen's status.

The operation of law upon definite spheres of social relations and behaviour, as well as its elimination and the transfer of its operation to other social norms and institutions, often provoke vital social consequences. This is a problem closely connected with the widely discussed question of the limits of law and the proper scope of legal regulation (Borucka-Arctowa, 1986, pp 129-37).

The concept of innovation I present is a description which has an axio-logically neutral character. Nevertheless, I realise that the assumption of neutrality is one that can hardly ever be fully accepted since some factors, such as some preferences in the presentation of problems, the vagueness of some characteristics (e.g., the criterion of novelty) might be treated more or less consciously in an axiological way. The adoption of a specific concept or innovation determines the selection of the analysed phenomena and this affects the relations between innovation and other phenomena.

The very analysis of the concept of innovation makes one consider its relation to the existing 'cultural heritage' and the extent of the conditioning of the emergence of innovation, its diffusion and adoption by the legal tradition of the milieu wherein it takes place.

When one considers the relation between innovation and tradition in the legal field, one has to think, first of all, of legal tradition and also of general tradition since the latter often has a significant effect on the course of innovation.

The term 'tradition' has not so far been precisely defined J Szacki (1971, pp 97-8) distinguishes three concepts of tradition to be found in the literature. The first is connected with the activity of the transmission of elements of a community's culture from one generation to another. The second, defined as objective tradition, concerns the object transmitted, called the 'social heritage'. The third, defined as subjective, refers to a generation's attitude to the past and the acceptance or rejection of the heritage.

In a society where significant and rapid changes are introduced by means of law and the majority of them have the character of innovation, the problem of the place of tradition in legal consciousness, i.e., tradition in subjective terms according to Szacki, requires special attention. Tradition is of interest to us as an attitude to connections with the past or, more precisely, as an attitude to legal norms and institutions that derive from the past. It can be expressed as a total acceptance of the social heritage in the field of law. This is because of the very fact of the 'pastness' by which one accepts as values the historical experience, continuity, stability and the sense of the reliability of law. It can manifest itself as proclaiming a disregard and sometimes even denial and disdain of the achievements of the past epoch (so called 'negaitve tradition', an attitude typical of the early and radical stages of revolutions). The third attitude is that of regarding the links with the past as an existing fact, the importance of which should be appreciated because of the continuity of the legal tradition. But a positive evaluation of some of the links requires additional axiological justification, not only referral to the 'pastness' of the norms and institutions. This attitude is related to the concept of 'progressive traditions' that is strongly stressed in the system of value of a socialist society. It ought to be noted that the content of these traditions undergoes some changes and is connected with both ideological and systemic transformations of these societies.

An attitude of openness to change, a readiness to accept innovation that is introduced by the legislator, must allow a critical appraisal of some past solutions and departure from them for the sake of new values.

Law is deeply rooted in tradition because of a number of factors. These have been discussed at length by M Krygier (1986, 1988). The thesis he puts forward is not only that law contains tradition (this would be a banal statement), but also that legal systems should be interpreted as traditions, albeit highly complex ones (Krygier, 1988, p 20).

Rather than argue against such an extreme view, I want merely to refer to the three characteristic features of tradition he mentions which also apply to law. The first is pastness, the second is authoritative presence—its traditionality consists in its present authority and significance for the lives, thoughts or activities of the participants in the tradition, the third is that it must have been passed down over intervening generations (Krygier, 1986, p 240). Krygier then continues:

> . . . Legal traditions provide substance, models, exemplars and a language in which to speak about law. Participation in such a tradition involves the sharing of a way of speaking about the world which, like language, shapes, forms and, in part, envelopes the thought of those who speak it and think through it (Krygier, 1986, p 244).

Therefore change is not independent of tradition. Language, legal rules and practice determine traditional ways of interpretation and application of new rules of an innovative character. Tradition can thus affect the process of diffusion and adoption of innovation. It can tone down and modify through interpretation and, in extreme cases of the discrepancy between tradition and innovation, can cause the failure of innovation. On the other hand, innovation can provoke some transformations and changes in the existing tradition and thus become a factor in the modification of traditional norms. This is especially true of creative innovation, the disclosure of the hitherto unperceived gaps in the received tradition and efforts to fill them in by means of far-reaching modifications in the whole system (Shils, 1971). It also applies to innovation as a response to the new needs and demands connected with political, cultural or scientific-technical revolutions.

As we have already stated, revolutionary changes in various fields of social life in general and law in particular are usually linked with innovation and departure from tradition. Is this view fully justified? What are the relations between innovation and tradition during periods of rapid changes and their immediate aftermath in the political system? What is the relationship during periods of relative stability in the political system? Do revolutionary changes have to be combined exclusively with rapid political transformations that lead to the complete severance of ties with the institutional framework of the system?

Let us answer the latter question first by presenting briefly some modifications of the concept of revolution (Baszkiewicz, 1981, pp 5–18).

Copernicus' treaty is called *De revolutionibus orbium coelestium*. In astronomers' language, the term revolution meant the quiet, cyclical and repetitive movements of heavenly bodies. Violent political changes were known and analysed by ancient authors. The Greeks used the expression 'statis', 'metabole ton politeion'; the Romans spoke of 'commutatio rei publicae'. It was only the Italian Renaissance authors who started to apply the term revolutions to the constant revolts and *coups d'état* of the time. The cyclical character of political changes might have reminded them of the cyclical movement of planets.

A more general outlook on revolution was shaped much later. For the naturalists of the eighteenth century, the history of the earth was made up of successive eras divided by 'revolutions'—great disasters that created new states of balance, i.e., total changes. The philosophers of the Enlightenment wrote about a great and thorough mental change 'revolution des esprits'. Voltaire and Rousseau interpreted revolution in terms of great breakthroughs in civilisation.

Some analyses of politial revolution also appeared. And yet, the English Revolution was referred to as the Great Rebellion or Civil War by its contemporaries while the term revolution was applied to the removal of James II in 1688. The 'Glorious Revolution' was bloodless and it stabilised the system after a long period of turmoil. The French Revolution introduced the idea of revolution as a total change and the writers of the epoch produced careful analyses of its causes and mechanisms.

The early bourgeois revolutions (in England and the Netherlands) were not, at their initial stages, devoid of conservative and traditional elements. They were directed against the authority that violated the good old traditional order. Revolution thus assumed a defensive and conservative character. The programmes formed by the owners' class were not in total rejection of the former society. Besides these moderate reform programmes, some expressions of the discriminated classes appeared, as expressed in the ideology of the levellers (radical representatives of the lower middle class) and the diggers (the movement of the poor from the towns and villages). They reverted to the idealised past of the 'return to the sources'. For the levellers this meant free ownership of land and for the diggers it was common ownership of land. This harking back to the past meant, as a rule, a utopian criticism of the present, destruction of the sinful social institutions and a promise of regaining the paradise lost (Borucka-Arctowa, 1957, pp 45–79; Baszkiewicz, 1981, p 210).

In the English Revolution, the parliamentary opposition was led by excellent lawyers who turned it into a great trial of law, a defence of the good old Common Law. They referred to the inviolable rules of the Magna Carta and did not wish for any innovation. However, on the threshold of the civil war, the new standpoint that the parliament as a superior authority and source of law might freely form the institutions and laws of the country paved the way for revolutionary innovations (Baszkiewicz, 1981, p 212).

In those early bourgeois revolutions, historical arguments tinted with conservatism were mixed with legal-naturalist, prospective and universal ones. The burden of attachment to traditional institutions, uncertainty as to the possibilities of the creative shaping of social reality left little room for innovation.

The mature bourgeois revolutions that followed gave up the idea of the 'return to the sources'. After the war with the English had broken out, America severed the ties with history. It was to be a truly New World, free of bad tradition and the 'baggage' of history. Thomas Paine defined the state of consciousness as a deeply-rooted conviction that we are able to start the world anew.

The French Revolution aimed at totally restructuring the society. From the very beginning, there were two clashing points of view: the first, moderate one was that realised by the Constituent Assembly proclaiming the need for the adjustment of old institutions to the revolution and the maintenance of a '*juste milieu*'. The other one, represented by the revolutionary left, advocated global change and disruption of continuity. The followers of Robespierre and the *sans-culottes* rejected the system created by the Constituent Assembly. They thought that the Republic was to introduce not only a new kind of government but also a new system of social relations, a realisation of the idea of equality and a propagation of new culture and manners. The downfall of the Jacobins' dictatorship and the failure of Babeuf's extreme concepts shattered the revolutionaries' hopes of completely transforming the society.

> The problem not only lies in the fact that after the victory of the new, the old cannot be abolished immediately, as the advocates of 'total' change soon realize, but also in the fact that the revolutionary 'rejection' of the old is always linked with the adoption of the live and stable elements of the old system. Because of the 'total' programme, the heritage can suffer some loss, however temporary it might be. And yet, confronted with the vitality of the old, the programme is usually defeated and modified (Baszkiewicz, 1981, p 220).

In my opinion, however, the problem ought to be taken up in relation to the changes of law in the states of the so-called 'socialist bloc', changes which were interpreted as revolutionary. I shall concentrate on the question of the extent to which the legal system that was introduced was able to reject the legal tradition and the European roots of legal culture. I shall consider especially the example of the Polish legal system. I shall also look at the general tendency of legislative policy and the lack of success in the economic field. The discrepancy between the planned economic aims and their implementation was one of the reasons which contributed to the general crisis of the whole system and to the fundamental changes of the political and economic structure that occurred first in Poland in 1989, then in Hungary and then in the other socialist countries of Eastern Europe.

It is noteworthy that the legislative activity of these countries, especially in the early stages of the new system, was characterised by faith in the power of law as a factor capable of transforming social relations, including economic ones. This view certainly differs from the Marxist concept of the socio-economic dependence of law.

Conviction as to the great power of law leads to the stressing of its organisational and innovative function. It is only after a period of some experience and disappointment that one begins to see problems connected with its implementation efficiency. More and more often law is said to create only some conditions for economic changes which, however, depend on many other factors and 'cannot be used as substitutive means to make up for the lack of other institutions' (Kulcsar, 1987, p 64, pp 124–5).

Another characteristic feature of all these legal systems is the huge growth of the number of legal norms. In the first period, they were linked with new economic, social and political changes but later on the increasing number of new regulations was linked, rather, with the correction of earlier economic-political stages. The 'momentary' instrumental nature of these legal norms, created quickly and without consideration, deprives them of a significant feature, stability (Kulcsar, 1987, pp 89, 90).

Penetration of some elements of legal tradition (both in terms of the achievements of the whole civilisation and of specific legal systems) as well as some elements of modern foreign law is characteristic of all the legal systems of socialist countries (although there is some difference as to the extent: Rot, 1984, pp 7–9).

The first Soviet codes were clearly based on western patterns and the civil code was quite close to the Russian civil code of 1913 (Gsovski, 1948, II, pp 24–6; Hazard, 1953, p 132). This has been stated not only by western lawyers but also by Soviet jurists who notice the influence of the Russian tradition and western legal culture and justify it by saying that 'communists are legitimate heirs to scientific, cultural and other achievements of mankind over the centuries of development' (Bratus, 1963, pp 179–80; Ioffe, 1957, pp 30–1).

The combining of tradition with innovation is apparent in the new codes of the Polish People's Republic such as the civil code and family code. They maintain the right proportions between the Polish legal tradition (closely linked with western tradition) and requirements resulting from the new social and political conditions. They have not departed from traditional legal constructions that often date back to Roman law, legal thinking of the preceding periods deeply-rooted in the legal consciousness of Polish society and the doctrine of other European countries. At the same time, the new codes contain the regulations that are required by a socialist economy and that are necessary to the development and strengthening of socialist relations between people. The basis for the institutions of property law has become Marxist theory about the differentiation of the forms of ownership where social property has been given the most important place. The different character of socialised economic transactions has also been considered by Ignatowicz and Sawczuk (1983, p 72). These same authors deal with the interesting and widely discussed problem of innovation in civil law. This field of law regulates the everyday life of an individual, especially that connected with traditional habits. At the same time, the role of civil law in the modern world consists in the introduction into it of the norms that correspond to the needs of modern civilisation. In other words, these are innovative norms concerning technical progress, production, ecological threats, protection of personal rights and the individual rights to privacy.

A well-known Polish jurist said that 'between the codes of the Enlightenment and the 1964 code of the Polish People's Republic there were many milestones but not a single break' (Longchamps, 1968, p 38).

In the socialist state, geared to rapid social changes and based, until recently, almost exclusively on central planning, the role of the initiator of innovation through law was held by the state. The process of diffusion and adoption of innovation depended, to a large extent, on the attitude of the advocates of innovation and the receivers of innovation. Their attitudes may be linked with deeply-rooted tradition or even stereotypes. We may often come across the opinion that the bureaucracy that should play the role of advocates of innovation may become a specific barrier for innovation, especially in the form of a kind of professionalistic traditionalism with very complicated and formal (bureaucratic) ways of changing the existing regulations.

An unfavourable disposition of the citizens—the receivers of innovation—may be bound up not only with an attachment to some tradition but also with a negative opinion of the way in which innovation is introduced, of the way in which the individual is manipulated and a feeling of threat to the individual's own personality. This is connected to the kind of planning carried out and the omission of the citizen from the process. It also results from depriving the citizens of the possibility of exerting actual influence on the direction of the changes introduced. The general tendency to decentralise planning and to share the state's legislative activity with social organisations (especially self-government) may help remove these barriers to innovation.

The great political, social and economic changes that have taken place, in most mature form, in Poland and Hungary and then spread to other socialist countries in Eastern Europe have taken a different course in each of them, despite many similarities.

It is generally believed that democracy and political pluralism have to be re-established and that the economies have to be thoroughly transformed since they cannot be reformed. The changes are fundamental and undermine the basic assumptions of the system. One could, therefore, justly apply the term 'peaceful revolution'. Effective steps have been taken in Poland and Hungary to introduce market economies. They have been accompanied by the view that the changes can soon take effect. The process of change is different in the Soviet Union.

What is the scope and nature of the Polish 'reforms'? They are different from the concept of reform used in this article and meaning gradual, evolutionary transformations that do not violate the basis of the system. What is the peaceful revolution like and what are the transformations of law against the background of tradition and innovation? The principal tendency is towards the return to the tradition of capitalism and market economy as regards ownership. Still, the point of departure is the current political and economic structure which requires a great deal of legal regulations to be introduced to change it in that way. The changes consist, to a great extent, in the return to the regulations that were binding in Poland in the period between the wars (there have been even suggestions that, with some modifications the whole of the commercial code of that period be restored) and the introduction of regulations and institutions modelled on the institutions of contemporary capitalist states. At the same time, there is a tendency towards the search for new solutions that results from the need to allow for the existing structures.

It is relatively easy to establish private enterprises based on individual capital, whereas privatisation of the state sector is complicated due to the great number of monopolist state enterprises (Kleer, 1989, p 4). In the system of socialist economy, such enterprises were justified not only economically but also because they were easier to manage centrally. If the privatisation of such enterprises is to follow normal market principles it is going to be a slow process. Introduction of foreign capital also has a limited range. Therefore, it is possible that in the economic model to emerge, significant roles would be played by both private and state sectors. State enterprises will have to undergo substantial transformations in order to achieve complete or almost complete independence and will have to apply market principles in their activities. The private sector will increase its influence on the economy where market principles are going to dominate even in such enterprises as co-operatives, shareholding enterprises, enterprises with workers' self-government and state enterprises.

It remains to be decided whether some forms of state interventionism will be preserved. So far, such a possibility has been ruled out since all the negative phenomena in the socialist system have resulted from the state's omnipotence. Hence the great hope placed in the free market that is to reshape the centralised socialist economy. However, the main problem is that the market is effective only if there exists a strong private economy. The transfer to market economy requires a transformation of social consciousness that has developed over the forty-five years of the rejected system. The significance of the changes that have been going on in Poland (and that have stimulated the changes in other East European countries) consists in the 'learning' of democracy, initiative and independence in the taking-up of economic activities.

Social acceptance of the great historical experiment is connected with all the negative consequences of the transition period of which the society is not always fully aware. The main problem is to change the idea of the protective role of the state that has been deeply-rooted in the society even though the standard of the protection has been low and has not met all basic needs.

The transformation of law against the background of political, economic and social change of the 'peaceful revolution' are characterised by the return to traditional forms of democracy and capitalist economy. Nevertheless, new solutions have to be searched for in the transformation of the rejected system and the construction of a new one. It must finally be noted that all of this creates the necessity for change and transformation in the whole of Europe as we approach the twenty-first century.

REFERENCES

H G Barnett, *Innovation, the Basics of Cultural Change* (New York, 1953).

J Baszkiewicz, *Wolnosc, Równosc, Własnosc. Rewolucje Burzuazyjne* (Liberty, Equality, Property. Bourgeois Revolutions) (Warszawa, Czytelnik, 1981).

M Borucka-Arctowa, *Prawo Natury jako Ideologia Antyfeudalna* (Natural Law as Anti-Feudal Ideology) (Warszawa, Panstwowe Wydawnictwo Naukowe, 1957).

——'The tasks of contemporary legislator and the proper frame of legal relation', *Archivum Iuridicum Cracoviense*, vol IX (1975).

——*Innovation Through Law in the System of Social Planning in Law and the Future of Society* (Warszawa, Polish Academy of Sciences, Institute of State and Law, 1973).

——'Can Social Sciences Help us in Determining the Limits of Law?' *Rechtstheorie*, Beiheft 9 (1986).

S W Bratus, *Predmet i sistema sovetsgogo grazhdansgogo prava* (Object and System of Soviet Civil Law) (Moskva, 1963).

W Friedmann, *Legal Theory* (London, Stevens and Sons, 1947).

V Gsovski, *Soviet Civil Law* (Ann Arbor, 1948).

P Hall, H Land, R Parker and A. Webb *Choice and Conflict in Social Policy* (London, 1976).

J Hazard, *Law and Tradition in the New Russian* (Oxford Slavonic Paper, vol IV, 1953).

J Ignatowicz, M Sawczuk, 'Postęp i Tradycja w Prawie Cywilnym' (Progress and Tradition in Civil Law) in *Tradycja i Postep w Prawie* (Tradition and Progress in Law), R Tokarczyk, ed (Lublin, Wydawnictwa Lubelskie, 1983).

O S Ioffe *Voprosy Kodifikatsü sovietsogo prava* (The Problems of Codification of Soviet Law) (Moskva, 1957).

M Krygier, 'Law as tradition', *Law and Philosophy*, 5 (1986) (Reidel Publishing Company).

——'The traditionality of statute', *Ratio Juris*, vol 1, No 1.

J Kleer, 'Co po socjalizmie Realnym?' ('After socialism what now?') *Polityka*, 48 (1989).

K Kulcsar *Modernization and Law* (Budapest, Institute of Sociology, Hungarian Academy of Sciences, 1987).

W Lamentowicz *Kapitalizm i Reformy Spoteczne* (Capitalism and Social Reforms) (Warszawa, Wydawnictwa Uniwersytetu Warszawskiego, 1987).

R T La Pierre *Introduction to H G Barnett, Innovation, the Base of Cultural Change* (New York, 1953).

F Longchamps *Problemow Poznania Prawa* (Problems of the Cognition of Law) (Wroclaw, 1968).

E M Rogers, *Diffusion of Innovations* (New York, 1962).

H Rot, ed, *Tradycja i Innowacja w Prawie Socjalistycznym* (Tradition and Innovation in Socialist Law) (Wroclaw, Acta Universitatis Watslaviensis, No 830, 1984).

E Shils, 'Tradition', *Comparative Studies in Society and History,* vol XIII, No 2, 1971).

J Szacki *Tradycja* (Tradition) (Warszawa, Panstwowe Wydawnictwo Naukowe, 1971).

CHAPTER 10

Revolutions and the Continuity of European Law

Adam Czarnota and Martin Krygier

I hope . . . to reinforce an insight that is threatened with oblivion in our swiftly changing age. What changes forces itself far more on the attention than what remains the same. That is a general law of our intellectual life. Hence the perspectives which come from the experience of historical change are always in danger of distortion because they forget the hidden constants. (Hans-Georg Gadamer, *Truth and Method,* New York, Crossroad, 1975, xiii-xiv.)

Two great revolutions, the French in 1789 and the Russian in 1917, have exerted a powerful influence on the very character of the historical process and have fundamentally modified the course of world events. (Mikhail Gorbachov, Speech to the United Nations, 7 December 1988.)

According to Voltaire, if you want good laws, you should burn the ones you have. In European history, as in human history generally, this advice has not been much followed. For the continuity of law is extraordinary. Much is law now because of what it was then. So too, what it will be depends significantly on what it happens now to be. This is true of every legal system that has endured. But revolutions are often thought to be the nemesis of such continuity. If nothing else does, *they* demolish the old and build the new. Or so it has been claimed, both by revolutionaries themselves and by those who oppose them.

    The truth is more complex and, with regard at least to law, typically less dramatic. This has not always been appreciated, nor have the reasons for it. Among those reasons we wish to focus on two: one having to do with the nature of legal continuity, the other with differences among revolutions. To understand the nature and depth of legal continuity one must attend to the *layered complexity* of legal traditions. To understand the interrelationships between law and revolutions, one must attend to important distinctions among the latter; in particular those flowing from differences between two types of relationship between state and society, and between the place and significance of law in these relationships, in the countries in which the revolutions occurred. These differences *preceded* revolutions, and they survived them too.

1 *Continuity and the Layered Complexity of Law*

What does it mean to speak of continuity within law? Most simply, there will be continuity when there is identity in the elements of law over time. But such identity is not necessary, and it certainly does not exhaust, the continuity of law. For continuity within enduring and complex traditions, such as the Judaeo-Christian tradition or the Western legal tradition is real and deep, but it is certainly not simply a matter of pure transmission of identical inheritances, unsullied or untransformed since the dawn of time. On the contrary it is compatible with great change. Indeed since such traditions require continual interpretation and reinterpretation by different people in different circumstances, their continuity—like that of all complex interpretive traditions[1]—necessarily involves and depends upon such change.

The present of any complex and enduring tradition is profoundly influenced by what comes down to it from the past, but little that is important remains without change. What has to be stressed is the constant *interplay* between inherited layers which pervade and—often unrecognised—mould the present, and the constant renewals and reshapings of these inheritances, in which authorised interpreters and guardians of the tradition and lay participants in it indulge, and cannot but indulge. So the traditionality of a highly traditional practice such as, say, the common law does not depend upon the identification of perennially enduring essential elements, objective carriers of meaning—the same meaning—from our distant forebears to us. Nor does the absence of such elements of itself point to the absence or unimportance of continuity in any social practice. Nor, finally, can traditions survive without continuous change, addition, innovation. Rather, '[t]he historical life of a tradition depends on constantly new assimilation and interpretation'.[2] As one of us has sought to show elsewhere, it is characteristic of such traditions to embody a continuing dialectic combining deep continuity and perpetual change.[3] They transmit traditional inheritances which, constantly interpreted, reinterpreted and transmitted, pass down to later generations in forms different from but linked to and decisively influenced by their predecessors. None of these elements of inheritance, transmission or reception is sovereign, none pure; all are essential to the amalgam, the palimpsest, that is tradition at any particular moment. The resulting traditions are more tangled, even mysterious, than pristine trans-mission or groundless, boundless, invention might appear to be. They are also more common and significant in social life. And law is an important one of them. Continuity is most obvious in legal systems based on sacred and canonical writings, where the canon has been closed, as in Talmudic and

Islamic law. For here at least central texts are identical over time. Of course the meanings attributed to passages from the Torah or the Koran have formed the subjects of countless controversies and have changed continuously and dramatically over the years of their interpretation. But it remains *these* texts that must be interpreted and applied. Yet even here continuity involves more than identity. Interpretation will occur in the light of a variety of traditional media of authoritative interpretation: secondary writings and traditional teachings which are also transmitted and considered to contain authoritative interpretations of the primary, sacred, texts; higher-order traditions about how to interpret and respond to those texts, writings and teachings; communities of authoritative interpreters, inducted and transmitted into the arcana of their craft or vocation, and continually adding to them; and institutions concerned with recording, preserving, protecting, transmitting the legal tradition. These higher-order traditions change and are supplemented continuously, and in terms of them new meanings are drawn from old texts. Moreover, even in secular legal systems, without strict canons or with canons open to revision, law commonly has an extraordinarily long life. This has certainly been true of Western law, at least since the twelfth century.[4] Within Western law such continuity is perhaps most obvious, and explicitly acknowledged, in English common law. Comparativists frequently stress this continuity as one of the central features which distinguish the common law[5]— with its relatively unbroken span over nine centuries—from European civil law, punctuated as the latter has been with receptions, revolutions and codifications.

Beginning with the surface, many contemporary *rules* of the common law can only be explained in terms of their ancestry, though—as is typical of traditions—the explanations that find favour among participants are often historically inaccurate.[6] (In the English case they are commonly also parochial, ignoring, for example, the extent of similarities and connections between developments in medieval English and European law.[7]) And what is true of those parts of the law which are manifest and relatively easily manipulable— explicit written rules—is all the more true of practices, understandings, conventions which are harder to identify from within for they seem so obvious and natural to initiates. Thus, of course, enormous changes have occurred in the common law, even if we confine our attention to the English common law—continuously over large tracts of time and with unprecedented rapidity over the last century and a half. Apart from incessant changes of detailed provisions, for example, Simpson points to five large changes within the common law: change in the *scale* of the system; the unprecedented importance of legislation as a source of law; the development of an academic law tradition in a hitherto practitioner-dominated legal order; modification in the structure of the courts and the decline of the jury as the characteristic method of trial.[8] Nevertheless, as Simpson shows, what is remarkable is the extent to which the 'common law system' has continued to be able to 'digest' these changes without discontinuity in fundamental aspects of the legal order itself.[9]

Inheritance matters across the Channel, too. It is true that there have been sharper discontinuities within the civil than the common law, but *within* is not a preposition without significance. For the continuities are remarkable, and deeper than the discontinuities as well. Thus, notwithstanding the significance of nineteenth-century codification, it remains true and important to remember that the *Code Napoleon* and the *bürgerliches Gesetzbuch* are relatively late appearances in the development of a civil law system that was already ancient at the time of Justinian—older then than the Anglo-American common law is today.[10]

Of course this genealogy needs to be enriched to take account of the eleventh-century Papal revolution,[11] the revival of juridical culture in Italy at the same time,[12] the importance of the universities in which Roman law was studied, glossed and propagated to students from throughout Europe,[13] the influence of medieval scholasticism,[14] and a great deal else within and without the law. Nevertheless, or all the more, it remains clear that some very old past has remained present in civil law. It remains in specific rules and categories, in the organisation of the legal system and areas of law, and in the ways in which lawyers approach the law.[15] And, as we shall see, it remains in much else besides. Here too, the law has not survived without persistent and drastic changes, but changes which were strongly affected by, and did not eliminate, enduring continuities within the tradition. As in all complex traditions, legal institutions, practices, techniques, ways of categorising legal problems, imaginable alternatives to these ways, all bear the weight of the inherited past.'

To understand the extent and depth of legal continuity, and the sources of legal resilience, one must appreciate two characteristics typical of legal traditions: their *complexity* and the intricately *layered and interconnected* nature of their parts. First of all, complexity. The plainest and crispest elements of law are its rules, particularly statutory rules. They are relatively easy to identify, and—for those authorised—to make, change and repeal. However, one particularly misleading inference often drawn from positivist emphases on rules has been that law is made up solely or at least primarily (rather than merely distinctively) of rules. This inference, of course, is the target of Ronald Dworkin's criticism of 'the model of rules' which he attributes to positivism.[16] Legal positivism, he claims, sees law as composed of a body of rules identifiable according to some supreme criterion of recognition; also, in H L A Hart's account,[17] a rule. Such legal theories, Dworkin argues, cannot account for the significant role in judicial decision of standards of a different kind, ones which operate differently from rules as ingredients in decision and which cannot be traced to any crisp identifiable ultimate rule. These Dworkin originally called 'principles, policies and other sorts of standards', which in his early critique of positivism he collapsed as 'principles' in contrast to rules. Later he narrowed his account of principles to include only standards concerned with individual rights rather than those which concerned collective goals.[18] Either way, the sources of the status of legal principles *as law,* are far less tidy than positivist accounts of law allow. Yet there are such sources and their relative indeterminacy does not diminish their power. Parallels to the principles of which Dworkin speaks can be found in every legal tradition. Indeed there are obvious analogies in other sorts of traditions than law, and in law itself the passage quoted applies to much more than principles of that sort that Dworkin later comes to focus on, those having to do with individual *rights*. Indeed it applies to elements of law which have no particular *substantive* import at all, but are nevertheless prerequisites of being able to think like a lawyer at all. For Dworkin might have said more about elements of law other than principles in the narrow sense, just as he might have given more thought than appears to the writings which introduced the distinction that he made famous, that between principles and rules. We here refer to the writings of Roscoe Pound.[19]

Pound repeatedly stressed the variegated character of law. Limiting himself to what he described as 'the body of authoritative materials prescribed or received as the basis of judicial decision',[20] Pound stressed that these materials were of several sorts, not all susceptible to easy identification or formal hierarchical ranking. He made the distinction in a variety of ways, but most commonly and importantly he distinguished between three elements of law: 'precepts', 'received techniques', and 'received ideals'. 'Precepts' include rules but also 'principles'—'authoritative starting points for legal reasoning, employed continually and legitimately where cases are not covered or are not fully or obviously covered by rules in the narrower sense';[21] 'conceptions', or 'authoritative categories' for picking out that in the world to which law will attach and 'in consequence of which a series of rules, principles, and standards become applicable';[22] 'doctrines' or 'systematic fittings together' of precepts, usually done by text-writers; and 'standards' or 'general limits of permissible conduct to be applied according to the circumstances of each case'.[23] Many of these latter precepts are in fact as authoritative as rules, though they receive far less clear formal recognition.

Nevertheless they are recognised by lawyers, on the basis of higher-order understandings, and in ways that lawyers within a particular legal order share and must share. Otherwise they could not invoke, interpret or deploy the substantive precepts they declare in ways that made sense to those whom they seek to persuade within a legal community. Yet they do. Among the sources of these shared ways of seeing and understanding are lawyers' 'received techniques'. These, Pound explained, 'are not legal precepts; they are modes of looking at and handling and shaping legal precepts. They are mental habits governing judicial and juristic craftsmanship'.[24] They are inculcated and deployed within every legal tradition, but of course they are not the same in every tradition. They are of many sorts, but particularly important among them are what Arthur Glass has described as 'the normative and regulative aspects of legal interpretation—viz. those culturally specific requirements that impose themselves upon, structure and give meaning to this interpretive practice'.[25] The provenance of these elements is typically less clear-cut[26] than that of, say, a statutory rule but their influence is typically more widespread, enduring and harder for initiates to evade. Just as many of them cannot simply be legislated, so—though their influence waxes and wanes over time—they cannot easily be repealed. And with regard to these elements particularly, as Pound observed, '[O]ne need not remark how much any institution is affected by its beginnings.'[27] Finally, Pound speaks of 'received ideals' which are 'quite as authoritative as the precepts themselves, which determine the starting points of legal reasoning, the course of that reasoning, and, indeed, often the whole process which we call interpretation and application'.[28] This point can be expanded, for it applies not merely to particular ideals such as, say, equality before the law. Comparative lawyers have noted that, beyond particulars of machinery and rules, legal traditions are associated with characteristic and distinctive 'styles'[29] and even 'visions'[30] of law. Recently, a number of authors have emphasised the extent to which particular legal orders embody and presuppose distinctive ideologies in a broad sense, distinctive 'ways of viewing both law and the world',[31] which incorporate particular constellations of values, particular 'legal views of reality' through which lawyers see the world, particular 'legal sensibilities'[32] which are pervasive and inform legal goals, means, doctrines and machinery. These sensibilities are not seamless or monolithic, and they are subject to strain and to change, but again it is typical that this change has deep roots in what has gone before. And finally it is not merely values and sensibilities *within* the law that matter. There are substantial differences *between* societies with regard to the importance and value placed *on* law, and such differences also endure, commonly over long periods. Thus it is true, significant and has widely been thought appropriate—even natural— that 'Western law has tended to be a pervasive element in Western society; that is, the extent to which social control is exerted through law rather than through other social forces has always been relatively large'.[33] This, as we shall see, has not always or everywhere been so.

Pound, of course, was not concerned merely to point to the existence of techniques and ideals in law, but to emphasise their importance. We tend to think of law as precepts, indeed as rules, but Pound explains, 'the technique of developing and applying the precepts, the art of the lawyer's craft, is quite as authoritative and no less important'.[34] And a legal tradition's body of received ideals 'handed down in the law books, read by students and taught consciously or unconsciously by law teachers as part of the fundamenta of legal thinking, is much more long lived than particular rules of law, and the ideals are much more far-reaching in their effects'.[35]

So an account of continuity in law must attend to authoritative substantive precepts other than rules and with significantly different roles in legal orders, and of environing sensibilities which inform every aspect of those orders. Moreover, not only are the elements of law complex; they exist in *layered* and interconnected relationships. Of course it is well-known that laws— particularly precepts—are hierarchically interrelated. For modern differentiated legal orders are not just bundles of laws, but legal *systems*, and part of the systemic quality of law stems from the fact that its norms are arranged in hierarchies of pedigree and validity. The hierarchies are not all clear or explicit, and those that are are at best incomplete. Yet they are crucial in legal systems. None of this is news to jurists, of course. Even at the explicit and readily recognised level, as analytical jurists have frequently stressed, legal systems are made up not merely of legal norms about behaviour but of hierarchies of derivation of lower from higher-order norms: norms about norms, norms about those norms, and so on.[36] And Hart[37] has emphasised that legal systems are full of rules about rules, which is one way of characterising the 'secondary rules' of recognition, change and adjudication that he considers essential for every institutionalised legal system, indeed for the transition from the 'pre-legal into the legal world'.[38]

However, we would like to draw attention to two less formalised and noticed, but no less important, ways in which legal traditions are layered, apart from the hierarchies of pedigree and validity. Roughly these categories correspond to Pound's second and third elements of law. One is what might be called an epistemological or hermeneutic hierarchy, which has to do with what it is to know and to understand within a legal tradition. For no legal tradition exists without developing and transmitting such a hierarchy of *higher-order* traditions,[39] which have to do with meaning, understanding and interpretation within the tradition. Legal traditions are full of traditions about traditions— second or higher-order traditions—and, given the complexity of legal traditions, these are not all rules. Indeed they cannot be, for rules and other precepts must be interpreted, and this will need to be done according to higher-order layers of legally authoritative material to be found, at the very least, above whatever level rules stop. Otherwise the interpretation of rules would have been left up for grabs—not a small thing and not commonly done in legal traditions, or indeed in other institutionalised normative traditions. As we have seen, some components of these higher layers are 'techniques', many are highly tradition-specific understandings about who in the legal system is important and why, who must defer to whom and to what, about the 'natural' way to proceed in marshalling arguments, arguing a case, delivering a judgement, justifying it, in developing the law, in changing it.

Moreover the *values* which have imbued, informed, moulded and guided the development of legal orders also are layered in deep, complex and important ways. It is obvious that values in and around law change continuously. But within the western legal tradition there are deeply embedded 'core values' which have shown astonishing persistence, resilience and indeed fertility, in that they have spawned numerous and different interpretations which are nevertheless related, often to each other and persistently to this core. Thus Harold Berman has shown the extent to which contemporary western law rests upon largely Roman and Christian foundations, which were incorporated in the western legal tradition which emerged in the eleventh and twelfth centuries, which have survived in recognisable—though often unrecognised— ways to this day,[40] and which have endured—under continual interpretation and reinterpretation—notwithstanding continual changes in social and political structure, and in the functions which law has been called upon to perform. Indeed the core values immanent in the western legal tradition have in turn affected the functioning of that law. These values influenced the perception and interpretation of interests articulated in particular historical epochs. In this way law maintained its identity as a significant element of social practice. Through changes in function and structure we can speak about legal *traditions*, and their continuity through changing historical epochs.

Any legal tradition, then, contains layers over and under its legal rules and they are among the reasons that '[t]he rule ordinarily symbolizes far more than its bare text states'.[42] These layers often work unmentioned in formal accounts of legal hierarchies.[42] They are no less observed in practice for being unobserved in theory.

These layers mould style[43] and they influence substance. They channel practice and they limit imagination. They change constantly but rarely abruptly and even more rarely in ways unrelated to or unconstrained by what went before. They pervade the central doctrinal, interpretive frameworks of thought and activity, and like them are passed down by the legal tradition, often over extraordinarily long periods of time. That they are not in any metaphysical sense natural is evident from the fact that despite their frequent longevity *within* legal traditions, these layered traditions differ strikingly *between* them. On the other hand, that they are not natural does not mean that they are easily dispensable or replaceable within any tradition which has grown up with a particular history, set and arrangement of them.

Of course, much of legal substance—particularly rules and other components of the first-order traditions of doctrine—is renovated generation after generation, often radically. Yet, as we have seen, so much of the law moves more slowly and provides the frameworks within which, and in terms of which, more rapid change typically occurs. Common among the slow movers in legal development are the particular kinds and categories of texts, authors and interpreters which are treated as authoritative; the higher-order traditions which guide lawyers in the reading, interpretation and manipulation of laws; the styles, visions, sensibilities and values, within which these activities take place and make sense. Short of social and political revolution, the institutions—or at least the types of institutions—which guard and sustain the law also commonly have long lives.

Within these enduring contexts of thought and action, the stuff of legal doctrine—statutes, judgements, interpretations, rules, principles, conventions, customs—is proclaimed, deposited, recorded, applied, dissected, interpreted, revised, rejected, supplemented and passed down; in and by authoritative legal agents and agencies.

Lawyers and all who use law inhabit and manipulate traditions whose general intellectual structures, underlying conventions and standards generally change glacially and in ways that individuals rarely have power to affect radically. There will be constant innovations within these traditional idioms, and of course in law it is possible to decree or legislate important elements of novelty, including rules, less often principles, and even new law-making or interpreting institutions. It is also possible to override law, even to discard large chunks of it. Particular rules and institutions might easily be abolished, though often they creep back. But higher-order traditions of dealing with rules and institutions in legal contexts—often unreflectively absorbed and hard to identify, let alone expunge—are harder to liquidate wherever law survives or to prevent from re-emerging wherever law re-emerges. At the level of unreflected-upon assumptions, procedures and presuppositions within legal traditions, change—though continuous—is generally a complicated, supra-individual and usually supra-generational affair. At *this* level, revolutions are rare in law, and more rarely still are they total. This, of course, is also true of many traditions outside the law, none of which is best understood in terms of the 'time-free' concepts prevalent in modern legal and social theory. What Bernard Rudden observes of judges is true more widely, and it is no small matter:

> . . . . not only is the individual judge conditioned by his background, but . . . the decades, or even centuries, of a traditional training, of particular methods of recruitment, even of the physical characteristics of the place where the job is done, create a corpus of professional habits and assumptions which affects judicial method and, through it, the legal order, and does so all the more strongly for being so rarely made articulate.[44]

None of this should be surprising, for to know and understand law is in many ways similar to knowing and understanding a language. That all of us can do whether or not we can articulate its rules, and to do it effectively requires more than mere knowledge of those rules.

Law embodies a language of density and complexity, and lawyers are expert speakers of it. And the creative lawyer who finds new and legally plausible things to say constructs not just in any idiom but in the—usually dense and heavily patterned—idiom of the legal tradition within which he works and thinks and in which those whom he seeks to persuade work and think. And this idiom encompasses not merely the explicit discourse of the law but also what James Boyd White calls its 'invisible discourse'.[45] As White remarks:

> Behind the words . . . are expectations about the ways in which they will be used, expectations that do not find explicit expression anywhere but are part of the legal culture that the surface language simply assumes. These expectations are constantly at work, directing argument, shaping responses, determining the next move, and so on. Their effects are everywhere, but they themselves are invisible . . .
> It is these conventions, not the diction, that primarily determine the mysterious character of legal speech and literature—not the 'vocabulary' of the law, but what might be called its 'cultural syntax.'[46]

As White emphasises, the fact that many conventions of legal discourse are frequently invisible, as much to those who employ them as to perplexed and bewildered laymen who do not know how to, is part of their power.

Thus legal traditions are not, as their explicit rules might be, some sort of machinery or coercive Esperanto, which can simply be isolated, identified, and shipped to operate identically wherever they are transported and assembled. Parts of them may well be shipped and very often are,[47] but something will be lost[48]—perhaps even gained[49]—in the process. For like any other complex and enduring tradition, legal traditions involve what Clifford Geertz calls 'local knowledge':

. . . local not just as to place, time, class, and variety of issue, but as to accent—vernacular characterisations of what happens connected to vernacular imaginings of what can. It is this complex of characterisations and imaginings, stories about events cast in imagery about principles, that I have been calling a legal sensibility.[50]

It is harder to invent or destroy such a sensibility than a rule.

2 *Revolutions*

The continuity of law, then, is typically long, dense, layered and complex. But what of revolutions? Do they not destroy what has been and build anew? Certainly revolutionaries have tried and claimed to do so. The *prehistory* of mankind might be full of continuity, but revolutionaries commonly proclaim a rupture between, on the one hand, the present which they inhabit and the future which they will create, and, on the other, the past which they have defeated. How significant a break do revolutions manage to achieve? How much do they contradict the continuity of law; how much do they confirm it?

It should already be obvious that a comprehensive break with past law is rather a tall order. Ditching a rule, an office, even a few officials takes neither imagination nor superhuman effort. Hunting down, let alone laying to rest, the layered complexes of precepts, techniques, sensibilities and values that comprise and mould legal traditions is a larger task than most people could think to attempt, let alone successfully carry through. And since no post-revolutionary society has been able to dispense with law for long, where are they to get it and how are lawyers to understand it? Secondly, it is important to stress the comparative rarity, historically and geographically, of revolutions. All social and national revolutions (those limited to a particular cultural-political unit) represent a possible—it is not clear to what extent necessary—road from what are loosely known as traditional to modern societies. They represent one episode in the process of social transformation, a peculiar quickening of social development, originally in the context of European civilisation broadly understood. From this observation it follows that a relatively rapid social change encompassing every area of social life is not a dominating phenomenon in history. If, following Max Weber, we compare the history of the great civilisations of our globe, slow spirals of development are more evident. Until the twentieth century, only European civilisation broke away from this pattern, from the tenth[51] century, with an ever greater acceleration of its development.[52] Even here contemporary historical and sociological research has laid increasing emphasis on the continuity of social development. Today one emphasises sources of the rapid development of Europe in elements constituting European civilisation around the tenth century, including specifics of social, political, cultural and geographical arrangements, which stimulated social changes in this area of civilisation.[53] Yet the pace, scale and spread of development of European civilisation has been extraordinary. It is conceptualised in various ways, depending on the theoretical position of the writer: the transition from feudalism to capitalism, the genesis of capitalism, the expansion of the market economy or the development of rationalism. Each of these conceptualisations draws attention to particular elements of the birth of modernity, but in each is implicit Marx's and Weber's perception that its sources had not existed often nor, until recently, in many places. What, then, is a revolution? It is common to distinguish and counterpose two phenomena: reform and revolution. Modern political movements have grown up, based on this distinction and on the different views of social reality and social possibility associated with each of its elements. And in the history of social thought, one can distinguish very broadly between two basic—and contradictory—approaches to revolution. The first recognises revolution as a critical and decisive—but linear—continuation of the historical process, qualitatively distinct from (mere) reform because it spells the transition from one social order to another. We find an example of such an approach in Marxism. In various versions and interpretations of Marxism, revolution is understood as an unblocking of existing contradictions in historical development, allowing a rise to a qualitatively higher stage of this development (a new socio-economic formation). The second approach, represented by conservatism, regards revolution as a phenomenon which rips a society from the continuity of historical development, breaking this continuity and building a new (usually worse) social order. Conservatives often acknowledge the need for reform; rather rarely for revolution. Yet in the light of their long-term social consequences, both contrasts between reform and revolution lose some of their sharpness. These contrasting conceptions can be seen to be complementary; two sides of the same coin. Such an approach appears particularly well-based if we look to the relations between law and revolutions.

What, then, distinguishes a revolution from a change, a reform, an innovation, within an ongoing social and political order? According to Theda Skocpol, '[S]ocial revolutions are rapid, basic transformations of a society's state and class structures; and they are accompanied and in part carried through by class-based revolts from below.'[54] This definition distinguishes social revolutions from other forms of conflict and processes of social change, such as, for example, coups, rebellions or other forms of political overturning. On such a general account of social revolutions, they are the turning points of history, marking and paving the way for new directions of social development. Yet if one looks at these 'historical turning points' from the point of view of the *longue durée*, then it turns out that revolutions do not necessarily inaugurate new and unprecedented directions in development. The above definition of revolution generalises certain characteristic traits of revolutions known in history, in particular the French Revolution and the Bolshevik Revolution. The effects of both these revolutions were quickened changes in social and political structure. Each also, we do not exaggerate in saying, represented a specific type of crowning of a long process of historical development within European civilisation. Whether the above definition exposes the specific traits of revolutions is open to doubt, however, if we compare precisely these two revolutions which are so often taken as paradigms of revolutions and revolutionary changes in society.

Not all revolutions are the same. In the 1950s there developed a basically ideological thesis about two types of social revolution, namely so-called Atlantic revolutions (the Dutch, English, American and French) and non-Atlantic, including the Russian and the Chinese.[55] The criterion for distinguishing these two types of revolution is not geographic: rather it is based on differences in the morphology of revolutions, in particular on differences in the amount of violence released and applied in the different types of revolution. Palmer argued that whereas Atlantic revolutions developed with a relatively limited amount of force and were followed by a relatively quick return to normalisation, the situation was different in the non-Atlantic revolutions. These deployed an incomparably greater amount of force and return to normalisation took incomparably longer. This analysis rests on a rather superficial analysis of events and does not try to explain the reasons for these differences between different types of revolution. Nevertheless, it draws attention to significant differences between the course that revolutions have taken. Why in fact did such differences occur?

Both the early revolutions (sixteenth to eighteenth centuries) and the later ones (twentieth century)—notwithstanding the different times and circumstances in which they occurred—can plausibly be portrayed as elements in the passage from traditional to modern society. Nevertheless, it seems to us that Palmer is right to stress that their course differed significantly. Even in the ideological projects of these revolutions we can find a characteristic difference in ideological justifications of revolutions and in projects for the future organisation of society. The ideologies of the earlier revolutions stressed demands for modifications, for changes limited in sphere and scope. Nowhere was this more manifest than in relation to law. The ideology of the English Revolution was backward-looking and stressed—where it did not manufacture—the continuity and legitimacy of its demands with the *good old [common]law*. Even in the American Revolution, ultimately justified in terms of Enlightenment perceptions of the world, the debates of the 1760s and 1770s centred on vindicating ancient rights (of Englishmen), which were allegedly being usurped. The Revolution ended and the Constitution was born, notwithstanding significant shifts of theme and rhetoric, within the frame of inherited constitutional debates.[56] In later revolutions the projects were different. The aims of the revolutions were to build a new social world, to realise a secular Utopia, on earth, here and now. And law played no important role in these aims. These revolutions were based upon different conceptions of rationality. They were not revolutions of lawyers nor revolutions which centred on law, but by social engineers centring on total social transformation. It might be argued that the French Revolution does not fit the model of Atlantic (Western) revolutions, for various reasons: for example, because of the enormous unleashing of violence or, even more important, because of the creation of new forms of social life. After all, contemporaries, and not only those across the Channel, saw the Revolution as a profound break with the past, one which was both dramatic and very sharp. One can point to the creation of a new social world in a new rationalist manner, for example in the new measures, calendar, clothing, social relations. Nevertheless we believe that in the internal dynamic of the revolution one must distinguish three phases: the first reformist phase, a second phase in which the creation of a new world was attempted, and a third neo-reformist phase. The only phase devoted to the 'creation of a new world' was that in which the Jacobins exercised power and unleashed the Great Terror. But after a relatively brief period where they exercised power between 1792–4, mainly as a result of the war and the need to mobilise the mass of the population, the Jacobins failed. What we will discuss below as civil society showed itself sufficiently strong to move the later development of the revolution along paths more acceptable to it. In the present text there is no room to develop this analysis in any depth, and we should emphasise that our analysis operates at a high level of abstraction involving theoretical rather than purely historical generalisations. Nevertheless the French Revolution clearly fits within the model of Western revolutions, to be developed below. In terms of their effects all the Western revolutions ended with changes in the political sphere which were responses to demands from— and changes within—society. None of them issued in a change in social relations imposed by the state. Hannah Arendt wrote that the French Revolution failed by comparison with the American, since the former tried to rebuild the whole society whereas the American was content to create a 'political framework for liberty'.[57] This thesis seems to us correct to the extent that it is applied to the second phase of the French revolutionary dynamic. This phase came to symbolise the Revolution for many, among them leading communists, but the Revolution's most enduring effects—particularly with regard to law—were not owed to that phase. Instead, they were the post-revolutionary codes, copied throughout Europe and elsewhere. In form, content and significance the Codes represented far less of a break with the past than appeared,[58] even at the level of surface detail. At deeper levels of precepts, techniques and values, the continuities—as we have suggested—are profound. As we shall see, Russia displayed a quite different type of continuity from those in the West.

What were the reasons for these differences in the course and effects of these two groups of revolutions, and what do they tell us about revolutions and legal continuity? It seems to us that one decisive element lay in a deep and very long-lived difference in relationships between state and society in the 'Atlantic' states, on the one hand and in the 'non-Atlantic' states, on the other. For it is not an accident that the earlier revolutions, connected with a smaller explosion of force, occurred in the western sphere of European civilisation and that they were radicalised with the passage of time and movement eastward.

Notwithstanding the many differences among them, one can point to many similarities in the arrangement of elements constituting the social and political arrangements of Western Europe, which differ from those found in Eastern Europe. The major difference lies in the different types of state which developed in Western Europe by comparison with other regions. This has long been noticed by observers and scholars and John A Hall has drawn attention to it again,[59] in distinguishing between differences in the relationships between state and society where the state is set as a 'capstone' above the society, as in the imperial states of China and Russia, and where its relationship to the society is 'organic' as in the West.

Capstone states are imperial in character, organising social resources in their terrain in an extensive fashion. They expand the resources at their command rather than improve their cultivation of them. Generally this type of state blocks social change. In states of this type the state is on the one hand arbitrary, politically without rival or limit, while on the other hand it is incapable of deep penetration into the social structure. It dominates the society but is unable to mobilise the society's energies and make use of its potential. The state's arbitrariness results in part from its social weakness. A capstone state in its activities can manage to eliminate independent channels of social communication; to dominate and control channels of horizontal communication; put simply, to eliminate independent and autonomous sources of social power. In sum we can say that this type of state was so strong that it was able to control society and so weak that it feared any changes within the state. In states of this type there develops a specific kind of gulf between the state apparatus and such social groupings as remain. The state dominates from above, but does little to contribute from within.[60]

Organic states, on the other hand, were linked with—indeed grew slowly out of—their societies, as slowly evolving parts of units, in which there existed various independent sources of social power. The process of formation of organic states began in western Europe again around the twelfth century. Far from forming the society,

> [t]he European state evolved slowly and doggedly in the midst of a pre-existent civil society . . . Civil society, for it deserves to be called nothing less, pre-existed the monarch. His only way of gaining money was to co-operate with his society. European pluralism was, in other words, based upon the strength and autonomy of the groups involved.[61]

The pluralism of centres of social power limited the arbitrariness of state power but on the other hand, by this limitation the state was capable of penetrating the social structure. Thanks to this the organic state was able to call upon greater reserves of social energy, and to preside over the development of new types of social relations, because channels of social communication were not liquidated. Whereas in capstone states there was a separation of state from society, in organic states there was an intermingling of sources of social and political power. These sources, depending upon the concrete historical situation, at times co-operated and at times rivalled each other. Organic states were states in which internal mechanisms of social change were not perpetually blocked and the organisation of resources was accomplished in an intensive, continually innovative manner. Within the framework of organic states, social changes, the rise of new types of social relations, occurred in a 'natural' way.

In other words, the state and political order did not block the possibilities of development of new types of social relations but also new types of social relations within civil society were created by the state only to a minimal degree. The states' major contribution was the provision of infrastructure—largely through law—not control. State organisation, institutions and legal guarantees provided by states became conditions for later developments within civil society. The organic state provided supports for the formation of an independent public sphere, which cannot be reduced theoretically, either to the private sphere or to the state. This is the sphere of 'civil society' composed of powerful groups independent of the state. It appears to us that the process of development of the organic state was inextricably linked with the process of development of civil society. For this reason we do not date the development of civil society with the development of the liberal-democratic state, but much earlier.[62] The situation was different in capstone states, in which the political order, only interested in reproducing itself, petrified only those limited social relations which ensured the reproduction of the political order, blocking at the same time the possibility of development of new types of social relations.

One can look at law in terms of this typology. The social functions and importance of law differed between the two forms of state. In organic states law developed as a practice which *counted* in social life and which was understood as a source of reciprocal rights and duties among those it affected. It was not seen purely as a repressive arm of the Crown against members of society; it had a relatively great sphere of autonomy from the central political order, and was to a greater degree created by everyday life, in other words with a greater role of customary law. The law provided a balance and a connection between civil society and the state. Using Habermas's distinction law was not merely a 'steering medium' but was also an 'institution', which 'belong[s] to the legitimate orders of the lifeworld itself and, together with the informal norms of conduct, form[s] the background of communicative action'.[63] In capstone states, on the other hand, the notion that power should be restrained by law, or that law should do other than transmit central orders, was alien. Nor was the notion of rights much in evidence. Rather, as Richard Pipes has observed of medieval Russia, '[T]here is no evidence . . . of mutual obligations binding prince and his servitor, and, therefore, also nothing resembling legal and moral "rights" of his subjects, and little need for law and courts'.[64]

In the organic states of the European continent the division between public and private law is a key element. For the organic state institutionalised public law in such a way that it allowed the process of natural social change. Public law in this type of state institutionalised a political order which allowed mobilisation of resources without the direct interference of political elements. And it did not obliterate the significance of private law.[65] This is even more evident in the English common law, which significantly did not recognise a separate sphere of public law. Things were different in capstone states where law remained under the tight control of the political order. In this type of state it is hard to speak of a division between public and private law, but not because the paradigm of law is private law—as in England—but because law merely serves the reproduction of the political system. Of course these are ideal types—categories which allow us to illuminate significant historical differences. They are nowhere fully realised but they are not idle fantasies. In organic states, revolutions were concerned primarily with transformation of the political order, with changing its institutional structure in favour of one more suited to demands coming from *within* civil society. New social relations *already existed—and even dominated*—in the framework of civil society and the old institutional structure. Before the revolution the political order allowed the development of new forms of civil society and for the reproduction of the whole social political order, but the existing politico-institutional structure was seen as blocking satisfaction of demands flowing upwards from civil society. It is thus hard in the case of organic states to speak of social revolutions in the strict sense, as revolutions which *effectively led to* new types of organisation of society. New types of organisation of civil society dominated before the revolution.[66]

Tocqueville's stress on the *continuity* of institutional reform in France from the *ancien régime* to the new seems apt to us of all the 'Atlantic' revolutions. After the dust (and it must be said blood) settled, the state again came to operate as an organic state able to draw upon independently mobilised social resources. Similarly in the other early revolutions, and with even less blood, there was relatively little use of force in the Dutch, English, American revolutions. It is not surprising that these revolutions drew on lawyers and were in a certain sense lawyers' revolutions. Law played a central role in the political and ideological debates of these revolutions. In the revolutions carried out in organic states it was not a question of the destruction of the pre-existing social order. Though one can speak of such an attempt—in the case of the French Revolution during its radical Jacobin phase—it was not carried through successfully.

The situation was different in the Bolshevik Revolution. The course of the revolution was different and so were its effects. It is possible to say that this revolution was a combination of a Western super-rational ideology with a different socio-political tradition than that which prevailed in the West. By super-rational ideology we understand an ideology proposing the rational reorganisation of the whole of society according to a presupposed (if not always confessed) ethical vision. It seems to us that it is possible to say, even more, that the realisation of such a super-rational vision was impossible (other than by military imposition) in the western sphere with a developed civil society but was historically possible in Russia. This is our reinterpretation of Lenin's famous thesis that Russia was the weakest point in the capitalist world, where communist revolution could be possible. Attempts were made to introduce reform, from the time of Peter the Great and particularly from the mid-nineteenth century. Typically reforms were imposed from above. They were also ambivalent and contradictory in their execution and effects. Moreover social groups were weak and underdeveloped and did not provide fertile social soil in which reforms might take root. The Russian Empire remained a capstone state, still blocking potential for natural development of forces within society. It is difficult to speak of the existence of a civil society in the sense of a community with centres of social power independent of the state. After the emancipation of the serfs in Russia we had to deal rather with disintegrating masses without an appropriate institutional support capable of organising them into a civil society. In contradistinction to the earlier revolutions, the Russian Revolution had the character of a real social revolution where the remains of the old social and political structure (though not all its institutions) were smashed. New social relations began to be built after the revolution but according to dispositions from above. The Russian Revolution was a 'planned' revolution, whose goal was to realise a certain ideological vision. The force responsible for building these new social relations was the organised Communist Party. The major instrument for the building of the new relations was the party-state. The state (under the control of the party) did not so much open the way for the development of the new social order as create one anew. However, it must be stressed that in the newly created social-political whole, the state performed functions comparable to those of the former capstone state, though in an incomparably more ruthless, brutal—totalitarian— manner. One can speak of a continuation—indeed intensification—of the ages-old functions of the Russian state. The basic goal of the state remained the reproduction of the existing political order, and the domination of society.

In France an attempt at the rationalist building of social relations, under the direction of the Jacobins, did not succeed against the strength and opposition of civil society. In Russia, where no civil society existed, this model succeeded. It is interesting that even the Bolsheviks were surprised with the effects of the Revolution and for a certain time tried to build a civil society (NEP 1922–28). Yet even this was not the work of a spontaneous social process, but a partial retreat by a monopolistic state in the face of weakness and the threat of failure. It did not last.

To conclude, in examining the nature of European revolutions we can distinguish two types of revolution according to the type of state involved. Only the later revolutions (Russian, Chinese) were revolutions in which the state introduced profound transformation in social relations. The transformations did not come from within the society but were imposed upon it by the state. The earlier revolutions (Dutch, English, American, French) were basically political revolutions which altered the structure of the state.[67]

3 Revolutions and the Continuity of Law

We conclude by drawing some connections between the themes of Parts One and Two of this paper. Our aim here is not to solve but to outline problems, according to the thesis that problems put well are half-solved.

In the first part we argued that legal continuity goes well beyond mere identity of elements, and indeed can occur in the absence of such identity. For legal traditions are both very complex and richly layered. Some elements and some layers are more easily dispensed with than others—if only because, but not only because, more easily noticed. And in the history of European law, continuity has been long, multi-layered and profound.

In the second part we sought to show, using quite simple categories, that it is impossible to put all the revolutions which have occurred in Europe in the same theoretical bag. In particular we stressed a distinction between two general types of revolutions. Thus notwithstanding our debt to him, we disagree with Harold Berman's treatment of all European revolutions on the same theoretical level, as we do with his thesis of a unified European legal tradition. We stress parallel but different developments. We can agree with him, however, that revolutions have had a limited impact on legal tradition.[68]

Our aim throughout has been to explore the interrelationships between historical continuity and revolutionary change. Our thesis needs further empirical elaboration, but at present we are ready to offer some theoretical outline of further research. From our arguments we can draw one general thesis, namely that in both Western and later revolutions as well we can see a continuity of law so great that even revolutions have had a limited impact on it. How limited one regards this continuity depends upon the level of law one takes into account. In both types of revolutions continuities of detail, notwithstanding frequent denials of them and strenuous efforts to avoid them, are easy to demonstrate[69]—though in view of the weakness of Russian legal traditions much Soviet legislation was borrowed from foreign sources (albeit the same sources that nineteenth-century Russian legal reformers borrowed from). Beyond that we stressed that at what might be called the deep structure of legal perceptions of the world, legal values, and the place, role and significance of law in social and political life, continuity is marked. This is as much the case in organic states, where that significance is as central and great as it is in capstone states, where it is not and remains not.

We suggested that these two continuous paths of development were related to differences in the interplay between state and society. But we could venture the hypothesis that a necessary if not sufficient element of the birth of the western type of social development was a specific kind of law. This never existed in our second historical example, Russia. In effect we can speak about two different traditions within one geographical unit. Traditions which survived not only political revolutions in the West but social revolution in Russia as well.

In the cases of Western development, political revolutions occurred as the realisation of demands which came out of civil society and the new form of state was a response to pressures from that society. In the second pattern revolution was the effect of weakness of the capstone, and a new society (but not a civil society) was created according to pressures from the political structure. Theda Skocpol put the thesis that one of the most important outcomes of revolutions was the strengthening of states. This thesis seems to us true but we should underline a distinction between different sources of state strength, according to the above models. In the first pattern states become more powerful because of the power of the civil societies within them, while on the second model the state becomes powerful because for a certain period it can harness society to the aims of the state. And on the first model power is socially grounded, whereas in the second model—as contemporary events in communist states reveal—it is not.

In the light of this distinction one can explain why in the Western legal tradition law was never reduced to a pure instrument of state power and on the other hand why the official Marxist legal ideology in communist countries remained 'vulgar socialist normativism'. In both cases we have to do with very different and very old legal traditions. At the present time hopes are developing, not so much for a meshing of these traditions as rather for a renaissance of the Western tradition in parts of Eastern Europe—particularly Poland—and for its grafting onto the Soviet Union. In Poland the pressures—typically—emanate from below, from a heavily bruised but regenerate civil society. In Russia, equally typically, they come primarily from a degenerate state in crisis. We do not speak of Poland, since it has not been our subject here. As to Russia, with some reservations we wish these efforts well, and it is no part of our aim to deny that new things can happen in history. Yet while hope springs eternal, and failure is a great educator, the precedents are not altogether encouraging.

NOTES

1   See esp. Gadamer, *Truth and Method, passim.*
2   Ibid. p 358.
3   Martin Krygier, 'Law as tradition' unpublished MS chs 2 and 5. See also Krygier, 'Law as tradition', *Law and Philosophy* 5 (1986), pp 237–62, esp. s.2; 'The traditionality of statutes', *Ratio Juris* I (1988), pp 20–39.
4   Harold Berman characterises Western law since the twelfth century as belonging to a common and continuing tradition, in the light of two characteristics. These are the combination of both the *fact* of continuous growth over centuries, 'with each generation consciously building on the work of previous generations' (*Law and Revolution. The Formation of the Western Legal Tradition* Cambridge Mass., 1983; p 5) and a shared conception of this growth as an organic development, 'an ongoing, growing body of principles and procedures, constructed—like the cathedrals—over generations and centuries'. Ibid. p 118).
5   See, for example, R C van Caenegem, *Judges, Legislators and Professors. Chapters in European Legal History* (Cambridge, 1987) chs 7–8 and also F H Lawson, *The Rational Strength of English Law* (London, 1951) p 19. Recently it has been argued that this continuity is equally a feature of English social and economic history. See Alan MacFarlane, *The Origins of English Individualism* (London, 1978); MacFarlane, *The Culture of Capitalism* (Oxford, 1987).
6   See S F C Milsom, *Historical Foundations of the Common Law,* second edition (London, 1981).
7   See Berman op. cit. pp 17–18 and David Ibbetson's review of this book, 'Law, religion and revolution in the twelfth century', *Oxford Journal of Legal Studies* 6 (1986), p 139.

8   See A W B Simpson, 'The survival of the common law system' in *Legal Theory and Legal History*, (London, Humbledon, 1987), pp 383–402.

9   Ibid. p 383.

10 John Henry Merryman, 'The Italian Style I: Doctrine', *Stanford Law Review* 18 (1965) p 41.

11 Cf. Berman, op. cit.

12 Cf. Charles M Radding, *The Origins of Medieval Jurisprudence* (New Haven, 1988).

13 Cf. Stephen Kuttner, 'The revival of jurisprudence' in *Renaissance and Renewal in the Twelfth Century*, Robert L Benson and Giles Constable, eds (Cambridge, Mass., 1982).

14 Cf. Berman, op. cit. p 123 and *passim*.

15 Cf. Watson, *The Making of Civil Law* (Cambridge, Mass., Harvard UP, 1981) p 179 and *passim*.

16 'The model of rules I' in *Taking Rights Seriously* (London, 1978).

17 *The Concept of Law* (Oxford, 1961).

18 See especially 'Hard cases' in *Taking Rights Seriously*, pp 81–130; *A Matter of Principle* (Cambridge, Mass., 1985); *Law's Empire* (London, 1986).

19 'Juristic science and law', *Harvard Law Review* 31 (1918) pp 1047–63; 'The theory of judicial decision I', *Harvard Law Review* 36 (1923), pp 641–62; 'The theory of judicial decision II', *Harvard Law Review* 36 (1923), pp 802–25; 'The theory of judicial decision III', *Harvard Law Review* 36 (1923), pp 940–59; 'The ideal element in American judicial decision', *Harvard Law Review* 45 (1932), pp 136–48; 'Hierarchy of sources and forms in different systems of law', *Tulane Law Review* 7 (1933), pp 475–87; 'A comparison of ideals of law', *Harvard Law Review* 47 (1933), pp 1–17; 'What is law?', *West Virginia Law Quarterly* 47 (1940), pp 1–12. For some recent uses of these writings see Julius Stone, 'From principles to principles', *Law Quarterly Review* 97 (1981), pp 224–57; *Precedent and Law* (Sydney, 1985), ch 13; A R Blackshield, 'The legitimacy and authority of judges', *University of New South Wales Law Journal* 10 (1987), pp 155–72.

20 'Hierarchy of sources and forms in different systems of law', p 476.

21 Ibid. p 483.

22 Ibid. p 484.

23 Ibid. p 485.

24 Roscoe Pound, 'The theory of judicial decision', *Harvard Law Review* 36 (1922–3), p 648.

25 Arthur Glass, 'Dworkin, Fish and legal practice', *Bulletin of the Australian Society of Legal Philosophy* 10 (1986), p 224.

26 '. . . except in cases within the four corners of rules in the narrower sense, the authoritative technique and the received ideals are at least quite as important elements in the process of decision as the authoritative precepts . . . The hierarchy of forms has no application to these. Everywhere the technique is traditional, and it is hardly set forth for what it really is even in doctrinal writing. The ideals are to be found in doctrinal writing, and in the English-speaking world in the decisions of the courts. But they are nowhere stated in such form as to call for the gradations of authority which obtain in the case of rules.' (Ibid.).

27 'A comparison of ideals of law', *Harvard Law Review* 47 (1933), p 4.

28 Ibid. p 477.

29 Zweigert and Kotz consider that 'the critical thing about legal systems is their *style*' (Konrad Zweigert and Hein Kotz, *Introduction to Comparative Law*, second revised edition, translated from the German by Tony Weir, Oxford, 1987, p 68).

They distinguish and discuss five factors which they regard as:
crucial for the style of a legal system or legal family: (1) its historical
background and development, (2) its predominant and characteristic mode
of thought in legal matters, (3) especially distinctive institutions, (4) the kind
of legal sources it acknowledges and the way it handles them, and (5) its
ideology (p 69).

30 P S Atiyah and R S Summers, *Form and Substance in Anglo-American Law* (Oxford,
1987), distinguish between characteristic English and American 'visions' of law,
defining 'vision' as 'a set of inarticulate and perhaps even unconscious beliefs held
by the general public at large and, to some extent, also by politicians, judges, and
legal practitioners, as to the nature and functions of law—how and by whom it
should be made, interpreted, applied, and enforced' (p 411).

31 Eugene Kamenka and Alice Erh-Soon Tay, 'Beyond bourgeois individualism: the
contemporary crisis in law and legal ideology' in *Feudalism, Capitalism and
Beyond*, Kamenka and R S Neale, eds (London, 1975) p 128. See also Philippe
Nonet and Philip Selznick, *Law and Society in Transition: Toward Responsive Law*
(New York, 1978); and Roberto Mangabeira Unger, *Law in Modern Society* (New
York, 1976).

32 Cf. Clifford Geertz, 'Local knowledge: fact and law in comparative perspective', in
Local Knowledge. Further Essays in Interpretive Anthropology (New York, 1983),
p 215.

33 Geoffrey Sawer, 'The western conception of law', in *International Encyclopedia of
Comparative Law*, volume II (Tubingen, 1975), pp 46–7.

34 'What is law?', *West Virginia Law Quarterly* 47 (1940), p 5.

35 'Hierarchy of sources and forms in different systems of law', p 477.

36 See Hans Kelsen, *General Theory of Law and State*, trans. by Anders Wedberg
(New York, 1961), ch XI, 'The hierarchy of norms', and *The Pure Theory of Law*,
trans. from the second German edition by Max Knight (Berkeley, 1970), p 35, 'The
hierarchical structure of the legal order'.

37 *The concept of Law* (Oxford, 1961).

38 Ibid. p 91.

39 See Karl R Popper, 'Towards a rational theory of tradition', in *Conjectures and
Refutations* (London, 1969), p 127.

40 Though Berman seems convinced the tradition is finally on the skids, his arguments
to this effect are the most impressionistic and least supported in the book.

41 John H Merryman, 'On the convergence (and divergence) of the civil law and the
common law' in *New Perspectives for a Common Law of Europe*, Mauro
Cappelletti, ed (Leyden, 1978), pp 195–233.

42 Cf. Pound, 'Hierarchy of sources and forms in different systems of law', p 486.
Everywhere the technique is traditional and it is hardly set forth for what it
really is even in doctrinal writing.

43 Cf. Jean Louis Goutal, 'Characteristics of Judicial style in France, Britain and the
U.S.A.', *American Journal of Comparative Law* 24 (1976), pp 43–72; Bernard
Rudden, 'Courts and codes in England, France and Soviet Russia', *Tulane Law
Review* 48 (1974), pp 1010–28.

44 'Courts and codes in England, France and Soviet Russia', pp 1014.

45 'The invisible discourse of the law. Reflections on legal literacy and general
education' in *Heracles' Bow. Essays on the Rhetoric and Poetics of the Law*
(Madison, 1985).

46 Ibid. p 63.

47 See Alan Watson, *Legal Transplants* (Virginia, 1973).

48 See J H Beckstrom, 'Transplantation of legal systems: an early report on the reception of western laws in Ethiopia', *American Journal of Comparative Law* 21 (1973), pp 557–583; idem. 'Handicaps of legal-social engineering in a developing nation', *American Journal of Comparative Law* 22 (1974) pp 697–712. See also O Kahn-Freund, 'On uses and misuses of comparative law', *Modern Law Review* 37 (1974) pp

49 See Watson, *Legal Transplants*; and idem. 'Legal transplants and law reform', *Law Quarterly Review* 92 (1976) p 79.

50 'Local knowledge: fact and law in comparative perspective', in *Local Knowledge. Further Essays in Interpretive Anthropology* (New York, 1983) p 215. Cf. Karl Llewellyn's observation of American judges:

> The judges are . . . not mere Americans. They have been law-conditioned. They *see* things, they see *significances* . . . Moreover, they *think* like lawyers, not like laymen; and more particularly like *American* layers, not like German lawyers or Brazilian lawyers (*The Common Law Tradition*, Boston, 1960, pp 19–20).

51 See Michael Mann's explanations in his short essay 'European miracle . . . historical explanation' in *Europe and the Rise of Capitalism*, J Beachler, J Hall, M Mann, eds (Oxford, 1988).

52 Cf. Michael Mann, *Sources of Social Power*, vol 1, *A History of Power from the Beginning to 1760 A.D.* (Cambridge, 1986).

53 See J Beachler, J A Hall, M Mann, eds, *Europe and the Rise of Capitalism*.

54 *States and Social Revolutions. A Comparative Analysis of France, Russia and China* (1979), 4.

55 R R Palmer, *The Age of the Democratic Revolution* (Princeton, NJ, 1959) vol I.

56 See John Phillip Reid, *Constitutional History of the American Revolution: The Authority of Rights* (Madison, 1986); John Phillip Reid, *Constitutional History of the American Revolution: The Authority to Tax* (Madison, 1987); Jack P Greene, *Peripheries and Center: Constitutional Development in the Extended Policies of the British Empire and the United States, 1607–1788* (Athens, Georgia, 1987).

57 Hannah Arendt quoted in Eugene Kamenka 'Revolutionary ideology and The Great French Revolution of 1789–?' in *The Permanent Revolution. The French Revolution and Its Legacy 1789–1989*, C Best, ed (London, 1988), p 99.

58 Cf. Peter Stein, 'Judge and jurist in the civil law: a historical interpretation', *Louisiana Law Review* 46 (1985), pp 241–57 at 253.

59 *Powers and Liberties. The Causes and Consequences of the Rise of the West* (London, 1985).

60 Cf. Ibid. p 35: 'Those who have written about empires have tended to stress either strength or weakness. But *both* were present, and the paradox (for it is not a contradiction) of empires is that their strength that is their monuments, their arbitrariness, their scorn for human life, hides, is based upon, and reflects social weakness. They are not able to deeply penetrate, change and mobilise the social order. Empires have . . . strong blocking but weak enabling powers'.

61 Ibid. p 137.

62 'First, much of Europe had a substantial predisposition toward representative, non-autocratic government by virtue of the peculiar institutions and power relations that developed during the medieval period. The decentralized and yet fairly stable political structures of Europe have no counterparts in China, Japan, the Ottoman Empire, or the Mongol successor states of Central Asia. In this respect we ought to be careful to avoid accounting for the outcomes of the modern world by processes developing only since beginnings of modernization. Nor can Europe

and non-European countries be utilized in a comparative study without making clear the importance of feudal assemblies, local government, and town charters'. Brian M Downing 'Constitutionalism, warfare, and political change in early modern Europe', *Theory and Society* 17 (1988) p 46.

63   J Habermas 'Law as medium and law as institution' in *Dilemmas of Law in the Welfare State*, G Teubner, ed (Berlin, 1986), p 212.

64   *Russia Under the Old Regime* (Harmondsworth, 1974), p 51.

65   'Public law—private law', in *Public and Private in Social Life*, S I Benn and G F Gaus, eds (London, 1983), p 69.

66   See the excellent analysis of the perception of *feudalism* by French bourgeoisie during the French Revolution made by J Markoff, 'Słowa i rzeczy: rewolucja burzuazyjna francuska definuje system feudalny' in *Interpretacje Wielkiej Transformacji*, A Czarnota and A Zybertowicz, eds (Warszawa, 1988), pp 357–82.

67   In these reflections we have ignored failed revolutions, such as the Hungarian and Spanish and the so-called post-war revolutions of Central Europe. In the first case this is because the revolutions ended in defeat. In the second because the first phase of these 'revolutions' depended on a completely different set of (geopolitical) factors.

68   Kalman Kulcsar in his articles 'Politics and law-making in Central-East-Europe' in *Legal Theory, Comparative Law*, Zoltan Peteri, ed (Budapest, 1984), pp 179–209, described the survival of traditions of perception of law after communist revolutions.

69   See Hubert Izdebski, 'Rewolucja i prawo w Europie w XX wieku', Part 1, *Czasopismo Prawno-Historyczne* 38, 2 (1986) pp 79–117; Part 2, *Czasopismo Prawno-Historyczne*, 39, 1 (1987) pp 111–58, Izdebski, 'La Tradition et le changement en droit. L'example des pays socialistes', *Revue Internationale de Droit Compare* 4 (1987) pp 839–88. Olympiad S Ioffe, 'Soviet law and Roman law *Boston University Law Review* (1982) pp 701–28. Rodolfo Sacco, 'The Romanist substratum in the civil law of the socialist countries', *Review of Socialist Law* 14 (1988) pp 65–86. Peter Stein, 'Judge and jurist in the civil law: a historical interpretation', *Louisiana Law Review* 46 (1985) pp 241–57. On the general issue of the heritability of law, see Alice Erh-Soon Tay and Eugene Kamenka, 'Marxism-Leninism and the heritability of law', *Review of Socialist Law* 6 (1980) pp 261–74.

CHAPTER 11

Legal Dogmatics and the Concept of a Scientific Revolution

Jyrki Uusitalo

1 The Importance of Factual Analysis

A number of philosophers and historians of science (Schelling, 1803/1974, Kuhn, 1970), in the context of the post-Kuhnian aftermath, have maintained that revolutions in scientific thought do occur. Nevertheless, the concept of a scientific revolution has usually been taken to be quite hard to define analytically. Some of the difficulties encountered may have resulted from the nature of the analysis undertaken. The typical conceptual analysis usually must assume that there is already something more or less well entrenched about the meaning of the concept or concepts under study, such as, in our case, the concept of a revolution in science. In those cases in which this initial assumption may not be particularly warranted, conceptual analysis should be augmented accordingly.

One way to do this is to recall and mobilise another kind (or, in fact, another and complementary dimension) of analysis—analysis of the sort that John L Mackie in his philosophical writings sometimes calls 'factual analysis', as distinguished from conceptual analysis in the elementary sense of the latter (cf. Stroud, 1986). A factual analysis of, say, revolutions in scientific thought would be, in Mackie's view, an important dimension of research, since it is this kind of analysis that puts theorising in touch with the realities of the states of affairs that are under scrutiny.

What, then, is factual analysis all about? It is a kind of learning process which is at issue here. When we are making use (or about to make use) of some concept, factual analysis advises us to reflect upon the nature of those things, states of affairs and processes that *de facto* exist and take place in the domain where we wish to make use of the concept or concepts in question. These states of affairs and processes often turn out to be different from what we first thought. Some of our received concepts perhaps are only weakly anchored in reality, some of them maybe not at all. And it is these exciting discrepancies between our assumptions about the furniture of the reality and the reality of that furniture itself that constitute both a natural point of departure for a deepened enquiry into that reality and, eventually, a re-evaluation and self-correction of our own assumptions.

This paper sets out to examine to what extent the concept of a scientific revolution makes sense in attempts aimed at a theoretical reconstruction of basic intellectual and cognitive processes in legal dogmatics. Although the title may easily give the impression that the orientation of the paper is largely fashioned in terms of conceptual analysis, the importance of a factual analysis of the sort just expounded is nevertheless to be noted here. In the case of legal dogmatics, the factual dimension of its meta-analysis may be mobilised by way of a comparison of the relative merits and demerits of 'revolutionary' vs. 'evolutionary' reconstructions of the basic processes of reasoning and the validation of results in legal dogmatic inquiry. It will be argued that it is indeed warranted to think that we may sensibly talk about revolutionary scientific processes in legal dogmatic inquiry, in a Kuhnian albeit somewhat additionally specified sense. And further, it will be argued that this is to an important degree due to the fact that a pure evolutionary framework of reconstruction is not enough from the viewpoint of social studies of science dealing with legal dogmatics as their subject matter.

It is, then, more or less in contrast with the notion of scientific evolution that the notion of a revolution in science will be understood in the present paper. This contrast is, admittedly, to some degree a relative one, and nor do I wish to maintain that accounts of science couched in terms of revolutions wholly can do without evolutionary assumptions. However, one of my glosses is that revolutions in disciplines such as legal dogmatics do have an irreducible role to play, and this I wish to substantiate in what follows.

2 Legal Dogmatics between Kuhn and Fleck

In legal theory, a number of arguments have been presented for the basic thesis that legal dogmatics—that is to say, the analysis of the substance and the content of valid law in any legal culture that has the framework of enacted statutes and agreed-upon legal sources as its underpinning framework—characteristically has a paradigm structure as its supporting skeleton. The viewpoints substantiating this idea may be divided, roughly speaking, into what I propose to call the internal and the external ones.

By the first designation, I mean a viewpoint of the sort that takes the constituting history and development of such a paradigm structure, for the purposes of the discussion, more or less as given and concentrates on elucidating the paradigm structure itself. Aarnio (1987, p 17 f) provides such a viewpoint by way of specifying the subject matter of normative regulation, the agreements on the sources of law, methodological rules and principles, and finally the interpretively relevant values and evaluations as the basic dimensions of what, following Kuhn, is termed the 'disciplinary matrix' of legal dogmatics—in other words, the basic furniture in the paradigm structure of the latter.

The interpretive activity of finding out the content of valid law is assumed to proceed under the guidance of such a structure, a structure which also makes possible a more or less friction-free communication between scholars as well as a common perception of problems, including such problem situations that posit themselves as anomalous and for the solution of which the paradigmatic structure functions as a resource.

On the whole, the internal perspective indeed admits that in agreeing upon some particular interpretation of the basic matrix, scholars do not accept it as a finished product but rather as something to be refined and elaborated in the (again following Kuhn) normal-scientific work of legal interpretation. It deserves to be added that this last-mentioned emphasis is in keeping with what some informed writers (e.g. Barnes, 1984, p 46 f), observe with reference to Kuhn's own basic stipulations.

What I have termed the external viewpoint functions in many respects as complementary to the internal one—in fact, to the extent that to talk of internal and external viewpoints in this particular context is to talk of two sides of the same coin. Important basic insights along the external dimensions of study are provided by Zuleta Puceiro (1985, p 129 f) as he observes that legal dogmatics itself should be seen as a historical notion the significance of which is based on the emergence of a larger socio-political 'culture matrix' itself: that is, on the historical consolidation of the legal positivistic image of a 'value-free' legal science which is significative of the rationalisation and formalisation of morality and civil society through law and the state (for a closer discussion of these developments, cf. Zuleta Puceiro, 1983, p 341 f).

The significance of these contextualities that have accompanied the emergence of dogmatic legal analysis in the form that is now familiar to us explains one feature of interpretive dogmatic legal analysis which should be observed by any attempts at such a factual analysis as was delineated earlier. This feature is the relatively active sensitivity to anomalies in dogmatic analysis. Cases that are 'hard', that is, those that involve legal gap situations in various forms, are usually detected quite sensitively at the level of the dogmatic scholars' professional consciousness, although attempts at solving them may be more or less routinised—albeit in such a way that does not automatically guarantee any 'algorithmic' success in solving them. But in any case, behind the inquiry itself there is the central pragmatic motivating need to 'succeed' in accommodating into the legal system those cases and those targets of regulation that are initially perceived as deviations from the normal and the routine.

I believe that it is in virtue of those historical viewpoints that I have above termed 'external', that we are now able to situate the paradigm framework of legal dogmatics, as it were, between two models of science in general, models not unrelated with each other. The first one of them is, in a rather Kuhnian fashion, any such model of a major natural scientific field the development of which may be conceived of in terms of phases of normal science whereby a paradigm is articulated in new domains and intermittently also reformulated or (as one particular interpretation of the basic matrix) even discarded in favour of another, as anomalous developments turn up and demand accommodation. Examples of such developments that classical history of science is able to marshal, concerning developments in physics or astronomy, may comparatively speaking shed light also on corresponding developments in dogmatic legal analysis. Problems and prospects of such a comparison in general have been discussed in legal theoretical literature (Villa, 1985).

There is, however, another aspect to be added to our picture of the continuities and discontinuities in legal dogmatics. And I believe that it is only by incorporating this aspect that we may be in a position to also *explain* how and why these continuities and discontinuities are intermingled in the way they are. When approaching this aspect, we should let ourselves be informed by a now classical analysis of the structure of a discipline other than physics and astronomy. I mean, of course, Ludwik Fleck's pioneering work on the dynamics of knowledge in medicine (Fleck, 1935/1980).

Fleck's interest in medicine was motivated by observations that have a number of consequences for any attempt at elaborating the paradigm framework to be used in studies of legal science. First of all, medicine combines theoretical and experimental aspects of science with such aspects as may be characterised therapeutic and practical. The structure of inquiry in medicine is collective and also interdisciplinary in the sense that previous premises of reasoning frequently must be reformulated in the light of information obtained in neighbouring fields. The research interests in medicine have to do with deviations from the normal (i.e., with pathological states of organisms) rather than with the normal *per se*. And finally, medicine is underpinned by a pragmatic need to succeed, through research and aided by it, in the solution of problems. On the basis of all these basic observations, Fleck concludes that medicine is characterised by an ever-present tension between attempts at a theoretical unification, only attainable through abstraction, and the necessity of concretising the results which, in turn, gives rise to a plurality of competing accounts when scholars are dealing with given topics.

To those familiar with the history of the literature on science studies, it is a well known fact that Kuhn's concept of a paradigm was more or less influenced by Fleck's basic intuitions, especially by his idea that on account of the above tension there emerges time and time again a dominant standpoint in a particular research field, which, however, sooner or later is challenged by new conceptions. (Cf. Kuhn, 1970, pp vi–vii). In our present context, what perhaps remains easily overlooked is the fact that almost all of the central charac-teristics that Fleck presents about the specific nature of medicine are more or less easily transferable into the description of dogmatic and interpretive legal science as well: the collective (or rather, in this case, auditory-relative) and argumentative structure of inquiry, the special motivation of centring inquiry on cases and situations that are interesting due to the very fact that they deviate from or remain outside of (routine) norms, as well as the pragmatic need to secure as much success as possible—in this case normative and regulative success, especially in view of the broader social setting of legal dogmatic inquiry. That is to say, Fleck helps us see some of those salient features of legal dogmatics that may serve as points of anchorage for a factual analysis which seeks to substantiate the claim that 'revolutionary' theoretical developments, which also have practical relevance, do have their place in the overall scientific field of dogmatic legal science.

It is for this reason that I have chosen to designate the position of legal dogmatics as a subject matter of social and philosophical science studies as a position 'between Kuhn and Fleck'. What should be borne in mind here is, of course, that the two emphases so designated are in no way incompatible with one another but rather complementary. For Kuhn, as a source for our more amplified frameworks of the dynamics of science, deserves (and needs) to be read through some of his most important predecessors as well, not only through all those debating paradigms in his aftermath.

3 *The Poverty of Purely Evolutionary Accounts of Science*

In the previous section it was mentioned that some particular and decisive characteristics of certain (not necessarily all) disciplines, such as those detected by Fleck in medicine and having obvious counterparts in legal science, might help us also explain the nature of actual scientific development in these disciplines. This point must now be substantiated. I propose to substantiate it by way of a short discussion of the following point: how would a 'purely' evolutionary view of scientific development (and, eventually, progress) be able to accommodate such characteristics in its overall picture of science as a process? If they seem to fit this picture only more or less poorly, this would then amount to an entrenchment of an essentially non-evolutionary view, that is, a view which emphasises the discrepancies between normal or routine inquiry and jumps in developments and which is better able to accommodate them. (Notice my terminological stipulation: I am treating evolution and revolution as, roughly speaking, concepts being the contrary of one another. This should be enough for our purposes. It would appear somewhat sweeping to talk of a relation of contradiction here.)

Evolutionary accounts of science, by and large, seem to suggest that scientific intuitions, innovations and theories may be (and, as a rule, are) able to secure their success if the scientists who are reproducing and replicating these intuitions and theories also manage to persuade other scientists to believe in these theories by any normal techniques of scientific communication. There have been several large-scale attempts to account for how this takes place, mostly within natural science (Hull, 1988). A sophisticated evolutionary perspective would probably also reserve a role for the 'genuine' cognitive properties of the scientific units undergoing the evolutionary process and claim that the success of some particular intuitions and theories is obviously also geared to their efficacy in this genuinely cognitive sense. However, what mostly seem to be missing in evolutionary accounts of this sort are an examination of the grounds of the theoretical success (and, respectively, with the more unfortunate cognitive units, their theoretical failure) as well as the ensuing inability to anticipate which *kind* of assumptions and theories *will* succeed. There have been critiques of, say, Hull in this regard (Ridley, 1989), as well as more general critical surveys of socio-biological accounts of scientific reason (e.g. Sintonen, 1988).

The above point can also be made in another way: evolutionary frameworks seem to be able to incorporate only very poorly (if at all) the dimension of an explicit (although metaphorically conceived) agenda of the critical problematic of any particular discipline. Alasdair MacIntyre has stressed the importance of such an agenda for any tradition-constituted inquiry which wishes to be able rationally to evaluate both its forwards- and its backwards-pointing developmental prospects: what is at issue is the agenda of unsolved problems and unresolved issues by reference to which scientific success or lack of it in making rational progress toward some further stage of development will be evaluated (MacIntyre, 1988, p 361). And as he adds, it may also happen to any tradition-constituted inquiry that by its own standards of progress it ceases to make progress.

This is an illuminating viewpoint, to which it should be immediately added that in order for this to be possible, within the tradition, discipline, or profession in question there must be some institutionalised mechanism through which evaluations of this sort may be undertaken. An essential part of the function of such a mechanism is to supply, at critical stages of conceptual and theoretical reappraisal , some explanatory account of how and why things went wrong. One is reminded of the Marquis de Condorcet's famous dictum that the explanation of the errors that have been made should be part and parcel of the progress of the human mind (Condorcet, 1793/1976, p 37). Purely evolutionary accounts of scientific advancement do not, as a rule, have a role for the operation of such a mechanism. (This is not to deny that upon their own premises, they might posit such a mechanism as an additional factor explaining the selection of the fittest alternatives. But this would not liberate them from the burden of evolutionarily explaining, again, the functioning of this mechanism.) In legal dogmatics, an evolutionary model of scholars' being able always to select the most feasible lines of interpretation would perhaps function well enough if we were able to make strong enough background assumptions concerning the operative context of legal inquiry—assumptions fashioning the social and political profile of legal dogmatics largely as informed by societal states of affairs that obtained several decades, even centuries, ago. Such assumptions would be, unfortunately, unencumbered by the factors of cognitive and normative uncertainty that *do* have a role to play in the development of modern law: we have come a long way since the emergence of the dogmatic matrix in its historically first forms.

4 *Revolutions and Their Role in Legal Dogmatics*

If purely evolutionary accounts, then, do not seem particularly feasible in social studies of legal dogmatics, there remains the natural alternative of granting revolutions a genuine role in the development of this discipline. Revolutions in this context, for all purposes of analysis, may be defined along the Kuhnian lines as shifts of professional commitments occurring during extraordinary research episodes (Kuhn, 1970, p 6) or as processes of displacement occurring in the conceptual network of viewing the world (ibid. p 102). The broader background context for revolutionary episodes is probably correctly surmised by Heller (1986, pp 187–8) as he writes that in situations where existing legal practices are disturbed, the resettlement of a (now altered) practice is not positively determined by the logical application of theoretically coherent rules but rather proceeds a-logically or *analogically* and may involve reference to other competing theoretical models of legal practice.

Heller seems to have a point in emphasising the analogical nature of legal interpretation (although I would be reluctant to talk about its a-logicality; analogy has its formal properties, after all). The most important dimension of such an analogy seems to be the conceptual and theoretical interaction that takes place between the received conceptions and the new ones: while the previously unfamiliar situations are fashioned as instances of the familiar, the familiar itself is also seen in a new light. Along this dimension, there is perhaps not so much drama about revolutions in doctrinal and scientific thinking. Rather they are the natural conclusion of developments that have been underway for some time. As Kuhn pointed out, a new theory, however special its range of application, seldom merely adds something that is already known: 'Its assimilation requires the reconstruction of prior theory and the re-evaluation of prior fact, an intrinsically revolutionary process that is seldom completed by a single man and never overnight' (Kuhn, 1970, p 7).

It seems to be in this very characterisation that Kuhn,—in one of his not so frequent conceptually completely lucid moments—catches an important point about what the revolutionary ingredient of scientific innovation in fact means. It is the new way of situating the contents of the past in relation to the present. In the context of acquiring legal understandings, this would amount to the conscious policy of letting the received legal conventions and the cases and topics of interpretation of the present confront each other in a conceptually interactive manner. It is never 'the past' as an allegedly unified and, in some sense, intellectually monolithic whole which is being encountered in interpretations as the so-called legal conventions are being resorted to. What is at stake in any talk about a legal 'convention' (or 'tradition', for that matter) is, for instance, a number of various sorts of precedents and other legal sources plainly and simply devised at a point of time clearly different from that of any conceivable 'present' case. To re-enact a tradition in law is to make a temporal and historical linkage between these sources and one's present interpretive situation. Some legal theorists have convincingly argued in favour of this inherently interactive and dynamic structure of any conceivable and typical legal tradition (Krygier, 1988).

The above specifications open up a perspective in which typically 'revolutionary' research ideas in a discipline underpinned by such (Fleckian) theoretical and pragmatic motives as I have argued legal dogmatics to possess, can best be seen as not-yet-wholly-realised, or simply unrealised, solutions that have to be made to work by scholars who are engaged in constructing, and showing the rational possibility of, results anticipated by such normative solutions. Thereby ingredients of the legal tradition—the latter understood in the above described 'non-essentialistic' sense—are activated as well. (A case in point might be the debate on the possibility of social principles incorporated in private law.) Such ideas are *not* depictable simply as *ex ante* conjectures to be subjected to test in a research process. Rather, legal dogmatic research in its periods of renewal seems to have a peculiar and interesting character since most of the research is conducted only after the solution has been arrived at.

That is to say, it is the potentialities of the unrealised capacities of normative and legal regulation that drive the research forward. (Points similar to this concerning any sort of laboratory research have been made in recent constructivist sociology of science; cf. Knorr, 1980.) And in order to gain an insight into what precisely it is that has remained unrealised so far, an evaluation of the sources delivered by the tradition (in the above described modest sense of the term) needs to be undertaken as well, since it is these sources that reveal the resources as well as the shortcomings of the past—*at the moment* they are brought in as data to situations that signify a conceptual dislodgement and reinterpretation in the law. (It should be fairly easy to draw a parallel to this from social and political revolutions: it is after all the latter that bestow a meaning on the periods leading up to them; and this seems to be a process which need not, and should not, involve any Truth Ministries as its midwives.)

The rational acceptability of interpretations and alternative ways of making the best out of the legal order, which has been considered to constitute a regulative principle of legal dogmatics (Aarnio, 1987, p 225 f), might be, in the light of the above viewpoints concerning the relatively mundane features of revolutionary phases in legal dogmatic interpretation, seen as its constitutive principle as well. Rational acceptability constitutes a yardstick for appraisal and acceptance as well as for criticism. The significance of this principle is also signalled by an additional, factually relevant point that has been emphasised (e.g. by Zuleta Puceiro, 1983, p 344 f): that the traditional ethos of uniform state-monopoly regulation, with which legal dogmatics was earlier imbued, is giving way to new publicly-grounded forms of securing consensus and political and social legitimacy. This would obviously call for the emergence of legal scholars' critically evaluative and non-contemplative relationship to the legal reality. Such a relationship would be, in principle, comparable, say, with the emergence of modern scientists' critical and experimental attitude as contrasted with contemplative and phenomenal ones (on the latter contraposition, cf. Bayertz, 1981, p 17 f). In view of such challenges, the notion of rational acceptability should perhaps indeed be seen not only as the regulative but also as the constitutive principle of legal dogmatics, since it can be seen as the kind of an institutionalisable medium and mechanism of self-evaluation whose significance is likely to be underrated by any purely evolutionary account. Maybe this kind of a medium may best serve as the link between rationality and revolution in legal dogmatics.

REFERENCES

Aulis Aarnio, *The Rational as Reasonable. A Treatise on Legal Justification* (Dordrecht, 1987),

Barry Barnes, *T S Kuhn and Social Science* (New York, 1984).

Kurt Bayertz, 'Über Begriff und Problem der wissenschaftlichen Revolution', in *Wissenschaftsgeschichte und wissenschaftliche Revolution*, Bayertz, ed (Köln, 1981), pp 11–28.

Antoine-Nicolas de Condorcet, *Entwurf einer historischen Darstellung der Fortschritte des menschlichen Geistes*, Wilhelm Alff, ed (Frankfurt am Main, 1976; orig. in French 1793).

Ludwik Fleck, *Entstehung und Entwicklung einer wissenschaftlichen Tatsache*, Lothar Schäfer–Thomas Schnelle, eds (Frankfurt am Main, 1980; orig. in 1935).

Thomas Heller, 'Legal Discourse in the Positive State: A Post-Structuralist Account', in *Dilemmas of Law in the Welfare State*, Gunther Teubner, ed (Wien/New York, 1986), pp 173–99.

David Hull, *Science as a Process. An Evolutionary Account of the Social and Conceptual Development of Science* (Chicago, 1988).

Karin D Knorr, 'The scientist as an analogical reasoner: a critique of the metaphor theory of innovation', in *Sociology of the Sciences Yearbook*, vol IV (Dordrecht, 1980), pp 25–52.

Martin Krygier, 'The traditionality of statutes', *Ratio Juris*, 1 (1988), pp 20–39.

Thomas S Kuhn, *The Structure of Scientific Revolutions*, 2nd, enlarged edition (Chicago, 1970).

Alasdair MacIntyre, *Whose Justice? Which Rationality?* (London, 1988).

Mark Ridley, 'Beastly success', *Times Literary Supplement* (12–18 May, 1989), pp 503–4.

Friedrich Wilhelm Joseph Schelling, *Vorlesungen über die Methode des akademischen Studiums*, Walter Ehrhardt, ed (Hamburg, 1974; orig. in 1803).

Matti Sintonen, 'Sociobiology helps—but not enough', *Science Studies* 1 (1988), pp 43–9.

Barry Stroud, 'Choices in an unreal world', *Times Literary Supplement* (18 April, 1986), p 424.

Vittorio Villa, 'Theories of natural sciences and theories of legal science. Models and analogies', *Archives for Philosophy of Law and Social Philosophy* (ARSP), Beiheft 25 (1985), pp 111–16.

Enrique Zuleta Puceiro, 'Scientific paradigms and legal change', in *Essays in Legal Theory in Honour of Kaarle Makkonen* (Vammala, 1983), pp 331–47.

Enrique Zuleta Puceiro, 'Scientific paradigms and the growth of legal knowledge', *Archives for Philosophy of Law and Social Philosophy* (ARSP), Beiheft 25 (1985), pp 127–34.

CHAPTER 12

Wechsel von Paradigmen und Stilen in der praktischen juristischen Argumentation: eine empirische Untersuchung von Argumentationen des Schweizerischen Bundesgerichts, 1881–1980

Fritz Dolder

Abstract Practical legal reasoning has the primary function of justifying judicial decisions in more or less logical and more or less persuasive terms. It does not contribute immediately to the growth of basic human knowledge and can thus not independently initiate or undergo Kuhnian changes of paradigms. It may, however, be compared to activities of applied science, and changes of the techniques of practical legal reasoning might therefore reflect changes of the cognitive or legislative dimensions of a legal system.

Isolated samples of practical judicial reasoning of the Federal Court of Switzerland in the field of private law (law of contract and law of tort) during the century 1881 to 1980 were characterised by the presence/absence of 13 standardised topics of reasoning. The general attitude of reasoning in different decades was judged on the basis of the relative frequency of occurrence of these different topics.

In contrast to what had been expected no significant difference in reasoning style between subsequent decades could be detected on the basis of this quantitative approach: the relative frequencies of each topic treated as binomial probabilities did not differ significantly in the single decades from their respective average frequencies during the entire century. Moreover, correlations between the rankings of frequency of each topic in single decades differed significantly from zero ($0.592^* < R_s < 0.895^{**}$), i.e. revealed a significantly positive correlation between the reasoning behaviour in different decades.

Although major issues of legal thought, like the impact of the purpose of norms

(Jhering: *Der Zweck im Recht,* 1877), the doctrine of *Interessenjurisprudenz* (Heck, 1912), *topische Jurisprudenz* (Viehweg, 1953) or the effect of practical consequences on statutory interpretation (*Folgenberücksichtigung*) were widely discussed in the professional community in the course of the century, none of these issues was apparently able to influence practical judicial reasoning to a significant extent. Thus, the systematic trend towards output determined methods of reasoning observed in judicial decisions of the years 1964 to 1978 in the Federal Republic of Germany in the context of the Münchener Projekt Rechtsprechungsänderungen (1982) could *not* be confirmed. Practical judicial reasoning of the Swiss Federal Court, as far as the indicated legal specialities and the century investigated are concerned, could rather be qualified as a highly conservative activity not significantly affected by a century of social and cultural change.

This conservative attitude in the choice of tools of reasoning is contrasted by major changes in the attitude of the Court towards citations of legal authors (widely used in Swiss judicial reasoning), which could be adequately described as *changes of style.* The frequency of citations in Court decisions has increased during the century by an impressive factor of $F \simeq 12.26$, while the ratio of foreign authors among the authors cited attained 80.5 per cent in 1891/1900, and decreased to 3.7 per cent in 1976/80 with a particularly dramatic loss in the percentage of German authors cited in the years following 1945, though not after 1933. This finding suggests an emotional dimension of the citation behaviour of the Court.

Einleitung

Praktische juristische Argumentation dient zur Begründung und Rechtfertigung von Einzelfallentscheidungen von Gerichten und Verwaltungsbehörden. Sie stellt die logische Verbindung zwischen dem Entscheid, den angewendeten Rechtsnormen und dem zu beurteilenden Sachverhalt her. Zwar geht die Argumentation im Einzelfall auf eine einzelne Person (Urteilsredaktor) zurück, doch es ist davon auszugehen, dass die Argumentation im Einzelfall kollektive sprachliche Verhaltensmuster einer professionellen Gemeinschaft zum Ausdruck bringt. Es ist die Vermutung geäussert worden, dass die praktische juristische Argumentation deutscher Gerichte in diesem Jahrhundert signifikante historische Veränderungen durchgemacht habe, wobei über die Einzelheiten dieser Veränderungen und deren Bewertung allerdings keine einheitliche Meinung besteht.[1] Die Aufgabe der vorliegenden Untersuchung besteht darin, die Übertragbarkeit dieser mehr oder weniger punktuellen Befunde auf das verwandte und in vielfacher Hinsicht historisch verbundene Rechtssystem der Schweiz in dem Jahrhundert 1881 bis 1980 mit dem verfeinerten Instrumentar nichtparametrischer statistischer Methoden zu überprüfen. In einem zweiten Schritt soll beurteilt werden, ob die gegebenenfalls beobachteten Einzelheiten mit den Kategorien Paradigma, Stil und Mode auf sinnvolle Weise beschrieben werden könnten.

Die Beurteilungskriterien: Paradigma, Stil, Mode

(1) Eine derartige Beurteilung der empirischen Daten hat dabei von folgenden charakteristischen Eigenschaften dieser Kategorien auszugehen: Der Begriff des *Paradigmas* in seinem ursprünglichen, an der historischen Entwicklung der Naturwissenschaften erarbeiteten Sinn charakterisiert Zustände und Vorgänge in den auf die kollektive Akkumulation menschlichen Wissens gerichteten kognitiven Wissenschaften. Er kennzeichnet Erkenntnisleistungen, welche für bestimmte wissenschaftliche Gemeinschaften Modellwirkung entfalten, weil und insofern sie beispiellos genug sind, um eine beständige Gruppe von Anhängern anzuziehen, und offen genug, um dieser Gruppe von Fachleuten alle möglichen weiteren Probleme zur Lösung zu überlassen.[2] Wechsel von Paradigmen erscheinen insofern als irreversibel, als altes und neues Paradigma sich gegenseitig inhaltlich ausschliessen[3] Dementsprechend hat der Fachmann für eine Leistungserstellung nach professionellen Standards nur in den kurzen Phasen von Krisen, in denen zwei Paradigmen nebeneinander koexistieren, die Wahl zwischen den beiden sich gegenseitig ausschliessenden Paradigmen und den mit diesen Paradigmen konformen Verhaltensweisen oder Gestaltungselementen, unter 'normalen' Verhältnissen aber niemals.

Dies beruht seinerseits auf dem Zusammenhang, dass den mit einem bestimmten Paradigma konformen Verhaltensregeln oder Gestaltungselementen in dem Sinne *ausschliesslich instrumenteller Charakter* zukommt, als sie sich im Rahmen des betreffenden Paradigmas als notwendige Instrumente zur Erzielung eines Leistungserfolges kennzeichnen, welcher Anspruch auf professionelles Niveau erhebt.[4] Zum Beispiel war es nach der Entdeckung des Sauerstoffs durch Lavoisier und seiner Erklärung der Verbrennungsvorgänge als Oxidationen nach professionellen Standards nicht mehr zulässig, Verbrennungsvorgänge nach der Phlogisthontheorie zu erklären. Oder es war nach der Erfindung des Transistors nach professionellen Standards nicht mehr zulässig, bestimmte Schaltungen mit den insoweit 'veralteten' Elektronenröhren zu bestücken. Aus diesem instrumentellen Charakter der paradigmakonformen Handlungselemente und der darauf beruhenden regelmässigen wechselseitigen Exklusion zweier auf dasselbe Erkenntnisobjekt gerichteter Paradigmen ergibt sich schliesslich, dass der Wechsel von Paradigmen mit derjenigen Verbesserung der Qualität der Leistungserstellung verbunden ist, welche gemeinhin mit dem Begriff des 'Fortschritts' umschrieben wird.[5]

(2) Demgegenüber charakterisiert der Begriff des *Stils* kollektiv determiniertes menschliches Verhalten als Ergebnis eines mehr oder weniger arbiträren Auswahlvorganges zwischen verschiedenen verfügbaren Ausführungs-oder Gestaltungsmitteln.[6] Bei der Erstellung einer stilbehafteten Leistung hat der Handelnde daher regelmässig die Wahl zwischen mehreren derartigen Gestaltungselementen. Diesen kommt (zumindest überwiegend) *expressiver Charakter* in dem Sinne zu, als sie sich nicht als notwendige Instrumente zur Erstellung einer stilbehafteten Leistung, sondern als echte

Handlungsalternativen kennzeichnen, die Leistung, also nach der einen oder der anderen Handlungsalternative nach professionellen Standards gültig erstellt werden kann.[7] Ein Kriminalroman über ein Tötungsdelikt kann sowohl in episch-realistischem Stil als auch in einem psychologisierend-barocken Stil geschrieben werden und in beiden Fällen seine Funktion zur Informationsvermittlung und Unterhaltung des Lesers nach professionellen Standards gültig erfüllen. Stilbildende Funktion kommt dabei den einzelnen Handlungselementen insofern zu, als sie eine 'expressive Identifizierbarkeit' von Handlungen bewirken und diese Identifizierbarkeit personenübergreifend aufrechterhalten.[8] Hinsichtlich der Erfüllung einer spezifischen Funktion bringt der Wechsel von Stilen keine funktionelle 'Verbesserung' der Qualität der Leistungserstellung und ist daher auch nicht mit 'Fortschritt' in dem hier verwendeten Sinne verbunden.

Moden unterscheiden sich von Stilen einzig durch die verhältnismässige Kurzfristigkeit ihres Wechsels. Auch sie charakterisieren kollektiv deter_ miniertes menschliches Verhalten in allen Lebensbereichen, wobei allerdings ein konventioneller Bedeutungsschwerpunkt in der menschlichen Bekleidung und Ernährung erkennbar ist. Es sollte allerdings nicht übersehen werden, dass auch Vorgänge in den kognitiven Bereichen von Moden beeinflusst werden und in diesem Sinne als 'modebehaftet' oder 'modisch' gelten können.[9]

Eignung der Kriterien zur Beurteilung der praktischen juristischen Argumentation

(3) Praktische juristische Argumentation dient zur Begründung und Rechtfertigung von Einzelfallentscheidungen von Gerichten und Verwaltungsbehörden. Sie ist nicht auf die Akkumulation des kollektiven menschlichen Wissens gerichtet und kann insofern auch kein Ojekt von Kuhnschen *Paradigmawechseln* im ursprünglichen Sinn sein. Es entspricht diesem Zusammenhang, wenn hervorgehoben worden ist, dass ein 'Fortschritt' in der Rechtsdogmatik zwar denkbar sei, aber eine 'erheblich kompliziertere Angelegenheit als der in den empirischen Wissenschaften' darstelle.[10]

Es liegt indessen näher, dass Paradigmawechsel in den kognitiven oder politischen Dimensionen eines Rechtssystems, also in der akademischen Wissenschaft vom Recht und in der Gesetzgebung, sich auf das praktische Argumentieren auswirken könnten, bzw. dass das praktische Argumentieren derartige Veränderungen rezipieren und nach aussen wiederspiegeln könnte. Praktisches Argumentieren wäre hierin mit Veränderungen in den angewandten, namentlich etwa den Ingenieurwissenschaften zu vergleichen. Auch diese profitieren bei Veränderungen ihrer praktischen Vorgehensweisen im Zeitablauf und damit hinsichtlich der Qualität ihrer Leistungserstellung unmittelbar vom Paradigmawechsel in den Grundlagenwissenschaften und verdanken diesen weitgehend ihren 'Fortschritt' im Sinne einer Verbesserung der Qualität der Leistungserstellung.

Was im Bereich praktischen juristischen Argumentierens Veränderungen in der Gesetzgebung betrifft, so stellt zumindest in den kontinentaleuropäischen Rechtssystemen jede Gesetzesänderung, also Veränderung der positiven Rechtslage, für die praktische Rechtsanwendung des betreffenden Sachgebiets einen Paradigmawechsel dar, indem alter und neuer Rechtszustand nicht oder gegebenenfalls nur für eine kurze Übergangszeit nebeneinander ko-existieren können. Ausnahmen dazu bilden Veränderungen der positiven Rechtslage durch Normen, welche lediglich einen faktischen Ist-Zustand fixieren und insofern als Normen mit reinem Symbolcharakter einzustufen sind, welche von 'vorneherein gar nicht darauf angelegt' sind, 'faktisch wirksam zu werden'.[11]

Versteht man indessen unter praktischer juristischer Argumentation ein von hinreichend allgemeinen Gesichtspunkten gesteuertes und insofern vom einzelnen Sachgebiet unabhängiges Handeln, so ist von derartigen 'lokalen' Paradigmaänderungen in der positiven Rechtslage nur dann ein unmittelbarer Einfluss auf dieses Argumentieren zu erwarten, wenn die veränderten positiven Normen den Prozess der richterlichen Begründung von Entscheidungen selbst betreffen. Derartige Normen sind indessen in den kontinentaleuropäischen Rechtssystemen des zwanzigsten Jahrhunderts selten ausgesprochen und sind in diesem Zeitraum noch seltener abgeändert worden.

Unmittelbare Einflüsse auf das praktische Argumentieren wären eher von einer akademischen Wissenschaft vom Recht zu erwarten, insbesondere, soweit sich diese mit der Methode der Rechtsanwendung beschäftigt. Inwiefern indessen Änderungen in diesem Bereich der Charakter von Para-digmawechseln zukommt, muss mit einiger Zurückhaltung beurteilt werden, da wie bei vielen geisteswissenschaftlichen Entwicklungen die strikte Inkom-patibilität von altem und neuem Zustand bei derartigen Vorgängen häufig nicht gegeben sein wird.[12]

(4) Dass praktisches juristisches Argumentieren in einer bestimmten Zeitperiode, von einem bestimmten Gericht oder einem bestimmten Urteilsredaktor durch einen bestimmten *Stil* charakterisiert werden und in diesem Sinne als 'stilbehaftet' oder 'stilgebunden' erscheinen könnte, erscheint als unvereinbar mit Vorstellungen, welche vom rein instrumentellen Charakter der Einzelfiguren einer juristischen Argumentation ausgehen. Aufgrund eines derartigen rein oder überwiegend instrumentellen Charakters der Einzelfiguren einer Argumentation würde nach dieser Vorstellung kein Raum für arbiträre und damit stilbildende Auswahlprozesse zwischen expressiven Argumentations- oder Begründungsalternativen bleiben. Zwar hat auch nach dieser Vorstellung die praktische Argumentation selbstverständlich den Wandel der Gesetzgebung und der in einer vorgegebenen Zeitperiode anwendbaren Rechtsnormen zu berücksichtigen. Als geradezu unstatthaft müsste es indessen nach diesen Vorstellungen erscheinen, dass die Begründung eines Entscheides auf einem Auswahlvorgang zwischen einzelnen Argumenten beruhen und dass dieser Auswahlvorgang durch expressiv determinierte Unwägbarkeiten bzw. das

persönliche Belieben des Argumentierenden gesteuert werden könnte, und dass daher im Ergebnis die Begründung von juristischen Entscheidungen in verschiedenen Zeitperioden einem Wandel des Argumentationsstils unterliegen könnte. Vollends inakzeptabel wäre es nach dieser Vorstellung, dass schliesslich gar der materielle juristische Entscheid von Veränderungen eines solchen 'Argumentationsstils' beeinflusst werden könnte.

Das Fehlen eines Stilwandels in der praktischen juristischen Argumentation erscheint nach dieser Vorstellung zur Gewährleistung gleichbleibender Qualität der richterlichen Entscheidungen und damit der materiellen Rechtssicherheit, das heisst aus funktionellen Gründen, als geboten und angesichts des rein instrumentellen Charakters der argumentativen Einzelfiguren auch als gesichert. Auf Grund dieses Zusammenhangs ist die dogmatische Jurisprudenz zusammen mit der Theologie als *stilrepugnantes* *Gebeit* der Geisteswissenschaften charakterisiert und dabei darauf hingewiesen worden, dass die Stilablehnung in diesen Fachgebieten eine inhaltliche Stabilisierungsfunktion erfülle.[13]

Im Gegensatz zu diesen stilablehnenden Vorstellungen sprechen vermittelnde Vorstellungen den Einzelfiguren der praktischen juristischen Argumentation lediglich *überwiegend,* nicht aber ausschliesslich *instrumentellen* Charakter zu. So ist etwa differenzierend angemerkt worden, dass nicht überall dem Stilcharakter des Handelns in gleicher Weise Aufmerksamkeit gezollt werde und dass deshalb eine explizite und eine implizite Stilbildung unterschieden werden müsste. Im Bereich juristischen Argumentierens sei es zwar so, dass 'jeder Richter einen persönlichen Stil der Urteilsbegründung verrate', dass aber 'sozial entscheidend' der sachliche Gehalt der Begründung, nicht deren Stil sei.[14]

(5) Schon seit längerer Zeit stehen derartigen 'stilrepugnanten' Vorstellungen indessen Ansichten gegenüber, welche den Begriff des *Stils* als geeignetes Instrument zur Erfassung verschiedener Einzelaspekte von Rechtssystemen verwenden.[15] Soweit sich derartige Ansichten auf das praktische juristische Argumentieren im Rahmen von Urteilsbegründungen beziehen, sprechen sie die im deutschen Sprachgebiet bekannte Unterscheidung zwischen 'Gutachten-' und 'Urteilsstil'[16] oder aber argumentative Einzelheiten, wie etwa die Berücksichtigung von empirischem Tatsachenwissen in der englischen Rechtstradition, die Berücksichtigung von Präjudizien oder die Offenlegung inhaltlich widersprechender Gesichtspunkte in der bundesdeutschen Rechtstradition an.[17] Ein veritabler 'Wandel' des Stils im historischen Zeitablauf ist der Begründungspraxis des deutschen Reichsgerichts und des Bundesgerichtshofs attestiert und damit die bevorzugte Berücksichtigung bestimmter Einzelfiguren der Argumentation, wie etwa 'offener' oder 'gebundener' Einzelargumente[18] oder situationsbezogenpragmatischer Einzelargumente[19] angesprochen worden. Schliesslich ist etwa dem Argumentationsverhalten des deutschen Reichsgerichts nach 1920 eine 'Wendung ins Allgemeingültige',[20] oder demjenigen des deutschen Bundesgerichtshofes nach 1945 eine Hinwendung zu 'problemgebunden-topischen Einzelargumenten unter vermehrter Berücksichtigung von Gesichtspunkten

der Brauchbarkeit des Ergebnisses, der Billigkeit und der Zumutbarkeit'
nachgesagt worden.[21]
Derartige Ansätze zur Fruchtbarmachung des Stilbegriffs für die
Beurteilung der praktischen juristischen Argumentation und die damit
verbundene Anerkennung eines Auswahlvorganges zwischen Einzelfiguren
mit zumindest teilweise expressivem Charakter erscheinen aus folgenden
Gründen als vertretbar: Schon Empfehlungen in den bekannten deutschen
Anleitungsbüchern, nur das, was dazu diene, den Entscheid zu rechtfertigen,
in die Entscheidungsgründe aufzunehmen,[22] unter mehreren sachlichen
Gründen den 'durchschlagenderen'[23] oder aus mehreren Gründen von
unterschiedlichem Wert den 'besten' oder 'denjenigen, der am weitesten trägt'
auszuwählen,[24] spricht zumindest gegen einen ausschliesslich instrumentellen
Charakter der Einzelargumente der praktischen juristischen Argumentation
und für eine (zumindest partielle) Auswahlmöglichkeit zwischen Figuren mit
(teilweise) expressivem Charakter. Auch der Praktiker der Entscheid-
begründung wird aufgrund seines persönlichen Erfahrungswissens
einräumen, dass im Rahmen der Einzelentscheidbegründung subjektiv
Freiräume der persönlichen Gestaltung wahrgenommen werden, welche sich
unter anderem in der Möglichkeit einer Auswahl zwischen verschiedenen
Einzelargumenten manifestieren. Derartige Gestaltungsmöglichkeiten bestehen dem Vernehmen nach zumindest hinsichtlich der Wahl zwischen
'Gutachten'- und 'Urteilsstil' für die Begründung ein und derselben
Entscheidung.[25] Schliesslich spricht auch die Kontroverse über die Rangfolge,
Auswahl oder Berücksichtigung von einzelnen Argumentations- oder
Auslegungsmethoden im Rahmen der diskursiven Argumentationstheorie
eher gegen einen ausschliesslich instrumentellen Charakter der Einzelfiguren
praktischer juristischer Argumentation und damit für die Existenz von
Auswahlmöglichkeiten   zwischen   Figuren   mit   expressivem   und
dementsprechend stilbildendem Charakter in diesem Bereich.[26]

Empirische Untersuching der Rechtsprechung des schweizerischen Bundesgerichts 1881–1980: Datenmaterial, Stichproben

(6) Zur Untersuchung der Zitatdichte wurde eine Stichprobe *REC
1881–1980* gezogen, in welcher die publizierten Entscheide des schweizerischen
Bundesgerichts zum Obligationenrecht (Schuldrecht) aus den Jahrzehnten
1881–90, 1911–20, 1941–50, 1971–80 anhand des Textes der amtlichen
Entscheidungssammlung (BGE) erfasst wurden.[27] Diese Stichprobe umfasst
5358 Seiten Erwägungen aus insgesamt 1218 einzelnen Entscheiden, wobei die
Darstellung des Sachverhaltes und des Verlaufs des Verfahrens streng
ausgeschieden und für die quantitative Auswertung der mehrmals geänderte
Satzspiegel berücksichtigt wurde.[28]

(7) Zur Untersuchung des Argumentationsverhaltens wurde die Ablehnung wissenschaftlicher Lehrmeinungen als stichprobenbildendes Kriterium eingesetzt. Dies bietet den Vorteil, dass die zu erfassenden Objekte (Argumentationen) verhältnismässig leicht anhand von äusserlichen Merkmalen, nämlich dem Zitat der betreffenden Lehrmeinung, zu identifizieren und vom restlichen Inhalt des Begründungstextes abzugrenzen sind.

Für die Untersuchung des Argumentationsverhaltens bei derartigen Ablehnungen wurde die Stichprobe *REC 1881–1980* auf das Jahrzehnt 1891 bis 1900 erweitert und dadurch eine grössere Datenmenge aus der Anfangszeit der Rechtsprechung zum Obligationenrecht gewonnen. Die derart gebildete Stichprobe *CLUS–152* erfasst alle in den fünfzig Jahren publizierten Entscheidungen zum Obligationenrecht und enthält in insgesamt 154 Ablehnungssituationen (cases)—wovon zwei ohne jede Begründung— insgesamt 434 Einzelargumente.

(8) Erfassungseinheit in der Stichprobe *CLUS–152* bildete das einzelne, bei der Begründung der Ablehnung einer Lehrmeinung eingesetzte Argument. Kriterium für dessen Abgrenzung und damit für die Aufteilung einer Gesamtargumentation in Einzelargumente bildet einzig dessen thematische Erkennbarkeit und Einheitlichkeit.[29]

Kategorien, Operationalisierung

Die Kategorien, die zur Beurteilung des Datenmaterials dienten, wurden nach folgenden Gesichtspunkten operationalisiert:

(9) Zitatdichte, Zitathäufigkeit (aktive Zitierfrequenz): Die Zitate in den als 'Erwägungen' gekennzeichneten Begründungstexten der amtlichen Sammlung der Entscheide des Bundesgerichts (BGE) wurden ausgezählt und auf 1000 Worte oder Wortäquivalente umgerechnet. Zitate aus dem gleichen Werk des gleichen Autors an derselben Stelle des Begründungstexts wurden einfach, Zitate mehrerer Autoren an derselben Stelle des Textes dagegen als mehrere Einzelzitate gezählt. Mehrfache Zitate des gleichen Autors an verschiedenen Stellen desselben Begründungstextes wurden an jeder einzelnen Stelle einmal gezählt.

(10) Argumentkategorien: Zur Charakterisierung der Argumentkombinationen zur Ablehnung von Lehrmeinungen wurde ein Raster von dreizehn Kategorien eingesetzt, welcher den von Schroth (1980) verwendeten Raster in verschiedenen Einzelheiten verändert und sich als besonders zweckmässig für das Gebiet des Obligationenrechts (Schuldrechts) erwies en hat.[30] Die eingesetzten Argumentkategorien wurden nach dem Vorschlag von Folke Schmidt (1976) als gebundene Argumente gekennzeichnet, soweit sie eine Grundlage in vorgeformten Rechtsquellen erkennen liessen, dagegen als offene Argumente, soweit eine solche Grundlage fehlte.[31] Die Unterscheidung dürfte ziemlich weitgehend, wenn auch nicht in allen Einzelheiten, mit der von Esser (1979) verwendeten in logisch/systematische und rhetorisch/topische Argumente, in ihren praktischen Ergebnis wohl auch mit derjenigen in

'fremdbestimmte' und 'eigenbestimmte' Argumente übereinstimmen.[32] Jedes Auftreten einer Argumentkategorie im Rahmen einer Begründung der Ablehnung einer wissenschaftlichen Lehrmeinung wurde erfasst, unabhängig davon, welche formale Funktion dieses Argument innerhalb der Ablehnung erfüllte.

Gebundene Argumente

W   Wortlaut, 'klarer Wortlaut'
A   Vorgeformte Rechtsnormen aus anderem Sachzusammenhang
B   Andere vorgeformte Erkenntnisquellen
    (Materialien, Präjudizien, Literatur, ausländisches Recht, alter
    Rechtszustand)
Z   Logische Konstruktionen
    (Analogieschluss, Umkehrschluss usw.)

Offene Argumente

X   Änderung der Verhältnisse
F   Folgenberücksichtigung (*argumentum ad absurdum*)
T   Zweck, 'Sinn und Zweck'
Pk Praktikabilität, Schwierigkeiten in der Rechtsanwendung
S   Schutz, Rechtsschutz

I   Interessen
G   Gerechtigkeit und Billigkeit
R   Rechtssicherheit
C   Andere Prinzipien
    (Vertragsfreiheit, Parteiautonomie usw.)

Auswertungsmethoden

(11) Rangkorrelationen nach Spearman: Die einzelnen Werte (Anzahl der Realisierungen) der Variablen (Argumentkategorien) wurden rangiert und die Rangkorrelationen R_s nach Spearman für die verschiedenen Variablenpaare (Rang einzelner Argumentkategorien in zwei verschiedenen Jahrzehnten) nach bekannten Methoden ermittelt. Der Einfluss von Bindungen auf die Rangkorrelationen wurde nach bekannten Methoden korrigiert.[33]

Die Signifikanz der derart erhaltenen Werte von R_s gegen Null wurde bei Signifikanzniveaus von 1% und 5% (2P $< =$ 0.01 und $< =$ 0.05) durch Approximation an die Normalverteilung getestet, sofern die Anzahl Daten pro Variable N $>$ 30 betrug, dagegen mit Hilfe einer t-Verteilung mit N–2[34]Freiheitsgraden, falls die Zahl der Daten pro Variable unter N $<$ 30 lag.

(12) Vergleich von Quotienten (Prozentzahlen): Die Unterschiede von Quotienten (Prozentzahlen) aus Stichproben mit unterschiedlichem Umfang wurde nach der von Neurath (1974) vorgeschlagenen Methode durch Vergleich zweier Wahrscheinlichkeiten im Rahmen einer Binomialverteilung gegen Zufallseinflüsse getestet.[35]

(13) Die partitionerende Cluster-Analyse wurde nach dem von Spaeth (1983) vorgeschlagenen Verfahren durchgeführt und dabei das Hauptprogramm BVPEXM für binäre Daten eingesetzt. Die Beurteilung der Zielfunktion D(n) sowie die Auswahl der optimalen Anzahl n Cluster für einen gegebenen Datensatz wurde nach den von Dolder und Buser vorgeschlagenen Kriterien vorgenommen.[36]

Ergebnisse und Diskussion

(14) In dem untersuchten Jahrhundert haben im Bereich der Rechsetzung, als dem politisch determinierten Teilbereich des schweizerischen Rechtssystems Veränderungen stattgefunden, welche aufgrund ihres irreversiblen Charakters, der inhaltlichen Unvereinbarkeit des alten und des neuen Zustandes und der Verbesserung der Regelungsqualität gemessen an den regelungsbedürftigen Verhältnissen durchaus als Paradigmawechsel gewürdigt werden können. Im engeren Bereich des Obligationenrechts dürften etwa folgenden Vorgängen die Qualität von Paradigmawechseln zukommen: die erste Kodifikation des Obligationenrechts durch den Bund 1881/1883, die Zuweisung der Zuständigkeit zur Gesetzgebung im Gesamtgebiet des Zivilrechts an den Bund im Jahre 1898 (Art. 64 Abs. 2 BV) und schliesslich das Inkrafttreten der Kodifikation des Zivilgesetzbuches (ZGB) und des neuen Obligationenrechts (OR) im Jahre 1912, welche die partikuläre Privatrechtsgesetzgebung durch die Kantone ablöste. Nur eine einzige Veränderung der positiven Rechtslage betraf dabei in diesem Zeitabschnitt die Methode der richterlichen Rechtsanwendung und damit unmittelbar die praktische juristische Argumentation: der berühmte Art. 1 Abs. 2 des Zivilgesetzbuches von 1907/1912 bestimmt, dass der Richter beim Fehlen von Gesetzes- oder Gewohnheitsrecht, nach der Regel entscheiden solle, die er als Gesetzgeber aufstellen würde, und dessen Abs. 3 ordnet an, dass er dabei 'bewährter Lehre und Überlieferung' zu folgen habe.

Die in dieser Norm enthaltene erstmalige positivrechtliche Verankerung der wissenschaftlichen Lehrmeinungen als Instrument richterlicher Rechtsanwendung hat keinen erkennbaren Einfluss auf das Argumentationsverhalten des Bundesgerichts in der untersuchten Stichprobe ausgeübt. Insbesondere lässt sich keine systematische Veränderung des Zitierverhaltens nach 1912 erkennen. Trotz des in Tabelle 3 dargestellten dramatischen Wachstums der Zitatdichte hat sich beispielsweise die *kritische Distanz* des Begründenden gegenüber dem Inhalt der zitierten wissenschaftlichen Aussagen nach 1912 erstaunlich wenig verändert: wie aus den dargestellten Ergebnissen hervorgeht, ist der prozentuale Anteil der abgelehnten Lehrmeinungen (Negativzitate) an den insgesamt zitierten Aussagen in den Zehnjahresstichproben mit einer Ausnahme nahezu konstant geblieben und erreicht im letzten Jahrzehnt 1971–80 erneut einen Wert von rund 7.5 %. Obschon der erwähnte Art. 1 Abs. 3 ZGB die Berücksichtigung wissenschaftlicher Aussagen ausdrücklich vorschreibt, unterscheidet sich die Ablehnungsquote des Jahrzehnts 1881–90 nicht signifikant von derjenigen der Jahrzehnte nach dem Inkrafttreten der neuen Kodifikation. Dies deutet darauf hin, dass diese Norm lediglich einen faktischen Ist-Zustand fixiert hat und—zumindest mit Bezug auf das Obligationenrecht—als eine der bereits erwähnten Normen mit reinem Symbolcharakter einzustufen wäre, welche von 'vorneherein gar nicht darauf angelegt' war, 'faktisch wirksam zu werden'.[37]

(15) Erscheint es nach dem Gesagten nicht als ausgeschlossen, dass praktisches juristisches Argumentieren in Urteilsbegründungen mindestens partiell 'stilbehaftet' oder 'stilgebunden' und damit ein Objekt von 'Stilwechsel' oder 'Stilwandel' im Zeitablauf sein könnte, so zeigen demgegenüber die empirischen Ergebnisse aus der Rechtsprechung des schweizerischen Bundesgerichts zum Obligationenrecht ein Bild auffälliger *Zeitunabhängigkeit* und Konstanz dieses Argumentierens.

TABELLE 1   Gebundene und offene Argumentkategorien in der Rechtsprechung des Schweizerischen Bundesgerichts zum Obligationenrecht, 1881–1980 (nach Rängen geordnet)

	1881/00	1911/20	1941/50	1971/80	TOTAL
Ablehnungssituationen	33 (–)	27 (–)	26 (1)	68 (1)	154 (2)
Einzelargumente total	81	69	96	188	434
Anteil gebundener	50	43	47	111	251
Argumente (W, A, B, Z)	61.7 %	62.3 %	49.0 %	59.0 %	57.8 %

Rang der einzelnen Argumentkategorie

Gebundene Argumente					
W	11.5	6	9.5	5	7.5
A	3.5	2.5	3	4	3
B	1	1	1	1	1
Z	2	4	2	2	2
Offene Argumente					
X	9	11.5	13	13	13
F	5	2.5	4.5	3	4
T	3.5	6	7	6.5	5
Pk	10	11.5	8	9.5	10
S	11.5	6	6	9.5	9
I	7	9	9.5	6.5	7.5
G	7	8	4.5	9.5	6
R	13	11.5	11.5	9.5	11.5
P	7	11.5	11.5	12	11.5

— Datenmaterial: Stichprobe CLUS 152
— Die Zahlen in Klammern bezeichnen die Ablehnungssituationen (cases) ohne Begründung.

Beurteilt man das Argumentationsverhalten anhand der Verteilung des argumentativen Aufwandes auf einzelne Argumentkategorien, so ergibt sich diese Feststellung aus den in (Tabelle 1 und 2) dargestellten empirischen Daten. Entgegen den Erwartungen bestätigen diese keine Verlagerung der juristischen Argumentation von 'gebundenen' zu 'offenen' oder von 'input-orientierten' zu 'output-orientierten' Argumentkategorien, wie sie mehrfach für die Entwicklung der Rechtsprechung in der Bundesrepublik Deutschland seit 1945 signalisiert worden ist.[38] Wie aus Tabelle 1 hervorgeht, war der Anteil 'gebundener' Argumente in unserer Stichprobe während des ganzen Jahrhunderts (mit Ausnahme eines Jahrzehnts) praktisch konstant bei rund

TABELLE 2   Rangkorrelationen nach Spearman zwischen den Rängen einzelner Argumentkategorien in vier verschiedenen Jahrzehnten, 1881–1980

	Früherer Rang		
Späterer Rang	1881–1900	1911–20	1941–50
1911–20	.681*		
1941–50	.718**	.864**	
1971–80	.666*	.895**	.786**

—Signifikanzschranken gegen Null: * 2P < 0.05, ** 2P < 0.01; vgl. Wissenschaftliche Tabellen Geigy, Band 3, 8.A. Basel 1980, S. 163 (t–Test mit N–2 Freiheitsgraden).
—Korrektur für Durchschnittsränge: S Siegel, *Nichtparametrische statistische Methoden* (Frankfurt, 1976), S. 197 ff.

TABELLE 3   Literaturzitate in der Rechtsprechung des schweizerischen Bundes-gerichts zum Obligationenrecht, 1881–1980

	1881/90	1911/20	1941/50	1971/80
Textäquivalente (× 1000 Worte)	421.05	621.42	241.43	359.15
Zitate	158	723	388	1651
Zitatdichte (pro 1000 Worte)	0.375	1.163	1.607	4.597
Indexzahl Zitatdichte	100	310	429	1226
Negativzitate (Ablehnungen)	11	47	52	122
Ablehnungsquote	6.96 %	6.50 %	13.40 %	7.39 %

—Grundlage: Stichprobe REC 1881–1980.

60% aller eingesetzten Argumente und auch die charakteristischen
Häufigkeiten der einzelnen Argumentkategorien haben sich in dem
untersuchten Jahrhundert nicht signifikant verändert. Die in Tabelle 2
dargestellten hoch signifikanten Rangkorrelationen zwischen den einzelnen
Jahrzehnten sprechen dafür, dass das Argumentationsverhalten einer
früheren Zeitperiode als Modell oder Programm auf dasjenige späterer
Zeitperioden einwirkt: Argumentationsverhalten wird darnach von einer
Generation von Urteilsredaktoren auf die nächste weitergegeben.

Diese Zusammenhänge werden durch die Ergebnisse der partitionierenden
Cluster-analyse bestätigt: Von Dolder und Buser (1987) ist vorgeschlagen
worden, die Argumentkombinationen einzelner cases mit Hilfe dieser
Methode in einer optimalen Lösung von n = 6 Cluster zu klassifizieren. Die
einzelnen Cluster sind nach diesem Vorschlag anhand ihres typischen
argumentativen Erscheinungsbildes als F-Typ mit durchschnittlichem
Aufwand, FS-Typ mit überdurchschnittlichem Aufwand, FZ-Overlap mit
höchstem Aufwand, ZAB-Typ, BZ-Typ mit unterdurchschnittlichem
Aufwand und als Rst-Typ charakterisiert worden. Die Verteilung der
untersuchten Argumentationen auf diese sechs Cluster im Zeitablauf zeigte
keine statistisch signikanten Veränderungen, welche als historisch signifikante
Entwicklung eingestuft werden könnten.[39]

Im Lichte dieser empirischen Ergebnisse erscheint das praktische juristische
Argumentieren des schweizerischen Bundesgerichts im Bereich des Obligationenrechts insgesamt als ein *erstaunlich konservativer Vorgang* an dem das
Jahrhundert 1881 bis 1980, ein Jahrhundert voll sozialen und kulturellen
Wandels, ohne nennenswerte Einwirkung vorübergegangen ist. Insbesondere
überrascht es den methodisch interessierten Praktiker, dass heftig umkämpfte
methodische Diskussionen in der deutschprachigen Rechtsdogmatik wie etwa
diejenige um die Zweckdeterminiertheit von Rechtsnormen (Jhering, *Der
Zweck im Recht,* 1877), um die Gedanken der Freirechtsbewegung mit ihrer
Betonung voluntativer Elemente in der Rechtsanwendung (Eugen Ehrlich,
Hermann Kantorowicz ab 1903), um die Lehren der Interessenjurisprudenz
(Philipp Heck, Problem der Rechtsgewinnung, 1912), der Topik (Viehweg,
1953) oder der Folgenberücksichtigung als Argumentform (z.B. Diederichsen,
1973)[40] keinen erkennbaren Niederschlag im Argumentationsverhalten des
Bundesgerichts gefunden haben. Die Vorstellung erscheint deshalb als
gerechtfertigt, dass Entwicklungen im akademisch-theoretischen Bereich
keinen (oder so gut wie keinen) unmittelbaren Einfluss auf das praktische
Argumentieren in der Rechtsprechung ausüben, sondern dass dieses ein mehr
oder weniger autonomes Dasein führt, in welchem nicht akademische Lehren,
sondern die Modell- und Programmwirkung des Argumentationsverhaltens
älterer Generationen und damit subsystemspezifische, professionelle
Traditionen dominieren.[41]

(16) Ein Erklärungsansatz für einen Teil dieser auffälligen Konstanz des
Argumentationsverhaltens ergibt sich möglicherweise aus dem
Zusammenhang, dass das schweizerische Bundesgericht bereits in den zwei
Jahrzehnten zwischen 1881 und 1900—nach modernen Masstäben—

verhältnismässig situationsbezogen und pragmatisch argumentiert hat und die begriffliche und 'doktrinäre' Verhärtung des Argumentationsstils nicht nachvollzogen hat, wie sie der Rechtsprechung des Deutschen Reichsgerichts zwischen 1879 und 1920 attestiert wird.[42] Damit befand sich das Bundesgericht im Einklang mit der schweizerischen Gesetzgebung und wissenschaftlichen Jurisprudenz, welche in der damaligen Zeitperiode ausgesprochen moderne und fortschrittliche Tendenzen aufwies, wie sie sich unter anderem im Zivilgesetzbuch von 1907/12 niedergeschlagen haben. Dementsprechend sind auch Stilveränderungen, wie sie für das deutsche Reichsgericht nach 1920 und den bundesdeutschen Bundesgerichtshof nach 1945 diagnostiziert worden sind, also etwa eine vermehrte Berücksichtigung 'allgemeiner Rechtsgrundsätze', 'problemgebundener' oder 'topischer' Argumente oder von 'plausiblen Gerechtigkeitsgesichtspunkten', in der Rechtsprechung des schweizerischen Bundesgerichts zum Obligationenrecht mit dem hier verwendeten Instrumentar der nichtparametrischen Statistik nicht erkennbar.[43]

So gehörte etwa der vergleichsweise moderne Gesichtspunkt der *Interessenberücksichtigung* und *-abwägung* bereits zwischen 1881 und 1900 zum argumentativen Instrumentar des schweizerischen Bundesgerichts in der untersuchten Stichprobe:

> BGE 19,821 (1893)
>
> Diese Frage ist in Doktrin und Praxis kontrovers; während nach der älteren gemeinrechtlichen Theorie (. . .) die Vorlage der Belege sich als unerlässlicher Bestandteil der Rechnungsablage darstellt, ist dieselbe nach anderer Ansicht gar nicht nötig (. . .) Entscheidend ist das *Interesse des Rechnungsherrn.* Bezüglich der Einnahmeposten, (. . .) , ist ein solches *Interesse nun zweifellos vorhanden;* der Rechnungsherr muss kontrollieren können, ob der Rechnungsführer die Einnahmen in vollem Umfange gebucht habe, und diese Kontrolle wird nur ermöglicht durch die vollständige Vorlage der Belege.

Wie aus Tabelle 1 weiter hervorgeht, hat sich die Beliebtheit des Interessentopos (Kategorie I) in dem untersuchten Jahrhundert insgesamt wenig auffällig entwickelt. Allerdings is dabei auf Grund der vorliegenden Daten nicht auszuschliessen, dass die Entwicklung dieser Kategorie vom 9.5-ten auf den 6.5-ten Rang zwischen 1941/50 und 1971/80 eine signifikante, wenn auch—gemessen am Erscheinungsjahr der Arbeiten Philipp Hecks (1912)—etwas verspätete Rezeption dieses argumentativen Gesichtspunktes eingeleitet haben könnte.

Auch das Argument der *Folgenberücksichtigung* (Kategorie F) als einer weitern typisch 'offenen' Argumentkategorie lässt sich bereits zwischen 1881 und 1900 regelmässig nachweisen. Es erscheint dabei nicht als ausgeschlossen, dass die argumentative Nutzung dieses Gesichtspunktes in jener Periode mit den zweckrationalen Lehren Jherings (*Der Zweck im Recht*, 1877) in Verbindung gebracht werden könnte. Ein schönes Beispiel einer derartigen Folgenberücksichtigung, bei der argumentiert wurde, dass die Folgen einer bestimmten Rechtsauffassung gegen den Gesichtspunkt der Gerechtigkeit—

also eines weiteren typisch 'offenen' Argumentationsgesichtspunktes—
verstossen würden, liefert der folgende Entscheid:

BGE 18, 915 (1892)
Die Befreiung des Inhabers des Baugewerbes von der Haftpflicht gegenüber der
Arbeit des Dachdeckermeisters usw. würde gegenteils gegen Sinn und Geist des
Haftpflichtgesetzes verstossen. (. . .) und es ist nun gewiss ein Grund nicht
einzusehen, warum er (sc. Bauunternehmer) hier von der Haftpflicht (. . .) befreit
sein sollte, während er haften würde, wenn es sich nicht um einen Kirchenbau (. . .),
sondern um eine Brückenbaute handelte.

BGE 20, 1120 (1894)
En effet, il serait inadmissible et immoral que l'assuré-responsable pût (. . .) se
soustraire en fait à la responsabilité civile (. . .) pour la faire peser sur l'assureur, de
telle sorte que les conséquences de lésions corporelles ou de cas de mort (. . .) se
trouvassent supportés, non pas par lui, mais par un tiers, l'assureur.

Auch der durchaus moderne Gesichtspunkt, dass eine bestimmte Ansicht zur
Folge haben könnte, dass die *Praktikabilität* einer bestimmten Norm
beeinträchtigt werden könnte, ist bereits in diesen beiden Jahrzehnten
argumentativ genutzt worden:

BGE 22, 572 (1896)
Denn wenn bei dieser Frage von den objektiven Kriterien abgesehen und einfach
auf die allgemeinen Verkehrsbegriffe oder die Zweckbestimmung der Waare
abgestellt würde, so ergäbe sich hieraus eine so einschränkende Interpretation des
Art. 246 OR, die mit dem Sinn und Geist dieser Bestimmung nicht in Einklang
gebracht werden könnte, und zu ganz bedenklichen praktischen Konsequenzen
führen müsste (. . .).

BGE 26 II 260 (1900)
Cette distinction est inconciliable avec la nature de la lettre de change et du chèque,
auxquels on enlèverait leur caractère propre et leur valeur particulière, si l'on devait
distinguer entre les acquéreurs successifs selon qu'ils ont connu le lieu réel de la
création de l'effet, et autoriser à l'égard de chacun la preuve de la connaissance ou
de l'ignorance de ce lieu.

Schliesslich wird in diesem Jahrzehnt auch das Argument mehrfach eingesetzt,
dass *veränderte tatsächliche Verhältnisse* (Kategorie X) bei der Interpretation
von Rechtsnormen berücksichtigt werden müssten, ein Gedankengang, der
zweifellos ebenfalls der Kategorie der 'offenen' Argumente zugerechnet
werden darf:

BGE 19, 930 (1893)
Eine ältere Theorie (. . .) geht dahin, dass der Offerent die Benutzung des
Telegraphen, . . ., nicht erwarten dürfe, . . . Allein heute, wo dieses
Korrespondenzmittel nicht mehr als ein ausserordentliches bezeichnet werden
kann, ist diese Auffassung nicht mehr haltbar (. . .) und es darf jedenfalls (. . .) eine
telegraphische Rückäusserung über eine ebenfalls per Telegraph aufgeworfene
Vertragsmodalität verlangt werden.[44]

Nach diesem Erklärungsansatz würde die beobachtete Konstanz des Argumentationsverhaltens des schweizerischen Bundesgerichts in der untersuchten Stichprobe nicht grundsätzlich gegen die Vorstellung einer Stilgebundenheit praktischen juristischen Argumentierens sprechen, sondern dafür, dass das schweizerische Bundesgericht stilverändernden Einflüssen in der untersuchten Zeitperiode weitgehend entgangen ist. Ob dazu neben der geschilderten modernen Argumentationsweise in den Jahrzehnten nach 1881 die Gunst der historischen Rechtsentwicklung beigetragen hat, welche der Schweiz zwar die erwähnten Paradigmaänderungen im Bereich der Rechtssetzung, aber keine mit der deutschen Entwicklung vergleichbaren politischen Veränderungen gebracht hat, kann an dieser Stelle offen bleiben.

(17) Der Entscheid darüber, ob im Rahmen einer praktischen juristischen Argumentation private wissenschaftliche Lehrmeinungen zitiert werden oder nicht, und welche Autoren gegebenenfalls dabei berücksichtigt werden, bleibt in der schweizerischen Rechtstradition zumindest teilweise dem persönlichen Belieben des Urteilsredaktors überlassen. Auf Grund der damit verbundenen Auswahlmöglichkeit erscheint daher das *Zitierverhalten* weniger als instrumentelles denn als expressives Gestaltungsmittel im Rahmen einer praktischen juristischen Argumentation und damit als Einfallstor für eine entsprechende Stilbildung. Dies ergibt sich nicht zuletzt daraus, dass andere nationale Rechtstraditionen stark divergierende Lösungen dieses Problems getroffen haben, welche von der völligen Ablehnung von Literaturzitaten in Gerichtsurteilen im angelsächsischen und französischen Rechtskreis bis zum Zitiereifer in deutschen oder österreichischen Urteilsbegründungen reichen.

Geht man von diesem Zusammenhang aus, so lässt sich die historische Entwicklung des Zitierverhaltens des schweizerischen Bundesgerichts in der untersuchten Periode kaum anders denn als *Stilwandel* interpretieren (Tabelle 3). Ein Wachstum der Zitatdichte (Anzahl Zitate pro Testeinheit) um einen Faktor von F = 12.26 in dem untersuchten Jahrhundert darf mit aller Zurückhaltung als dramatisch bezeichnet werden und lässt den Schluss zu, dass zumindest der formelle Einfluss publizierter Lehrmeinungen auf die Urteilsbegründungen des Bundesgerichts in dieser Zeit entscheidend gewachsen ist. Dieses Ergebnis entspricht einigermassen den wenigen semi-empirischen Äusserungen zum Zitierverhalten von Gerichten in der Bundesrepublik Deutschland nach 1945.[45]

Es liegt nahe, das beobachtete dramatische Wachstum der Zitatdichte neben dem Wachstum der zitierfähigen Literatur auf eine wachsende Bedeutung zeremonieller Aspekte des Zitiervoranges zurückzuführen, wie beispielweise der Vorstellung, durch Zitieren 'einen Teil der Verantwortung loszuwerden', durch Zitieren 'Gelehrsamkeit' oder die Internalisierung gemeinsamer professioneller Verhaltensnormen anzudeuten.[46] Dabei sollte indessen nicht übersehen werden, dass das Zitieren von Lehrmeinungen in der Tradition des mittelalterlichen *argumentum ab auctoritate* immer auch einen Verzicht auf eigenes Argumentieren bedeutet.[47]

(18) Wenn man davon ausgeht, dass der Stilbegriff wesentlich durch das Element des Auswählens zwischen verschiedenen, nicht ausschliesslich

instrumentellen Gestaltungsmitteln bestimmt ist, so verkörpert auch die in Tabelle 4 dargestellte dramatische Abnahme des *Anteils ausländischer Autoren* an den Literaturzitaten einen Stilwandel besonderer Art. Vier verschiedene Einzelheiten erscheinen bei dieser Entwicklung als bemerkenswert: Einmal das Ausmass des Rückganges des Ausländeranteils von 84.1 % (1881/85) auf 3.69% (1976/80), welches dafür spricht, dass sich in dem untersuchten Jahrhundert das schweizerische Obligationenrecht von den vielen kontinentaleuropäischen Rechtsordnungen gemeinsamen römischrechtlichen Grundlagen weg zu einer von der nationalen Gelegenheits- und Massnahmengesetzgebung geprägten Spezifität entwickelt hat, in der der ausländischen wissenschaftlichen Aussage nur noch sehr geringe argumentative Überzeugungskraft (persuasive authority) beigemessen wird.

Zum zweiten beeindruckt der hohe Anteil deutscher Autoren vor dem ersten Weltkrieg, welcher nur mit dem ungewöhnlich hohen Ansehen der deutschen Rechtskultur bei den schweizerischen Juristen jener Zeitperiode erklärt werden kann[48] und der die schweizerische Entwicklung der Jahrzehnte nach 1880 in die Nähe *kultureller Entkolonialisierungsvorgänge* rückt.

Dabei treten im Rahmen dieser Entwicklung *interessante Diskontinuitäten* auf: der Anteil deutscher Autoren an den Zitaten weist zweimal einen dramatischen Rückgang auf, nämlich von 36 % zwischen 1911/15 auf 27 % zwischen 1916/20 und einen noch stärkeren von 29 % zwischen 1941/45 auf 19.6 % in den Jahren 1946/50. Dagegen blieb der Anteil zwischen 1920 und 1940 praktisch konstant. Es ist dabei unverkennbar, dass diese beiden Diskontinuitäten mit den bekannten traumatischen Ereignissen der deutschen

TABELLE 4 Anteil ausländischer Autoren an den Literaturzitaten in der Rechtsprechung des Schweizerischen Bundesgerichts zum Obligationenrecht, 1881–1980 (in Prozenten)

Jahre	Ausländer Total	Deutsche Sprache		Französische Sprache		Andere	N = 100 %
1881/85	84.1	63.5	75.5	19.1	22.7	1.59	63
1886/90	78.2	60.0	76.7	14.9	19.1	2.97	101
1911/15	42.3	35.8	84.6	5.07	12.0	1.45	414
1916/20	36.3	27.0	74.4	9.00	24.8	.33	300
1941/45	29.0	28.5	98.3	.48	1.65	—	207
1946/50	23.8	19.6	82.4	2.98	12.5	1.19	168
1971/75	4.88	4.46	91.4	.28	5.73	.14	717
1976/80	3.69	3.24	87.8	.45	12.2	—	894

—DATENMATERIAL: Stichprobe REC 1881–1980;
—Bei den deutsch- und französischsprachigen Autoran bedeutet die erste Zahl deren Anteil an den Literaturzitaten insgesamt, die zweite deren Anteil an den Literaturzitaten ausländischer Autoren der betreffenden Zeitperiode.

Geschichte dieses Jahrhunderts (Zusammenbruch des Kaiserreiches 1918 und des Nationalsozialismus 1945) zusammenfallen, welche jeweils mit einer ebenso dramatischen Verminderung des Ansehens der deutschen Kultur im Ausland verbunden waren.[49] Obschon also—wie bereits dargestellt—das praktische juristische Argumentieren des schweizerischen Bundesgerichts in der untersuchten Zeitperiode kaum von den fachlichen Vorgängen im wissenschaftlich-theoretischen Bereich beeinflusst worden ist, so konnten sich doch die argumentierenden Personen den *emotionellen Einflüssen* des jeweiligen historischen Kontexts nicht vollständig entziehen.

ANMERKUNGEN

1 Josef Esser (1976), 'Argumentations- und Stilwandel in höchstrichterlichen Zivilentscheidungen', *Etudes de logique juridique* (Bruxelles) 6 (1976) S. 53–77, vor allem 66 ff; Josef Esser (1979), 'Juristisches Argumentieren im Wandel des Rechtsfindungskonzepts unseres Jahrhunderts', *Sitzungsberichte der Heidelberger Akademie der Wissenschaften, Philophisch-historische Klasse*, 1979, Nr 1 vor allem S. 12 und 19 ff; Uwe Diederichsen, 'Die "reductio ad absurdum" in der Jurisprudenz', in *Festschrift für K Larenz* (München, 1973) S. 157, spricht von einem 'fast epidemisch anmutenden Befund' einer Häufung folgenorientierter Argumentstrukturen in einer Stichprobe aus den Jahren 1953 bis 1957; Arthur Kaufmann, Ulfrid Neumann, Jochen Schneider, Hg., *Schlussbericht zum Münchener Forschungsprojekt 'Argumentationstheoretische Aspekte höchstrichterlicher Rechtsprechungsänderungen'* (München, 1982) S. 80 ff. konstatieren eine 'Umorientierung der Rechtsprechung von der Input- auf die Output-Seite' bei der Begründung von Rechtsprechungsänderungen.

2 Thomas S Kuhn, *Die Struktur wissenschaftlicher Revolutionen* (Frankfurt/M., 1973) S. 28 und 44.

3 Kuhn, a.a.O. S. 128, 135 und 142.

4 Zur Unterscheidung von instrumentellen und expressiven Handlungselementen Alois Hahn, 'Soziologische Relevanzen des Stilbegriffs', in *Stil; Geschichten und Funktionen eines kulturwissenschaftlichen Diskurselements,*, Hg. H U Gumbrecht *et al.* (Frankfurt/M., 1986) S. 603/4 (Referate des Internationalen Kolloquiums in Dubrovnik, Frühjahr 1985).

5 Kuhn, a.a.O. S. 21 und 212 ('Fortschritt durch Revolutionen').

6 Vgl. zu diesem Wahlvorgang als konstitutivem Element des Stilbegriffes Stephen Ullmann, *Sprache und Stil* (Tübingen, 1972) S. 14 und 149; Rudolf Heinz, *Stil als geisteswissenschaftliche Kategorie* (Würzburg, 1986) S. 92.

7 Zu diesem expressiven Charakter von Handlungselementen bei der Stilbildung vgl. Hahn, a.a.O. S. 603 wonach ein Stilelement eine fixierbare Haltung darstelle, welche 'eher expressiver als instrumenteller Natur' sei, sowie a.a.O. S. 604, wonach Stil eine Formung von Handlungen sei, welche für einen Handelnden, eine Gruppe oder eine ganze Kultur typisch sei, 'ohne dass diese Formen eindeutig "technisch bedingt" seien'.

8 Erving Goffman, *Frame Analysis* (Cambridge, Mass., 1974) S. 288, bezeichnet als eine Funktion des Stils 'the maintenance of expressive identifiability'.

9 Vgl. Karl Popper, 'Die Normalwissenschaft und ihre Gefahren', in *Kritik und*

Erkenntnisfortschritt, Imre Lakatos/A Musgrave Hrsg. (Braunschweig, 1974) S. 57 (mit Bezug auf Soziologie und Psychologie); auch Ferdinand Fellmann, 'Stile gelebter Philosophie', in *Stil*, a.a.O. S. 585, spricht von 'geistigen Moden' und kontrastiert sie mit 'Denkstilen'.

10   Robert Alexy (1983), *Theorie der juristischen Argumentation* (Frankfurt/M., 1983) S. 328; Hans Doelle, 'Juristische Entdeckungen', in *Verhandlungen des 42. Deutschen Juristentages* (Düsseldorf, 1957), Band II (Tübingen, 1959), bezeichnet das Gestaltungsrecht (S. B 10) und die sog. Doppelwirkungen (S. B 12) als 'Entdeckungen'; auch Mario Jori, 'Revolutions in Legal Science: Back to the Concept of Law', in *Enlightenment, Rights and Revolution*, Neil MacCormick and Zenon Bankowski, eds (Aberdeen, 1989) S. 341 f, verwendet den Begriff des Paradigmas mit Zurückhaltung und beschränkt ihn auf methodische Aspekte der Rechtsentwicklung.

11   Vgl. Peter Noll, *Gesetzgebungslehre* (Reinbek, 1973) S. 157 (Normen mit Symbolcharakter).

12   Vgl. Jori, a.a.O. S. 342 f.

13   Heinz, a.a.O. S. 42, 48 und 92.

14   Hahn, a.a.O. S. 610.

15   Vgl. etwa Ernst Zitelmann, 'Die Jurisprudenz als Kunst', *Juristische Blätter* (Wien) 33 (1904) S. 123–5; Heinrich Triepel, *Vom Stil des Rechts. Beiträge zu einer Aesthetik des Rechts* (Heidelberg, 1947); Adalbert Erler, 'Zeitstil und Rechtsstil', *Studium Generale* 7 (1954) S. 612–18; die beiden bereits zitierten Aufsätze von Josef Esser (1976) und (1979); Hein Kotz, 'Über den Stil höchstrichterlicher Entscheidungen', *Konstanzer Universitätsreden* Bd. 162 (Konstanz, 1973); Hans-Wolgang Strätz, 'Notizen zu "Stil" und Recht', in *Stil*, a.a.O. S. 53–67.

16   Strätz, a.a.O. S. 53/54; vgl. Kurt Schellhammer, *Die Arbeitsmethode des Zivilrichters* (Karlsruhe, 1976) S. 375–7.

17   Kotz, a.a.O. S. 15 ff (England), S. 19 (Präjudizien) und S. 23 ff (Diskurs).

18   Esser (1979), a.a.O. S. 14 f.

19   Esser (1979), a.a.O. S. 19 ff, besonders S. 22.

20   Esser (1976), a.a.O. S. 68.

21   Esser (1976), a.a.O. S. 70.

22   Sattelmacher/Lüttig/Beyer, *Bericht, Gutachten und Urteil* (25. A. Berlin/ Frankfurt, 1968) S. 201.

23   Sattelmacher/Lüttig/ Beyer, a.a.O. S. 206.

24   H Berg, *Gutachten und Urteil* (Stuttgart/ Düsseldorf, 1974) S. 147.

25   Vgl. dazu die längere Diskussion bei Schellhammer, a.a.O. S. 375 ff.

26   Statt vieler Robert Alexy, a.a.O. S. 305 f (Regeln J.7, J.8 und J.9), sowie Joachim Rahlf, 'Die Rangfolge der klassischen juristischen Interpretationsmittel in der strafrechtswissenschaftlichen Auslegungslehre', in *Juristische Dogmatik und Wissenschaftstheorie*, Eike von Savigny, Hg. (München, 1976) S. 14 ff, vor allem S. 22/23 (Leugnung einer Rangfolge).

27   *Amtliche Sammlung der Entscheidungen des Schweizerischen Bundesgerichts (BGE), Teil 2 (Zivilrecht)* (Lausanne, 1875 ff).

28   Vgl. für die Einzelheiten: F Dolder, *Rezeption und Ablehnung wissenschaftlicher Lehrmeinungen in der Rechtsprechung des schweizerischen Bundesgerichts zum Obligationenrecht, 1881–1980* (Diss. Basel, 1986) S. 40 ff.

29   Vgl. Joachim Rahlf, a.a.O. S. 16, 'Argumente, also Festellungen und Behauptungen, die andere Behauptungen stützen oder schwächen'.

30   Ulrich Schroth, 'Eine Methode der formalen Rekonstruktion von Gerichtsurteilen', *ARSP Beiheft* Nr 14 (1980) S. 122 ff.

31 Folke Schmidt, 'Gebundene und offene Argumente in der Rechtswissenschaft', *Schriften zur Rechtstheorie, Heft 48: Zur Methode der Rechtsfindung* (Berlin, 1976) S. 218 ff; zu dieser Kategorienbildung vgl. Esser (1979), a.a.O. S. 16.

32 Esser (1979), a.a.O. S. 17.

33 Einzelheiten bei Sydney Siegel, *Nichtparametrische statistische Methoden* (Frankfurt, 1976) S. 197 ff. sowie Herbert Büning/Götz Trenkler, *Nichtparametrische statistische Methoden* (Berlin/New York, 1978) S. 256 f.

34 Siegel, a.a.O. S. 202; Büning/Trenkler, a.a.O. S. 257; *Wissenschaftliche Tabellen Geigy* (6.A. Basel, 1960) S. 170. 12, Tabellen S. 66/67.

35 Paul Neurath, *Handbuch der empirischen Sozialforschung*, René König, Hg, Band 3/b (3.A. Stuttgart, 1974) S. 74 ff.

36 Fritz Dolder/Mauro W Buser (1987), 'Klassifizierung von Argumentkombinationen in Gerichtsurteilen mit der partitionierenden Cluster-Analyse', *Rechtstheorie* 1989 (Nr 3). S. 380–401.

37 Peter Noll, a.a.O. S. 157 (Normen mit Symbolcharakter).

38 Esser (1976), a.a.O. S. 68 (nach 1918), 70 (nach 1945); Esser (1979) S. 22 und 26; Schlussbericht, a.a.O. S. 79 ff; zum Begriff der 'offenen' und 'gebundenen' Argumente Esser (1979) S. 14 ff. Folke Schmidt (1976), a.a.O. S. 218 ff. Per Olof Bolding, 'Reliance on authorities or open debate?', *Scand. Stud.Law* 13 (1969) S. 68 ff; zum Begriff der 'input'- und 'output-orientierten' Argumentkategorien, Schlussbericht, a.a.O. S. 80/81.

39 Dolder/Buser (1987), a.a.O. S. 155 ff.

40 Uwe Diederichsen, a.a.O. S. 155 ff.

41 Hahn, a.a.O. S. 609/610, stellt fest, dass Stilbildungen eher durch die subsystemspezifischen Traditionen erklärbar seien und bezieht diese Aussage ausdrücklich auch auf das Rechtswesen.

42 Esser (1976) a.a.O. S. 65–8.

43 Esser (1976), a.a. O. S.68–70 (Weimarer Republik) bzw. 70 ff. (Entwicklung nach 1945).

44 Ähnliche Argumentation in BGE 18,970 und 20, 1203.

45 Egon Schneider, 'Belege in den Entscheidungsgründen', *Zeitschrift für Zivilprozess ZZP* 77 (1964) S. 222–53; Spiros Simitis, *Informationskrise des Rechts und Datenverarbeitung* (Karlsruhe, 1970) S. 40 ff und 81.

46 Schneider, a.a.O. S. 225 f, Simitis, a.a.O. S. 41 und 81.

47 Vgl. zur mittelalterlichen Entwicklung Norbert Horn, 'Argumentum ab Auctoritate in der legistischen Argumentationstheorie', *Festschrift Wieacker* (Göttingen, 1978) S. 261 ff.

48 Vgl. Klaus Urner, *Die Deutschen in der Schweiz* (Frauenfeld/Stuttgart, 1976) S. 15, 64–8, 558 ff.

49 Vgl. zu dieser emotionellen Dimension der deutsch-schweizerischen Beziehungen nach 1945 beispielsweise Max Frisch, *Tagebuch 1946–1949* (Frankfurt/M., 1950) S. 140 und 407.

CHAPTER 13

Can We Speak of an Economic Revolution in Legal Reasoning?

Pierluigi Chiassoni

Among the different approaches American legal scholars developed in the last thirty years, the legal-economic approach is still one of the most successful.

On the one hand, legal scholars generally acknowledge what has been dubbed 'economic imperialism in the law', namely, a pervasive use of economic concepts, tools, and reasoning to rethink (several branches or the whole of) positive law, and devise legal reforms. On the other hand, lawyer-economists claim economic reasoning can turn a hardly rigorous legal science, wandering from one problem to another without any firm methodological foundation, into a legal science able to devise legal policies which are informed, oriented to precisely defined goals and rationally testable.[1]

One way to appreciate the impact of the law and economics movement on legal reasoning would be to compare legal-economic reasoning as employed by legal scholars, with standard conceptualistic and realistic legal reasonings.

Section 1 contains two tentative models of legal-economic reasoning, namely: a model of legal-economic casuistic reasoning, or the reasoning employed to solve specific problems according to the existing law, and a model of legal-economic conceptual reasoning, or the reasoning employed to transform the basic legal concepts of a given law-field.[2]

Section 2 surveys some of the main differences between legal-economic reasonings, on the one hand, and standard conceptualistic and realistic legal reasonings on the other.

Section 3 offers some tentative remarks about the revolutionary character of legal-economic reasonings. For the present purposes, a way of legal reasoning is revolutionary if it either represents a sweeping technical improvement over different ways of reasoning, or embodies values which upset conventional private and public morality, or both.

1 *Legal-Economic Reasonings*

1.1 Legal-economic casuistic reasoning

In Rongovia, the smoke of Acme, a widgets factory, spoil the laundry of Miss Bee. The problem is who has what rights. To provide an answer to this problem, lawyer-economists would follow a reasoning which can be divided into three stages: the input stage, the output stage, and the justification stage.

The input stage of legal-economic casuistic reasoning. At the input stage, besides the *prima facie* statement of facts above, lawyer-economists take into account three different kinds of inputs, namely: legal inputs, methodological inputs, and normative inputs. These inputs are the premises of legal-economic casuistic reasoning.

In the case at hand, *legal inputs* are mainly information about Rongovian nuisance law, torts law, and property law, traditional ways of legal interpretation and argument included.

Methodological inputs are the tools to be used to solve the problem at hand, Lawyer-economists would employ bargaining theory, the theory of price, the Coase theorem, statistical techniques, and notions like productive efficiency, wealth maximisation, negative externalities, etc.

Normative inputs are the goals which, according to lawyer-economists (be they acting on their own, or on behalf of a hypothetical policy-maker), should be achieved by the answer to the problem at hand. Accordingly, a proposed answer is good if, but only if, it is likely to promote such previously chosen goals. Suppose in this case lawyer-economists pick the following two goals: economic efficiency (i.e., the overall goal of minimising public and private costs, or maximise social wealth), and the minimisation of government interference in the relationships between individuals. Suppose, further, that lawyer-economists rank efficiency over the minimisation of government interference.

The output stage of legal-economic casuistic reasoning. At the output stage, lawyer-economists identify the right answer to *Bee v. Acme* with regard to hypothetical social and economic settings of implementation. They would roughly proceed as follows.

Identifying tentative legal answers. After a survey of Rongovian law, lawyer-economists realise that three different legal answers are available. (a) Acme has a right to spoil Miss Bee's laundry as it likes. Any claim for damages or injunction by Miss Bee should be turned down according to the principle: Leave the losses where they fall. (b) Acme has a right to spoil Miss Bee's laundry provided it pays for the damages she suffers. That is to say, Miss Bee has a right, protected by damages only, not to be polluted by Acme. (c) Miss Bee has a right, protected by an injunction, not to be polluted by Acme. If Miss Bee sues Acme for polluting her laundry, a judge could order Acme to shut down its plant.

Identifying the right legal answer according to economic tools and normative inputs. Lawyer-economists employ economic tools to ascertain which answer, if any, among the three listed above is the right one from the viewpoint of efficiency and the minimisation of government interference. To do so, they predict which impact each available legal answer is likely to have on efficiency and the minimisation of state interference in a given hypothetical economic setting (suppose they assume that the market for Acme's widgets is perfectly competitive).

To begin with, lawyer-economists reject the first answer available (Acme has a right to pollute Miss Bee as it likes) because, at least *prima facie,* it poorly affects efficiency in a competitive market. They argue as follows.

Efficiency requires widgets to be offered to consumers at their true price, namely at a price that perfectly mirrors their actual costs to society. Accordingly, allowing Acme to produce widgets without bearing all costs of production (its negative effects on Miss Bee included) has three undesirable consequences. First, the price of an Acme widget does not reflect its entire cost because Acme is being subsidised by Miss Bee. The social cost of Acme's output is greater than its private cost. Second, lawyer-economists assume that Acme may be driven out of the competitive market for widgets, were it to pay for the social cost of its output. Accordingly, so far as Acme is being subsidised by Miss Bee, it would be kept in the market despite its inefficiency. Third, until Miss Bee bears part of Acme's production costs, Acme will have no incentive to improve its productive processes so as to minimise their overall costs: Acme will not care about dynamic productive efficiency (research and development).

On the basis of the reasoning above, lawyer-economists conclude that, at least *prima facie,* efficiency requires imposing some liability on Acme. To find out which form of liability is better, they turn to the other legal answers available.

The second legal answer available states that Miss Bee should be granted a damages-protected right not to be polluted by Acme.

Apparently, this answer is efficient: it makes Acme internalise its negative externalities. However, as soon as lawyer-economists also take into account the goal of minimising state interference, the so-called Coase theorem, bargaining theory, and administrative efficiency (the costs of running the government machinery), they conclude that such an answer will not always do. Three points make them hesitant about granting Miss Bee a right to damages against Acme.

Which damages? Lawyer-economists have to decide which damages to award and calculate their amounts. Should they award Miss Bee past damages only, or rather provide for Miss Bee's future damages as well? Apparently efficiency requires Acme to internalise all its present or future negative externalities.

Liquidating damages. Lawyer-economists have to decide whether to compensate Miss Bee for her future damages by a lump sum award, or set up a compensation mechanism, by means of which Miss Bee can be exactly compensated for her future losses. Lawyer-economists hesitate to award Miss

Bee lump sum damages. Indeed, in such a case, this will have a negative effect on dynamic productive efficiency and social wealth. Once it has paid the lump sum damages to Miss Bee, Acme will have no incentive to reduce the pollution due to its production process, even when technological improvements would make it cheap and easy. Furthermore, Acme would be granted a right to keep indefinitely polluting its immediate environment. This is clearly a social waste: are we really sure that, in the long run, Miss Bee's laundry will be the only damaged item? Besides, such a policy would be hardly acceptable to an environmentalist public. Finally, lump sum damages call for difficult calculation and/or decision as to how much compensation is due (problems of overcompensation or undercompensation arise). Nonetheless, lawyer-economists also hesitate to make Acme pay for the damages it inflicts upon Miss Bee: periodically, at the end of each year, for example. Here there is no apparent problem of overcompensation or undercompensation, but an inquiry into the amount of damages to be paid to Miss Bee is to be held each year. Suppose Miss Bee claims her laundering during the past year has been damaged more than Acme is willing to admit. Periodical damages solutions are likely to call for a continuous involvement of courts (or arbitrators) over years, and, accordingly, cause greater administrative costs, provided they never completely dispose of the dispute *Bee v. Acme.* To conclude: lawyer-economists realise that granting Miss Bee a right to damages against Acme is not necessarily an efficient policy, and apparently involves either difficult calculations, or a heavy involvement of government officials, or both.

Escaping calculations. On the basis of bargaining theory and the so-called Coase theorem, lawyer-economists think they might avoid the riddle of calculating Miss Bee's damages efficiently. Perhaps a different legal answer would allow Miss Bee and Acme to solve their problem in a mutually satisfactory way by themselves. Lawyer-economists turn then to the third legal answer available to see whether it could do.

The third legal answer available states that Miss Bee should be granted an injunction-protected right against Acme.

Lawyer-economists claim that, if transaction costs (strategic behaviour included) are low, such an answer is efficient and promotes the minimisation of government interference. They argue as follows.

Minimal intervention by the government. Granting Miss Bee an injunction against Acme does minimise government interference in the relationship between Bee and Acme. On the one hand, if Miss Bee sues Acme, and the judge finds Acme actually spoils Miss Bee's laundry, she will grant Miss Bee an injunction against Acme. The judge will react almost mechanically to Miss Bee's complaint, and accordingly the administrative costs of the dispute are likely to be very low. On the other hand, if both Miss Bee and Acme know a judge may grant an injunction, they might get round the bargaining table. Here, courts' behviour affects individuals' relationships only indirectly. The degree of government interference is the lowest possible.

Furthering efficiency. The indirect governmental influence considered above would promote economic efficiency. Suppose Acme, a prosperous widgets firm, wants to avoid an injunction. Accordingly, Acme will attempt to buy off Miss Bee. Provided low transaction costs (strategic behaviour included) are assumed, Acme and Miss Bee will reach a mutually satisfactory, efficient agreement. Suppose, on the other hand, that Acme, a firm on the verge of bankruptcy, cannot buy off Miss Bee. In this case, Miss Bee will obtain an injunction against Acme. The outcome is efficient too: Acme, an inefficient firm, will be driven out of the market.

At the end of the output stage, lawyer-economists reach the following conclusions. (a) Given their normative and legal inputs, and assuming a competitive market for Acme's widgets and low transaction costs (strategic behaviour included), the right answer is granting Miss Bee an injunction against Acme's pollution. (b) Given their normative and legal inputs, and assuming a competitive market for Acme's widgets, high transaction costs (strategic behaviour included), and low administrative costs, the right answer is granting Miss Bee a right to damages against Acme. (c) Given their normative and legal inputs, and assuming a competitive market for Acme's widgets, high transaction costs (strategic behaviour included), and high administrative costs, the right answer is granting Acme a right to pollute Miss Bee's laundry.

The justification stage of legal-economic casuistic reasoning. At the justification stage, lawyer-economists consider which of the three right answers above, designed for hypothetical settings, is the most acceptable in the real world, namely, with regard to their economic, political and legal settings of implementation.

Economic and political justification. If the Rongovian widgets market is close to a competitive market, and transaction costs (strategic behaviour included) are low. lawyer-economists would conclude that, from an economic point of view, Miss Bee should be granted an injunction against Acme. If the Rongovian widgets market is close to a competitive market, transaction costs (strategic behaviour included) are high, and administrative costs are low, lawyer-economists would conclude that, from an economic point of view, Miss Bee should be granted a right to damages against Acme. If the Rongovian widgets market is close to a competitive market, transaction costs (strategic behaviour included) are high, and administrative costs are also high, lawyer-economists would conclude that, from an economic viewpoint, Acme should be granted a right to pollute Miss Bee's laundry. If, finally, the Rongovian widgets market is not competitive, lawyer-economists would go back to the output stage and check the likely performance of each of the three tentative legal answers in a monopolistic or oligopolistic widget market.

Suppose lawyer-economists find out that, from an economic point of view, granting Miss Bee an injunction is the right answer. Suppose, furthermore, that such an answer is also acceptable from a political point of view. They turn, then, to whether such an answer can be argued to be legally justified, not only with regard to the legal instrument employed (an injunction is, *ex hypothesi,* an acceptable tool in Rongovian law), but also with regard to the specific goals, or principles that instrument is made to serve.

Legal justification. Following conventional legal scholarship, lawyer-economists assume that an answer is justified according to positive law if it can be shown to be the outcome of some reasonable interpretation and manipulation of existing legal materials. On the basis of this assumption, lawyer-economists claim their answer is legally justified if it passes what may be called 'the legal-economic internal justification test'.

The legal-economic internal justification test states that a legal answer is justified according to a given positive law if, but only if, the goal or goals it serves are already being served by some positive legal rule or institution. the legal-economic internal justification test works as follows.

(I) By means of economic analysis (statistical inquiries, storytelling, economic matters of course, etc.), lawyer-economists see whether the actual effects of some positive legal rule and institution promote efficiency and the minimisation of government interference (lawyer-economists do not care about legislative intent, or the so-called objective purpose of rules and institutions, or goals different from those they select). (II) If that is the case, lawyer-economists claim that those rules and institutions can be regarded either as explicit embodiments of the principle of efficiency and the principle of minimising government interference, or as being implicitly grounded on such principles. (III) If that is the case, lawyer-economists argue that the principle of efficiency and the principle of minimising government interference are positive legal principles, be they explicit principles, or implicit principles, or both, according to the standpoint from which one looks at them. (IV) If that is the case, lawyer-economists comclude their proposed answer is legally justified, since it clearly promotes two positive legal principles like the principle of efficiency and the principle of minimising government interference.

1.2 Legal-economic conceptual reasoning

Lawyer-economists employ economic tools not only to solve specific legal problems, but also to transform the traditional legal concepts of a given law-field. Suppose the law-field is Rongovian nuisance law. Suppose, furthermore, that lawyer-economists assume that economic efficiency and the minimisation of state interference are the goals to be pursued. Legal-economic conceptual reasoning would then proceed through three stages: the goals-reduction stage, the concepts-transformation stage, and the justification stage.

The goals-reduction stage of legal-economic conceptual reasoning. At the goals-reduction stage, lawyer-economists assume that efficiency and the minimisation of government interference are the only, or the dominant, goals of Rongovian nuisance law. In so doing, they perform a normative selection of the goals Rongovian nuisance law should serve. They either overlook other possible goals, or rank such goals lower than efficiency and minimising government interference. Such a reduction is the prerequisite for lawyer-economists rethinking Rongovian nuisance law, and transforming it according to their goals.

The concepts-transformation stage of legal-economic conceptual reasoning. Lawyer-economists apply economic notions and theories to re-define the basic concepts of Rongovian nuisance law, so as to make them systematically serve efficiency and the minimisation of state interference.

For instance, following Learned Hand, lawyer-economists may claim that Acme's activity is not a nuisance to Miss Bee if, but only if, $B > PL$ or $B = PL$, where B is the costs of precautions incurred by Acme to avoid damaging others, P is the probability that a loss will occur unless Acme takes precautions B and L is the loss actually suffered by Miss Bee. In this case, lawyer-economists turn a vague concept like 'nuisance' into a concept that is quantitative and operational (whether an activity is, or is not, a nuisance becomes a matter of empirical research). Lawyer-economists see many advantages in turning legal concepts into quantitative and operational ones. (a) Quantitative and operational concepts leave judges no (strong) discretion about whether they do, or do not, apply to a situation at hand, and, accordingly, about whether a situation at hand does, or does not, violate the criteria they are related to. (b) Quantitative and operational concepts are easily manageable by decision-makers: they do not require 'reasoned elaboration'. (c) If constantly employed by decision-makers, quantitative and operational concepts positively affect the predictability of official decisions and systematically serve the goal they are meant to promote. (d) If regularly employed by decision-makers, quantitative and operational concepts allow for technical criticism of decision. These advantages represent as many reasons lawyer-economists offer to adopt their transformed concepts.

The justisfication stage of legal-economic conceptual reasoning. Lawyer-economists offer both an internal justification and an external justification for the transformation of the concept of nuisance they have performed.

Internal justification is meant to show that the outcome of courts using a quantitative and operational concept of nuisance (like the one lawyer-economists propose) are wholly compatible with positive legal principles. Here lawyer-economists use the legal-economic internal justification test as a basis for explanations of Rongovian nuisance case-law ('positive analysis of Rongovian nuisance case-law').

External justification is meant to show that, if courts use the quantitative and operational concept of nuisance lawyer-economists propose, their decisions will not only be according to the law, but also substantially improved as to their precision, predictability, and instrumentality.

2 Legal-economic Reasonings, Conceptualistic Reasonings, Realistic Reasonings

2.1 Legal-economic reasonings v. conceptualistic reasonings

In the light of the models above, the difference between legal-economic reasonings and standard conceptualistic reasoning are obviously striking (many analogies between old and new conceptualists notwithstanding).[3] I shall mention only a few of them.

Interdisciplinary v. monadic approach. Legal-economic reasonings are interdisciplinary. Their inputs, outputs, arguments, concepts and systems are partly drawn from economic theories, moral philosophy, and political philosophy. By contrast, conceptualistic reasonings are monadic. Their inputs, outputs, arguments, concepts and systems are specifically legal (this is what Richard Posner means by 'law as an autonomous discipline').[4] This difference is apparent as soon as one compares casuistic legal-economic reasoning, as outlined above, and casuistic conceptualistic reasoning. In easy cases, conceptualists employ a logical reasoning (statement of facts, self-evidently relevant legal materials, subsumption of facts under the relevant materials, decision). In hard cases, conceptualistic reasoning is analogical (it proceeds on analogies and disanalogies between cases). In any case, conceptualists believe their ways of reasoning, logical and analogical alike, lead to legally right answers firmly embedded in positive law.

Care v. indifference about actual consequences. Legal-economic reasonings test the correctness of legal rules, standards and concepts against their working in the real world. Conceptualistic reasonings, by contrast, test the correctness of legal rules, standards, and concepts against other more important, rules, standards and concepts. Furthermore, these more important rules, standards and concepts are *paper* rules and concepts, namely: (a) they work as argumentative chips in the process of justifying full-blown decisions, rather than as guidelines in the decision-making process with regard to some specific problem; (b) they establish purely linguistic standards of criticism, rather than substantive standards of criticism: according to them, any decision is justified if its formulation sounds good with regard to their usual formulations.

Instrumentalism v. neutralism. Legal-economic reasonings display the view that law, legal concepts and legal systems are instruments of legal policy, to be shaped by scholars for the use of judges and legislators. By contrast, conceptualistic reasonings display the assumption that law, legal concepts and legal systems are to be treated *as if* fixed entities 'out there', waiting for scholars' discovery.

Quantitative and operational concepts v. vague concepts. Legal-economic reasonings works with quantitative and operational concepts. By contrast, conceptualistic reasonings works with qualitative, vague concepts.

Judicial discretion and scholars' preferences. Legal-economic reasonings are meant to expose official discretion (and scholars' preferences) at each point of their stages. By contrast, conceptualistic reasonings conceals official discretion (and scholars' preferences) under the literally taken veil of 'law-finding' and 'fact-finding'.

2.2 Legal-economic reasonings v. realistic legal reasonings

In the light of the models above, the differences between legal-economic reasonings and the reasonings of American legal realists seem a matter of degree and variation on the same methodological and jurisprudential themes, rather than a matter of incompatible fundamental views about law, legal science, and legal reasonings.[5]

Instrumentalism. Legal-economic reasonings and realistic reasonings are both grounded on the view that law, legal concepts and legal systems are instruments of legal policy, to be shaped by scholars for the use of judges and legislators. The realist maxim 'the problems of law are problems of social engineering' holds for lawyer-economists as well.

Clear and informed legal thinking. Legal-economic reasonings and realistic reasonings both oppose vagueness, metaphors and ignorance in legal thinking. Both legal-economic reasonings and realistic reasonings display the view that legal scholarship should provide goal-informed analyses (and reinterpretation) of existing legal materials in order to state more clearly what the law is (or how the law actually works), and what to do if one wishes to change it.

Official discretion. Both legal-economic reasonings and realistic reasonings display the view that official discretion can be controlled by means of scientific scholarship, but never ruled out.

Interdisciplinarity. Legal-economic reasonings and realistic reasonings are both interdisciplinary ways of reasoning. In fact, besides political science and sociological influences, the works by legal realists display the influence of economic theories. Like lawyer-economists, realists use economics not only to collect data about interests which might have shaped legal institutions, but also to identify some purpose or purposes of legal institutions on the basis of which they test their actual working and design their reform.[6] Unlike lawyer-economists, however, realists (so far as I know) did not transform any qualitative legal concepts into a quantitative one, nor did they invent any legal-economic argument like the internal justification test.

Economic imperialism. If the similarities and differences between legal-economic reasonings and realistic reasonings I listed above are correct, what accounts for much of the differences between the two ways of reasoning is the differences between institutional economics and the social sciences methodologies, employed by the realists, on the one hand, and neoclassical price theory Chicago-style, applied welfare economics, transaction costs economics, Austrian economics, neo-institutional economics, and econometrics, employed by lawyer-economists, on the other. In particular, economic imperialism, the idea that economics provides a general study of human behaviour to be used by any other social science, legal science included, accounts for the most striking difference between legal-economic reasonings, on the one hand, and realistic reasonings on the other: the sweeping role of efficiency and costs notions in legal-economic thinking.

3 *Are legal-Economic Reasonings Revolutionary?*

In the light of the two sections above, it is possible to make some (tentative) remarks about whether legal-economic reasonings are revolutionary, i.e., according to the definition provided at the outset, either they represent a sweeping technical improvement over different ways of legal reasoning, or they embody values which upset conventional private and public morality, or both.

Do legal-economic reasonings represent a sweeping technical improvement over different ways of legal reasoning? Obviously, the answer depends on how we define 'technical improvement'. A fairly acceptable definition of 'technical improvement' would be the following: a way of legal reasoning represents a technical improvement over different ways of legal reasoning if it better responds to three kinds of criticism, namely, empirical or theoretical criticism of its factual premises, moral criticism of its value premises, and instrumental criticism of its conclusions. Empirical or theoretical criticisms of the factual premises of a given legal reasoning are better responded to by more detailed information about the real world which is being collected in the process of reasoning. Indeed, the more facts are accounted for in detail and differentiated as against other facts, the more it is possible to criticise a line of reasoning not only for those facts it accounts for, but also for the facts it keeps out of the screen. Moral criticisms of the value premises of a given line of reasoning are better responded to the more the particular values it argues for are clearly exposed as to their actual bearing on individuals. Instrumental criticisms of the conclusions of a given line of reasoning are better prompted to the more the means-to-end relationship between a given value and its purportedly appropriate means is clearly exposed in the reasoning.

If we accept the definition of 'technical improvement' (of legal reasoning) above, we may conclude that legal-economic reasonings are revolutionary: they clearly represent a sweeping technical improvement over conventional forms of legal reasonings.

Legal-economic reasonings surely represent an improvement over standard conceptualistic reasonings, where facts are always prequalified *legal* facts, value judgements are hidden behind vague clauses, and, accordingly, it is difficult, if not impossible, to make instrumental criticisms.

Legal-economic reasonings also represent a technical improvement over standard realist reasoning, at least from the viewpoint of the techniques for stating facts.

Do legal-economic reasonings embody values which upset conventional private and public morality? This question, at least *prima facie,* commands no clear-cut answer. As a matter of fact, different lawyer-economists, different users of what I have dubbed legal-economic reasonings, are commited to different (or even very different) values: from extreme *laissez-faire* or libertarian values (like those endorsed by James Buchanan and Richard Epstein), to moderate *laissez-faire* values (like those endorsed by Richard Posner), to social-democratic values (like those endorsed by Guido Calabresi). Accordingly, whether legal-economic reasonings do, or do not embody values which upset conventional private and public morality is a question that cannot be answered once and for all, but requires us to focus on the particular values actually endorsed by particular lawyer-economists in particular situations.

Such an answer highlights one point about legal-economic reasonings which, though very evident, is often overlooked by those questioning 'the moral worth' of the law and economics movement as a whole, namely: there is no necessary (or logical) connection between the tools and techniques of legal-economic reasonings, on the one hand, and some specific set of values or goals, on the other. Different sets of values can be argued for by using the same tools and techniques, and vice versa.[7] Furthermore, the tools and techniques of legal-economic reasonings spring from a range of different economic theories. An inquiry into the tools and techniques actually employed by particular lawyer-economists to serve particular values, though mostly worthwhile, goes beyond the scope of the present paper.

NOTES

1   See Bruce A Ackerman, *Reconstructing American Law* (Cambridge and London, Harvard University Press, 1984), pp 46 ff.

2   See Guido Calabresi, 'Some thoughts about risk distribution and the law of torts', *Yale Law Journal* 70 (1961) pp 499–553; Ronald H Coase; 'The problem of social cost', *Journal of Law and Economics* 3 (1960), pp 1–44; Guido Calabresi and John T Hirschoff; 'Toward a test for strict liability in torts', *Yale Law Journal* 82 (1972), pp 1055–85; Richard A Posner, 'An economic theory of criminal law', *Columbia Law Review* 85 (1985), pp 1193–231; Robert Cooter, 'Unity in tort, contract, and property: the model of precaution', *California Law Review* 73 (1985) pp 1–51; Robert Cooter and Thomas Ulen, *Law and Economics* (Glenview and London, Scott, Foresman and Company, 1988).

3   See Grant Gilmore, *The Ages of American Law* (New Haven and London, Yale University Press, 1977) pp 107–9.

4   See Richard Posner, 'The decline of law as an autonomous discipline: 1962–1987', *Harvard Law Review* 100 (1987) pp 761–80. See also Hessel E Yntema, 'The hornbook method and the conflicts of law', *Yale Law Journal* 38 (1928) pp 468–83; Underhill Moore and Theodore S Hope, 'An institutional approach to the law of commercial banking', *Yale Law Journal* 38 (1929) pp 703–19.

5   A different view is argued for by Bruce A Ackerman, *Reconstructing American Law* (Cambridge and London, Harvard University Press, 1984) pp 6–22.

6   See, e.g., Edwin W Patterson, 'The apportionment of business risks through legal devices', *Columbia Law Review* 24 (1924) pp 335–59; K N Llewellyn, 'The effect of legal institutions upon economics', *American Economic Review* 15 (1925) pp 665–83; William O Douglas, 'Vicarious liability and administration of risk'. *Yale Law Journal* 38 (1929) pp 584–604, 720–45; Lon L Fuller and William R Perdue, 'The reliance interest in contract damages', *Yale Law Journal* 46 (1936) pp 52–96, 373–420.

7   See, e.g., Richard A Posner, *Economic Analysis of Law* (Boston and Toronto, Little, Brown and Company, 1986[3]) pp 24–5.

CHAPTER 14

Critical Legal Studies: A Revolution in Legal Thought?

David Jabbari

Introduction: The task of critical legal studies

The American Critical Legal Studies (CLS) Movement is the most influential critical movement in law since Legal Realism.[1] A noteworthy characteristic of CLS is its aim to translate legal criticism into a programme of radical social transformation.[2] Unlike previous critical movements in law, CLS attempts to show that this programme of social transformation may be engineered by developing the potential for such transformation that lies within existing legal rules and doctrines, and not by other non-legal means.[3] This paper examines this novel contention.

Two intricate hurdles confront CLS in its task. For want of less awkward terms, I call these hurdles 'legal nihilism' and 'circularity'. The problem of legal nihilism takes two forms.[4] Firstly, it manifests itself in a loss of hope in moving beyond criticism of law to the creation of a new conception of law. The criticisms of legal adjudication made by the Legal Realists, for example, were not confined to the application of existing legal rules but extended to all possible exercises of judicial discretion.[5] Secondly, it is represented by a scepticism of the law's potential to bring about social transformation. An example is found in the writings of the celebrated Marxist legal theorist Pashukanis who suggested a system of 'technical regulation' as a replacement for the opposition of interests which he felt characterised law.[6] In so arguing he denied that law could have a role in bringing about and regulating social transformation. The consequence of legal nihilism is that proposals for transforming society cannot be pursued through the conventional modes of legal challenge, and thus are conditional upon the occurrence of fundamental social change. In the absence of this extra-legal change, orthodox legal scholarship may either accommodate critical insights without major revision of prevailing legal values, as in the case of Legal Realism, or deny them as utopian, as in the case of Marxist theories of law.[7]

If the Scylla for the reconstructive aims of CLS is legal nihilism, the Charybdis is the problem of circularity. 'Circularity' is the term I shall use to describe the following problem.[8] Since a major component of the critical side of the critical theory project is to demonstrate that 'classical' conceptions of law rest upon a highly restrictive set of values, it is clear that critical legal theorists are thereby estopped from postulating an equally value-laden but different conception of law as a replacement for the old; for example that the law of contract is premised upon altruism rather than individualism.[9] A critical theory of law which attempts to reconstruct law simply by replacing existing legal values by ones diametrically opposed, through more acceptable, will not truly refute the conception of law which it is criticising. As a result, such a theory will remain vulnerable to precisely the same criticisms that it has made in attacking the value-laden character of existing law.[10]

Through an evaluation of the reconstructive component of CLS, I shall argue that the movement does not provide a solution to the problems of legal nihilism and circularity. For the purposes of interpretation and explanation of the fundamental differences that exist within the confusing welter of contemporary CLS, I have employed Weberian ideal types as the means by which to identify its pertinent themes.[11] I have identified three levels at which CLS has sought to establish new conceptions of law: the method of criticism, the relationship of law to society, and the strategy for reconstructing the law. Section One, 'The Method of Criticism', shows how contemporary Critical Legal Theorists derive their new conceptions of law from their critique of existing law, thereby responding to the first limb of the problem of legal nihilism. Section Two, 'The Relationship of Law to Society', analyses the attempts of Critical Legal Theorists to overcome the second sense of legal nihilism by demonstrating that law can be an agent of social change. Section Three, 'The Strategy for Reconstructing Law', addresses the question of whether the theorists' new conceptions of law can avoid simply negating and replacing the values of existing law, the problem of circularity.

I *The method of criticism of CLS: deconstruction*

An essential constituent in any theory which seeks to move beyond legal nihilism and circularity is a method of criticism which can indicate the basis for a new conception of law without departing from the values of existing law. In this regard, the method of deconstruction is currently enjoying a vogue amongst Critical Legal Theorists.[12] The method has non-legal origins however, in the work of the French philosopher Jacques Derrida, whose writings focused predominantly upon problems of literary interpretation. In sharp contrast to those literary theorists who purported to enable the reader to understand the meaning of a text, Derrida's aim was to render it impossible to read it—to deconstruct rather than reconstruct its meaning.[13] For Derrida an attempt by a text to recreate a reality external to it is an illusion, an illusion perpetuated by certain rhetorical devices that are cunningly imported into any such interpretation.

A deconstructive reading of a text is similar to the method by which a psychoanalyst probes the mind of his patient in order to discover those aspects of the patient's subconscious that have managed to deceive the super-ego and thus gain admission to the conscious mind. Perhaps the most important means by which a text can deceive the mind is found in the device of the 'conceptual dualism'.[14] When deconstruction has 'interrogated' a text, it will break through the defences and reveal a set of binary oppositions, or 'conceptual dualisms': public/private, masculine/feminine, same/other, true/false, central/peripheral etc. Critical Legal Theorists make great use of this aspect of deconstruction. An example of the operation of the device of conceptual dualism is provided by Tushnet in his description of the way in which liberal constitutional theorists have attempted to confine the insights of the Legal Realists to a 'peripheral' rather than 'core' application of rules:

> ... whenever someone worried about the relation between Realism and the core, the arguments that seemed to work on the periphery seemed to work on the core as well. This has led to successive efforts to redefine what the core is ... Whenever the centre locates the core, it will find critical scholars ready to demonstrate that that's not it either.[15]

Since any text, legal or other, will implicitly favour the validity of one of the poles of these dualisms at the expense of the other, the text can have coherence only to the extent that it begs the question as to the validity of the pole it favours. For example, Unger has attempted to show that the law of contract possesses coherence only in so far as it implicitly assumes the validity of the principle of freedom of contract and excludes the principle, also found in the law, that freedom of contract will not be permitted to subvert communal relationships such as marriage.[16] Similarly, the principle of freedom of contract is accorded more significance than the many instances where the law affirms a paternalist motivation, for example unfair contract terms and sale of goods legislation, the doctrine of mistake etc.

The process of constantly favouring the validity of one of the poles of a conceptual dualism results in the establishment of a hierarchical relationship between the poles in a given text, or body of legal doctrine. The permanently disfavoured pole is called the 'dangerous supplement' and is dangerous because it can threaten to undermine the unity of the text which constantly disfavours it. Thus for the deconstructionist, a body of law is only ever an apparent unity and is better viewed as a means of implicitly establishing hierarchy. In terms of the socially transformative potential of law, deconstruction can indicate a new conception of law without going beyond the values of existing law, even if some of these values have previously been suppressed. This requires us to discover the dangerous supplements in an area of law, and to use them as a basis on which to argue for a radically different interpretation of the law. Remaining with contract law, it would be possible to rewrite the law of contract as a paternalist body of rules, which exists to protect those with inferior bargaining power, without departing from principles found in existing law.[17] As we shall see later, the CLS strategy for reconstructing law, 'deviationist doctrine', is simply this positive aspect of deconstruction. It should be noted that the reconstructed conception of law provided by deconstruction draws its being from existing yet disfavoured legal authority. It therefore avoids the problem of circularity described in the Introduction.[18]

The main problem with the method of deconstruction concerns the degree to which it views the dilemmas at the level of law and legal theory as resulting from dilemmas at the level of social and economic systems. To illustrate this problem, consider Unger's deconstructive reading of the law of contract.

It will be remembered that for Unger contract law can be understood in terms of the operation of a favoured principle of freedom to contract and a disfavoured counter-principle that such freedom will not be allowed to subvert traditional or communal patterns of life. The operation of the disfavoured principle explains the legal invalidity of all contracts that offend public morality, such as contracts to commit a crime or contracts contra bonos mores. It also explains the unwillingness of contract to enter certain 'private spheres' such as the marital relation.[19] The crux of the problem is the question of to what extent the law's reluctance to subvert communal life or to intrude into the private spheres of social life, is a result of the whim of legal doctrine or of pressures exerted by the economic system. For example, Marxist theories of law would explain failure of the law to regulate these areas in terms of the need of the economic system to rely upon certain non-legalised codes in order to ensure the overall effectiveness of that system.[20] Thus it often is argued that the non-contractual nature of marriage allows men to exert authority over women, thereby ensuring the stability of traditional family life. The problem is that Unger, like other deconstructionists, presents his favoured principles and disfavoured counter-principles as universal: he gives no indication of their genesis or the conditions for their existence.[21] Deconstruction displays a doctrine-centredness, a belief that conceptual dualisms are on a par with social contradictions. By assuming the existence of conceptual dualisms in legal doctrine rather than providing explanations for them, deconstruction implies that the problems encountered at the level of legal doctrine are not a product of the economic and social environment. In doing this, deconstruction further implies the belief that legal doctrine possesses its own evolutionary logic. In the next section we shall see that this position impairs CLS attempts to establish the capacity of law to transform social relationships.

II   *The relationship of law to society: the constitutive theory of law*

In the last section we considered the success of CLS in overcoming the first sense of legal nihilism. In this section we are focusing on the second sense of legal nihilism and so will be asking whether the model of the law and society relationship formulated by CLS can show law to be capable of changing society. In looking at the relationship between law and society, we are examining how the theorists believe that law influences and is influenced by its social and economic environment. The theorists need to show that law is not merely a reflection of some causally antecedent economic or social force but has a degree of autonomy from such forces which allows it to modify the character of those forces.

In their fervour to show that law can be taken seriously as a means of effecting social transformation, Critical Legal Theorists attack what they label 'crude instrumentalism'. There are three main senses in which Critical Legal Theorists use this term: all or most legal rules reflect the interests of the ruling economic class; the social relations generated by economic production determine the substance of legal rules; and law operates exclusively through a coercive apparatus.[22] All these accounts of crude instrumentalism have a common core. They conceive of law as being part of a social 'superstructure' which is determined by an economic 'base'. Since law is part of this superstructure it cannot change except through changes in society, which in turn are caused by changes in the economic base. The consequence of this is that law cannot be used as a tool of social transformation for it is itself a product rather than a determinant of society. To overcome instrumentalisation, Critical Legal Theorists have employed a position known as 'the relative autonomy of law' whereby law can be viewed as influenced by economic forces, but still possessing such a degree of autonomy in relation to those forces that it may in turn be able to influence them. Such a theory is attractive for it allows one to take law seriously as a means of social change and to assert its intimate connection to economic forces. There is, however, a distinct problem with the thesis of the relative autonomy of law:

> unless it is capable of being linked to some account which specifies the boundaries or limitations of autonomy it can only be understood as constantly running the danger of lapsing into the assertion of either autonomy or determinism coupled with an expression of faith that on the one hand autonomy is limited and has determined limitations, or on the other, that determinism is limited or postponed.[23]

In order to demonstrate that law can transform society, a critical theory of law must then demonstrate that law has the abiliy to influence wider economic and social relationships without lapsing into either legal autonomy or crude determinism. On the one hand, if law is conceived of as autonomous from social forces, as evolving purely according to its own characteristics, then the nexus between law and society is broken, and thus one cannot show how law could effect social change. On the other hand, if law is seen as being determined by social or economic forces it cannot then be said to influence or direct those forces. Thus the problem is one of finding the right balance of autonomy and determinism.

The CLS attack on crude instrumentalism attempts to demonstrate that legal doctrine does not possess sufficient determinacy to be used as an instrument for the furtherance of economic interests. To believe that law could be used in such a way is, for the Critical Legal Theorists, to believe that economic interests can be directly translated into law. Gordon summarises the CLS position:

> . . . if the critiques of legal belief structures are accurate—that even in their theoretically ideal forms they are contradictory and incoherent, and that in practical application they depart constantly from the ideal in wildly unpredictable fashion—it follows that no particular legal regime of legal principles could be functionally necessary to maintain any particular economic order. Similarly, no given economic order can be thought of as requiring for its maintenance any particular bunch of legal rules, except of course those that may be part of the definition of that economic order, as 'private property' of some sort is to most people's definition of capitalism.[24]

The theorist who has perhaps contributed most to this line of thought is Duncan Kennedy. In his essay on paternalism in the law of contract, Kennedy employs a detailed economic analysis to show that far from being determined by economic relations, law evolves according to a pattern of its own.[25] The brunt of his attack is unleashed on the economic analysts of law who have attempted to rationalise implied warranties in contracts as efficient from the perspective of wealth-maximisation. Kennedy attempts to defeat these positions by showing that for these interventions in contract to be efficient, it would be necessary to show that law is a vehicle for the translation of economic interests into legal rules. He argues that legal doctrine is radically indeterminate *vis-à-vis* the advancement of particular economic interests; that is, nothing in the principles of contract law is definite enough to tell a legislator or judge what to do when asked to change the existing law of agreements to the advantage of a particular economic interest. To illustrate his case Kennedy identifies two sterotypical policy arguments which he believes recur endlessly in different legal contexts. In the 'altruist' mode, the decision-maker resolves a gap or ambiguity in the law by requiring a party who injures the other to pay compensation, and by allowing a liberal law of excuse when the injuring party claims to be not really responsible. In the 'individualist' mode, the injured party should, it is thought, have 'looked out for himself' and the party seeking excuse should have avoided binding himself to an obligation he could not fulfil. Kennedy's point is that these policy arguments are purely rhetorical and therefore any legal rules modelled upon them cannot be shown to have any effect on the distribution of wealth without a mass of additional assumptions. To give an example, if an implied term is inserted into contracts for the sale of goods for the purposes of ensuring fitness for purpose and merchantable quality of the goods, there is no way of knowing the economic effects, in terms of distribution of wealth, caused by this implied term. Whereas altruist policy-makers would see such a term as being in the best interests of the economically under-privileged, the fact is that the person invoking the term may be wealthy. Since on Kennedy's analysis law is too indeterminate to be a bearer of economic interests, it follows that it cannot be used in an instrumental fashion. The upshot of this position is to deny causal priority to the economic system, for law evolves according to its own logic. In this way US Critical Legal Theorists refute instrumentalism. We must now move on to discover how Critical Legal Theorists view the relationship between law and society. The positive contribution of CLT in this respect can be found in 'The Constitutive Theory of Law'.

The nascent and rudimentary character of the Constitutive Theory of Law places significant limits on the detail with which we can describe it. The term originates in the work of US Critical Legal Theorist, Karl Klare, in his essay 'Law Making as Praxis'.[26] Many Critical Legal Theorists have recognised the Constitutive Theory of Law to be an attempted solution to the problems of instrumentalism. The method by which the theory seeks to resolve this problem possesses a great similarity to Pashukanis' approach in one respect:[27] it denies that law can be conceived of as existing independently of wider social relations. The law is not 'the armed receptacle for values and priorities determined elsewhere' but is better understood as part of a complex social totality 'in which it constitutes as well as is constituted, shapes as well as is shaped' by society.[28] The Constitutive Theory of Law appears to resemble the theory that law is relatively autonomous of social and economic factors because it suggests that law both determines and is determined by the wider social totality. But this superficial resemblance between the two theories is misleading. Those who believe that law is relatively autonomous of society nevertheless maintain that economic forces ultimately shape and constrain the law. By contrast, Critical Legal Theorists who support the Constitutive Theory of Law have given up any belief that the economy has causal priority *vis-à-vis* the law, but instead believe that both form a 'seamless web' in which each determines the shape and character of the other. Since law is not in any sense upon an economic leash, the Constitutive Theory of Law is not a position of relative autonomy. Legal development is seen as resulting from law's internal characteristics, not from the characteristics of society. As we shall see later, this belief in the power of law *vis-à-vis* the economy leads to the naively optimistic claims made by deviationist doctrine, claims which impair its ability to establish the transformative potential of law.

The Constitutive Theory of Law blurs the essential connection between law and the economic and social system. Such a theory cannot establish the transformative potential of law because it does not allow us to conceptualise how it is possible for programmes of social change to be pursued through law. Although law does shape and is shaped by society, law's development depends principally upon its own characteristics. Since the way law interacts with society is unclear, the effect law has on social relations is indeterminate.

Further the belief in the autonomy of law *vis-à vis* economic relations is one of the central features of the orthodox view of law Critical Legal Theorists are seeking to criticise. The Constitutive Theory, relating legal doctrine to a nebulous social whole as it does, is so general as to be practically unworkable. The results of work done on the premises of such a theory would be at best *ad hoc* and unsystematised and would leave the reformer with a sense of powerlessness to change any aspect of the totality. Without providing a point of entry for critical analysis of legal doctrines, the Constitutive Theory does more to generate a nihilistic attitude of resignation than to establish the transformative potential of law. If it were the case that the Constitutive Theory of Law was oriented to describing the principles of law's relation to society, the notion that 'the Constitutive Theory of Law is an aspiration towards a theory which does not, as yet exist'[29] would be correct.[30]

III   *The strategy for reconstructing law: deviationist doctrine*

In his essay on the Critical Legal Studies Movement Unger presents the best description of the features of deviationist doctrine.[31] Unlike more nihilistic critical legal theorists, Unger is committed to taking existing law seriously and accepts its claims to normative authority. However, in place of traditional legal doctrine, Unger argues for a system of 'deviationist' legal doctrine which would embody explicitly 'controversy over the right and feasible structure of society, over what the relations among people should be like in the different areas of social activity'. The way in which deviationist doctrine would achieve this is by a development of 'the disharmonies of law. [T]he conflict between principles and counter-principles that can be found in any body of law.' Unger urges us to see that these principles and counter-principles represent rival visions of human association. We saw earlier that in the law of contract Unger identifies a dominant principle of freedom of contract and a counter-principle that freedom of contract will not be permitted to subvert the communal aspects of social life. Whereas the principle of freedom of contract represents an individualistic politics, the counter-principle rests upon more communitarian values. Thus for example, the legal invalidity of contracts *contra bones mores* helps to protect elements of communal morality. It is by taking the counter-principles as the basis for a new vision of law and society that deviationist doctrine seeks to reconstruct law.

It is clear that deviationist doctrine can be viewed as the positive expression of the method of deconstruction, since it takes those values which have traditionally been disfavoured by law and argues that these values rather than the favoured ones could constitute a new understanding of a particular area of law. An example of deviationist doctrine can be found in Collins' *The Law of Contract*,[32] a work which explicitly cites Unger as its inspiration. Collins mounts an assault on standard contract law textbooks for their favouring of values of freedom, minimal market regulation, and a divorce between private economic transactions and public control over the social order, at the expense of the social values of fairness, trust and co-operation which infuse the content of the law of contract. Collins argues that these standard texts have concealed their advocacy of the former values by exhibiting formal and technical reasoning, which gives the law of contract the appearance of 'an ahistorical embodiment of natural reason'. Thus Collins' reconstructive aim is to restate the law of contract as being the regulation of the market according to ideals of social justice. These ideals embody, for Collins, 'communitarian values' namely, 'assistance to the weak and handicapped, fairness in the distribution of wealth, and altruistic concern for the interests of others which give birth to the Welfare State'. He proceeds then to give many examples of cases drawn from the law of contract which embody these values.

This paper is not concerned to focus on the intricacies of deviationist doctrine. Rather, it is concerned to evaluate the role of deviationist legal doctrine as a means of social transformation. It is clear from Unger's writings that the strategy of deviationist doctrine is seen by him as a means of procuring a larger ideal of social transformation. Unger's ideal for a transformed society is rooted in 'the great secular doctrines of emancipation' of the past which were united in a belief that a 'weakening of social divisions would reveal deeper individual and collective identities and liberate productive and creative powers'.[33] Employing the strategy of deviationist doctrine in the widest sense Unger argues from the system of rights generated by liberal individualism for a counter programme to the maintenance or re-emergence of any scheme of division or hierarchy that 'can become effectively insulated against the ordinarily available forms of challenge'. Unlike liberal notions of rights which are usually phrased in negative terms as prohibitions against state interference, Unger argues for a disfavoured conception of rights as positive claims for social advantage. The aim of deviationist legal doctrine would be to give content to these rights and thereby bring about a transformed society. 'Immunity rights' would give individuals the power to resist interference and domination; 'destabilization rights' would entitle individuals to demand the disruption of existing social institutions; 'market rights' would give a conditional claim to divisible portions of social capital, and 'solidarity rights' would foster mutual reliance, loyalty and communal responsibility. This system goes under the grand title of 'the structure of no structure' and represents a 'super-liberalism' for it takes liberal premises about the state and society to 'the point at which they merge into a larger ambition: the building of a social world less alien'.[34] Thus just as Collins believes that his restatement of the law of conract will create a social order in which law regulates the operation of the market according to ideals of social justice, Unger believes that deviationist doctrine can bring about a transformed society. There are, however, two major problems in the strategy of deviationist doctrine, relating respectively to the problems of legal nihilism and circularity.

The first problem with deviationist doctrine concerns the implicit belief of

Unger that changes at the level of legal doctrine can bring about changes in wider social relationships. The problem here is that unless deviationist doctrine can be joined to an account of the relationship between law and society which demonstrates that law relates to society in a determinate fashion, there is no reason for us to believe that deviationist legal doctrine is anything other than an academic exercise in interpretation. The Constitutive Theory of Law certainly establishes a nexus between law and society but it gives no indication of how doctrinal legal concepts influence that reality. Indeed, on Kennedy's thesis of the radical indeterminacy of law, deviationist legal doctrine could affect society in only a chaotic and unprincipled way. The problem ultimately reduces to one that we identified earlier as casting its shadow over deconstruction: to what extent are ideals and conflicts at the level of legal doctrine conditioned by social conflicts. It is arguable that deviationist doctrine confuses legal principles and counter-principles with actual contradiction:

> ... [for the Critical Legal Theorists] the conceptual categories through which liberalism seeks to understand the world become converted into real relations, it comes to appear as if the dualities of liberal thought are sociological categories through which we can make sense of contemporary society.[35]

This is all part of a doctrine centeredness of CLS, a tendency which leads some Critical Legal Theorists to view the enterprise of legal scholarship as akin to that of literature.[36] Even if legal doctrine possesses no internal coherence one must explain why law manifests a determinate relation to economic and social life, why we have a law of 'contract' or 'property'. The crucial problem from our perspective is that if legal doctrine cannot be shown to have a determinate influence on society, deviationist doctrine cannot establish the transformative potential of law.

There is a second major problem which confronts deviationist doctrine as a strategy for reconstructing law, a problem which relates to the issue of circularity described in the Introduction. Although we have said that deconstruction and deviationist doctrine solve the problem of question-begging circularity by starting out from the counter-principles within the area of law being criticised, this can generate a new problem. Once the disfavoured pole of an area of law or theory becomes, through the operation of deviationist doctrine, as firmly established as its dominant predecessor there is no reason why it may not itself be criticised on the same grounds as its predecessor: that it represents both a value laden and partial account of the possible forms of human association. Indeed Unger concedes the weakness of deviationist doctrine in this respect when he acknowledges its 'dependence upon the starting points provided by a particular tradition'.[37] Thus if Unger is to sustain any definite vision of law and society, he must give way on any commitment he has to the subjectivity of legal values. If Critical Legal Theory is to avoid being 'hoisted on its own Critical petard' therefore, it must discover some resolution to these problems.[38] What is needed is a progression beyond the search for ultimate justification of the law, in favour of a conception of law which would seek to obtain the most democratic determination of legal disputes. We can cite the German social theorist, Habermas, as authority for this proposition. Habermas' contention is that modern principles of legitimation must be procedural: 'Since ultimate grounds can no longer be made plausible, the formal conditions of justification themselves obtain legitimating force.'[39]

Conclusion

So what are the prospects for Critical Legal Theory? The major implication of our discussion of US Critical Legal Theory is that it does not realise the aim which sets it apart from previous critical movements in law: to demonstrate that existing legal rules and doctrines can generate new conceptions of law which show law to be capable of both effecting and regulating social transformation. The likely outcome of this is that US Critical Legal Theory will develop in a way similar to Legal Realism. While the more theoretical proposals of the Realists were adopted by mainstream legal scholarship, 'The tradition of textbook and casebook jurisprudence survived the challenge of realism with relative ease and only minor reform.'[40]

NOTES

1   The best introduction to this tradition is: D Kairys, ed, *The Politics of Law: A Progressive Critique* (Pantheon, New York, 1982); R M Unger, 'The Critical Legal Studies movement', *Harvard Law Review* 96 (1983) p 561; A Hunt, 'The theory of Critical Legal Studies', *Oxford Journal of Legal Studies* 6 (1986) p 1.
2   See Hutchinson and Monahan, 'Law, politics and the critical Legal scholars: the unfolding drama of American legal thought', *Stanford Law Review* 36 (1984) p 199.
3   This is explicit in Unger's seminal work 'The Critical Legal Studies movement' where he describes his 'willingness to take the extant authoritative materials as starting points and to accept their claims to normative authority': *Harvard Law Review* 96 (1983) p 561 at p 577.
4   The issue of nihilism in law is the subject of much contemporary discussion in legal theory. See: G Rose, *Dialectic of Nihilism: Post-Structuralism and Law* (Oxford, 1984); J Singer, 'The player and the cards: nihilism and legal theory', *Yale Law Journal* 94 (1984) p 1; R Gordon, 'Nihilism and academic freedom', *Journal of Legal Education* 35 (1985) p 1; J Stick, 'Can nihilism be pragmatic?', *Harvard Law Review* 100 (1985) p 332; and P Goodrich, 'Law and modernity', *Modern Law Review* 49 (1986) p 545.
5   On the relation between Legal Realism and nihilism see: P Goodrich, *Reading the Law* (Blackwell, 1986) pp 210–15.
6   E Pashukanis, *Law and Marxism* (Inklinks, 1978) ch 7. For a criticism of Pashukanis' system of technical regulation see R Warrington, 'Pashukanis and the commodity form theory', *International Journal of the Sociology of Law* 9 (1981) p 1.

7   Thus according to Tushnet, classical jurisprudence survived the challenge of Legal Realism with only minor reform: 'Legal scholarship; its causes and cure', *Yale Law Journal* 90 (1981) p 1205.

8   I formulated the problem of circularity as a variant of a related methodological problem labelled by Unger 'the problem of language'. He describes it thus: 'The methods of proof and argument are part of the theory to be criticised. In what form then is total criticism to bring its suit, and by what law are its claims to be judged?' *Knowledge and Politics* (Free Press, 1976) p 12.

9   See H Collins, *The Law of Contract* (Weidenfeld and Nicolson, 1986).

10 Authority for this argument can be drawn from Hegel's *Science of Logic*, trans A V Miller (London, 1969) p 581: '. . . The refutation must not come from outside, that is, it must not proceed from assumptions lying outside the system in question and inconsistent with it. The system need only refuse to recognise those assumptions . . .'

11 Weber's ideal types can be defined as follows: 'An ideal type is constructed by the abstraction and combination of an indefinite number of elements which, although found in reality, are rarely or never discovered in this specific form . . . Such an ideal type is neither a "description" of any definite aspect of reality, nor, according to Weber, is it a hypothesis, but it can aid in both description and explanation': A Giddens, *Capitalism and Modern Social Theory* (CUP, 1971) pp 140–2.

12 See M Tushnet, 'Critical Legal Studies and constitutional law: an essay in deconstruction', *Stanford Law Review* 36 (1984) p 623; D Hoy, 'Interpreting the law: hermeneutical and post-structuralist perspectives', especially section 28: 'Deconstruction and the CLS movement', *Southern California Law Review* 58 (1985) p 135; C Dalton, 'An essay in the deconstruction of contract doctrine', *Yale Law Journal* 94 (1985) p 1114; M F Katz, 'After the deconstruction: law in the age of post-structuralism', *University of Western Ontario Law Review* 24 (1986) p 51.

13 For a good basic introduction to Derrida's thinking, see D Hoy, 'Jacques Derrida' in *The Return of Grand Theory in the Human Sciences*, Q Skinner, ed (CUP, 1985).

14 See J Ree, 'Metaphor and metaphysics: the end of philosophy and Derrida', *Radical Philosophy* 38 (1984) p 21. See also C Dalton, 'An essay in the deconstruction of contract doctrine', *Yale Law Journal* 94 (1985) p 1114 at p 2007.

15 M Tushnet, 'Critical Legal Studies and constitutional law: an essay in deconstruction', *Stanford Law Review* 36 (1984) p 623 at p 628.

16 R M Unger, 'The Critical Legal Studies movement', *Harvard Law Review* 96 (1983) p 561 at pp 616–25.

17 For an example of this strategy see H Collins, *The Law of Contract* (Weidenfeld and Nicolson, 1986).

18 This is subject to a criticism of deconstruction which I shall discuss later in this paper. Namely, that when deconstruction is used to reconstruct law, as I suggest Unger uses it, it simply begs the question as to the validity of the disfavoured pole, or 'dangerous supplement', thereby falling foul of the problem of circularity. In this, it fails to live up to Derrida's attack on the 'whole absolutist habit of thinking in binary terms': see J Ree, 'Metaphor and metaphysics', *Radical Philosophy* 38 (1984) p 21 at p 31.

19 See *Lowe v. Peers* (1768) 4 Burr. 2225, and *Spiers v. Hunt* [1908] 1 K.B. 720.

20 See K Renner, *The Institutions of Private Law and their Social Function* (Routledge and Kegan Paul, 1948) at pp 105–22.

21 It is interesting to consider the parallels between Unger's theory and the jurisprudence of R M Dworkin in this respect.

22 See Beyleveld and Brownsword, 'Critical Legal Studies', *Modern Law Review* 47 (1984) p 359. See also H Collins' *Marxism and Law* (Oxford, 1982).

23 A Hunt, 'The theory of Critical Legal Studies', *Oxford Journal of Legal Studies* 6 (1986) p 1 at p 29.

24 R Gordon, 'New developments in legal theory', in *The Politics of Law*, D Kairys, ed (Pantheon, New York, 1982).

25 D Kennedy, 'Distributive and paternalist motives in contract and tort law with special reference to compulsory terms and unequal bargaining power', *Maryland Law Review* 41 (1982) p 563.

26 *Telos* 40 (1979) p 1.

27 See E Pashukanis, Law and Marxism (Iukenk Links, 1978).

28 See A Hunt, 'The theory of Critical Legal Studies', *Oxford Journal of Legal Studies* 6 (1986) p 1 at pp 39–40.

29 A Hunt, 'The theory of Critical Legal Studies', *Oxford Journal of Legal Studies* 6 (1986) p 1 at p 40.

30 Since the Constitutive Theory of Law renders it almost impossible to make general statements about how precisely law relates to society, it might be thought that its inevitable direction is towards a particularisation of legal study. If it is impossible to theorise about law in the abstract, it may be possible to lay out the relationship of law to society in extremely narrowly defined concrete situations. Interestingly, such a method is present in Kennedy's recent thought: 'You can't plausibly describe "being" except in the vaguest and most general way . . . you can plausibly describe relatively contextualised, non-abstract, rich human situations', D Kennedy, 'Roll over Beethoven', *Stanford Law Review* 36 (1985) p 1 at p 48. This method also seems present in Unger's recent writings on 'formative contexts': see R M Unger, *False Necessity* (CUP, 1987). The great risk of this model however is that of lapsing back into naive empiricism, in which every situation is uniquely the result of specific causal factors: see A Hunt, 'The theory of Critical Legal Studies', *Oxford Journal of Legal Studies* 6 (1986) p 1 at p 40.

31 R M Unger, 'The Critical Legal Studies Movement', *Harvard Law Review* 96 (1983) p 561 at p 577.

32 H Collins, *The Law of Contract* (Weidenfeld and Nicolson, 1986). See preface.

33 R M Unger, 'The Critical Legal Studies movement', *Harvard Law Review* 96 (1983) p 561 at p 584.

34 R M Unger, 'The Critical Legal Studies movement', *Harvard Law Review* 96 (1983) p 561 at p 602.

35 A Hunt, 'The theory of critical Legal Studies, *Oxford Journal of Legal Studies* 6 (1986) p 1 at p 10.

36 See in particular C Dalton, 'An essay in the deconstruction of contract doctrine', *Yale Law Journal* 94 (1985) p 1114.

37 R M Unger, 'The Critical Legal Studies movement', *Harvard Law Review* 96 (1983) p 561 at p 580.

38 See Hutchinson and Monahan, 'Law, politics and the Critical Legal scholars: the unfolding drama of American legal thought', *Stanford Law Review* 36 (1984) p 199 at p 234.

39 Cited in G Teubner, 'Substantive and reflexive elements in modern law', *Law and Society Review* 17 (1983) p 239 at pp 269–70.

40 P Goodrich, *Reading the Law* (Blackwell, 1980) at p 210.

CHAPTER 15

Self-Regulation and Need-Orientation as Models for Legal Dogmatics

Thomas Wilhelmsson

I   *The Problem*

The critical discussion concerning the possibilities of developing an alternative legal science during the 1980s, at least in Finland and Scandinavia, has rediscovered legal dogmatics (legal doctrine). Whereas a critical lawyer, in the 1960s and 1970s, tended totally to deny the scientific character of legal doctrine, he is now prepared to recognise it as a legitimate field of study, which, however, may and should be developed in a critical way. The alternatives for such a development are, of course, numerous. Two of them will be discussed in this paper: it focuses on the doctrinal tools offered by the theories concerning *reflexivity* and self-regulation as a basic trend in modern legal development, on the one hand, and a Finnish analysis of the emerging *need rationality* in law, on the other.

The analysis of both theories—or rather both groups of theories—is facilitated by the fact that they have a striking structural resemblance. Both contain an empirical as well as a normative component. What is wanted is extracted from something which already is considered to be emerging. We are said to be in a phase of radical changes in legal thought and the authors of the theories want to press these changes further.

Some of the theories discussed are not elaborated primarily to be used by legal dogmatics. However, in this paper I will focus on that aspect. The question to be analysed is: what can a critical legal dogmatics gain from these theories? The answers to that question will, of course, be very tentative; the theories concerned are not very precise and may be interpreted in very different ways.

II *Presentation*

The three-stage-model for legal development in modern society presented by Gunther Teubner (1983) hardly requires any thorough presentation. The rather intense international debate concerning that theory is well-known. This debate shall not be presented here (see hereto, e.g., the book edited by Born-Bredsdorff-Hansen-Hansson, 1988); it has concentrated mainly on questions other than ours (the impact of reflexive law on legal dogmatics). It seems sufficient for our task to note very briefly the three stages of rationality which Teubner presents as characterising the development of modern society:

> —The *formal rationality*, within which the law is justified with reference to the values of individualism and autonomy, forms the basis of a rule-oriented, deductive legal thinking.
> —The *substantive rationality* designates the need to regulate economic and social activity in order to compensate for market inadequacies as the justificatory basis of the law and the application of law is purpose-oriented, implemented 'through regulations, standards and principles'.
> —The *reflexive rationality* is the emerging type of rationality replacing the two former.

The reflexive rationality sees *self-regulation* as an ideal. The legal thinking is, therefore, oriented towards *procedure*. The primary task for the law is not to give content to the solutions but to create structural premises for self-regulative processes. The law only has to 'decide about decisions, regulate regulations, and establish structural premises for future decisions in terms of organization, procedure and competencies' (Teubner, 1983, p 275).

This reflexive rationality does not yet represent the dominating way of thinking. It is in the process of evolving through particular self-regulative elements in the law. On this basis, however, a progressive policy of law is thought to be able to formulate new demands. The reflexive rationality represents the future, Utopia, the direction in which the development should be linked. This normative aspect is obviously the interesting part of the theory of reflexive law. As a pure historical theory it is probably not correct (see, e.g., Reich, 1984, pp 280-1, Hydén, 1984, p 43 and Pöyhönen, 1985, p 134) and it would certainly have caused a lot less debate.

It seems clear that the phenomena to which the theory of reflexive law draws our attention are in some way essential when interpreting the development of modern legal thinking. This assertion is supported by the fact that quite a few theories pointing in the same direction have been put forward at the same time or even earlier than Teubner's. Especially in German legal thinking many similar dialectical 'three-stage-models' have been presented. The analysis is not as thorough as by Teubner but the lines of thought seem to be quite parallell. The following table shows the connections:

	I	II	III
Teubner	formal rationality	substantive rationality	reflexive rationality
Schmidt (1980)	*Privatautonomie*	*Materialisierung*	*Sozialautonomie*
Wiethölter (1982, 1984)	*Formalisierung*	*Materialisierung*	*Prozeduralisierung*
Brüggemeier (1982)	contract I	conract II	organisation

These theories are, of course, not identical, although the concept of *Prozeduralisierung* in the debate often is used more or less as a synonym for reflexive law (see, e.g., Hart, 1984, p 75). Teubner (1984, pp 91–2) points out an important difference between these two concepts: whereas Wiethölter is primarily interested in creating procedures through which consensus on the level of the society as a whole can be reached, reflexive law is interested in self-regulation within social subsystems.

Also the Finnish analysis of the evolution of *need-rationality* in law shows some striking similarities with the theories just mentioned. In his sketch concerning the development of the *models of legal argumentation* in capitalist society Lars D Eriksson (1979; 1980, pp 108–10) also distinguishes three stages, the first two of which could very easily be put into the table above.

> —The exchange value rationality of early capitalism forms the basis of the argumentation model of *subsumptional logic*. The legal norm itself is the starting point for the argumentation and the foreseeability of legal decisions is a central value.
> —In late capitalism use-value rationality has attained a dominating position. This kind of rationality, however, forms the basis of two different models of legal argumentation. The first one is the *goal-rational* model (or system-oriented goal-rational model), in which the social content of the legal decisions comes to the foreground. One starts from the goals of the legal regulations and evaluates the social consequences when making decisions. The decision-maker strives at getting socially balanced results which can contribute to the preserving of the system.

Use-value rationality also lies behind the *need-rational* model (or need-oriented goal-rational model) of argumentation. The social content and consequences of a legal decision are also emphasised in this model. The aim, however, is not to care for the needs of the system (its cohesion), but for the needs of the members of society. In evaluating the rationality of a decision the crucial question is what effects the decision has on the *concrete and real needs* of the members of society.

This last state is presented by Eriksson partly as a description of a new rationality structure which can already be seen in some elements of the law. It is, however, in the same way as the theory of reflexive law also, and perhaps predominantly, a theory with a normative content, a legal Utopia.

III   Comparison

The theory of reflexive law does not delimit its object very clearly. In the discussion a lot of quite disparate phenomena have been placed under the heading reflexive law (see, concerning private law Teubner, 1983, pp 276–78). A traditional example is the regulation model of labour law (the collective agreement), another one the new models in the field of consumer law (*Stiftung-Warentest*; cfr in Scandinavia the Consumer Ombudsman negotiating with business organisations and enterprises on the basis of very open-ended general clauses). In the field of public law different forms of institutional democracy have been mentioned in this context (see, e.g., Eriksson, 1986, p 287). Many different kinds of tendencies seem to have been dragged into the realm of reflexive law. An analysis of the question, what kind of Utopia reflexive law offers us, may against this background lead to rather different results depending on the preferences and the specialities of the respective author.

In order to achieve a better view of the similarities and the differences between reflexive rationality and need-rationality we have to look closer into the components of these conceptions of rationality. Teubner (1983, p 257) distinguishes three dimensions of legal rationality: justification of law, external functions of law and internal structures of law. For our task, that is an analysis of the implications of the said theories for legal dogmatics, these distinctions are not very well suited. Teubner's three dimensions seem to be more useful in describing the empirical-theoretical basis of his theory than its instrumental aspects. When analysing the normative perspective for future doctrine offered by the theories discussed here, the comparison seems to be easier when distinguishing the *goal, content* and *method* of both rationalities. What kind of Utopia do we strive for (a), what content should the legal rules have in our Utopia (b) and what kind of methods should legal dogmatics and legal practice use here (c)?

(a) *The goals.* The great interest of progressive lawyers and social theorists in the theory of reflexive law is probably primarily explained by its potential to back up demands on new forms of direct democracy. The theory has, at least in Finland, brought some new fuel to the democracy debate. At first glance this emphasis on self-regulation and democracy seems to have very little in common with the thoughts concerning need-rationality, which stresses the goal of caring for the concrete and real needs of the members of society. Depending on how one interprets the theory of reflexive law, the differences, however, might not be so deep as they seem to be.

The democracy concept is not a goal in itself in Teubner's theory. His idea of self-regulation is also founded on reasons of efficacy or, more specifically, on the striving to create a regulation which has the desired effects without being destructive. The law

> seeks to identify opportunity structures that allow legal regulation to cope with social problems without, at the same time, irreversibly destroying valued patterns of social life (Teubner, 1983, p 274).

In one connection, when describing examples of reflexive patterns in the law of private organisations, Teubner even states that the main goal

> is neither power-equalization nor an increase of individual participation in the emphatic sense of 'participatory democracy'. Rather, it is the design of

organizational structures which makes the institutions—corporations, semi-public associations, mass media, educational institutions—sensitive to the outside effects of their attempts to maximize internal rationality. Its main function is to substitute for outside interventionist control an effective internal control structure (Teubner, 1983, p 278).

The cited passages clearly indicate that reflexive law is also seen as a tool for effectively coping with social problems and not only as an instrument for achieving the self-determination of the individual. Still, the way in which the problems are dealt with differs from the methods of substantive law: one should, to as large an extent as possible, increase the participation of the people concerned in the process in which the problems are dealt with. This, however, will in turn mean that these involved persons gain greater possibilities to articulate their concrete and real needs and get these needs recognised as legally relevant. If one looks at reflexive law from this perspective, its goals seem to lie rather close to those of the normative theory of need-rationality.

(b) *The content.* Also on this level, at the outset, there seem to be rather deep differences between the demands for need-rationality and for reflexive law. A law dominated by the thought of need-rationality clearly has a substance: as Eriksson (1979, p 46) puts it, a 'Marxian jurisprudence' should take seriously the social needs and interests which the legal order of late capitalism contains. It seems self-evident that according to this view law should not be made an empty space, which only has to be reflexively filled out by the involved persons. The primary task for a need-rational lawyer would instead be the task of extracting from the existing legal material new principles and rules which may serve the concrete and real needs of the citizens.

Although reflexive law, which as noted earlier emphasises regulations 'in terms of organization, procedure and competencies' (Teubner, 1983, p 275), seems to strive for a law without material content, it reveals itself, by a closer study, to have rather important material implications, too. The proponents of reflexive law talk about the possibilities of a 'reflexive logic' within legal doctrine, a logic which implies a *simulation* of reflexive processes in cases where assymetric power and information structures obstruct a genuine reflexivity. The tools for effecting this reflexive logic are certain general clauses, which contain concepts like 'good faith' or 'public policy'. With the help of these general clauses one may reach 'reflexive' norms with a material content. Or as Teubner put it:

> This means that, in the case of 'interaction deficiencies' between contracting parties, objective purposes and duties are defined authoritatively by virtue of law; in the case of 'market deficiencies', commercial customs are replaced by the judicial definition of market behavior rules; and in the case of 'political deficiencies' the judicial process defines standards of public policy (Teubner, 1983, pp 277–8).

The differences and similarities between reflexive rationality and need-rationality, when one analyses the material content of their rules, is thus to some extent dependent on which kinds of processes reflexive law is thought to 'simulate'. In case the simulation reflects processes in which the concrete and real needs of the parties would be articulated, the resemblance between the rationality models is rather evident.

(c) *The method*. In all theories considered in this paper the *flexible* character of the new elements of law is emphasised. The simulation process described above is founded on such a postulate. The new law is, and ought to be, open-ended, giving the courts—and evidently as a consequence also legal doctrine—a rather large discretion. Teubner has also in other connections—even before developing the theory of reflexive law—strongly emphasised the need to avoid unflexible solutions: in applying the general clauses of civil law one should not, as the traditional theory suggests, try to continuously through so called '*Fallgruppenbildung*' make the content of the law more precise; one should instead see the general clauses as a form of 'learning law' designed to allow flexible legal reactions on social changes (Teubner, 1980). Also a need-rational argumentation is characterised by flexibility. Within this form of rationality the value of legal foreseeability no longer has a dominating position in legal decision-making, as the relevant arguments are primarily drawn from the concrete situation (see, e.g., Eriksson, 1979, p 44).

IV *Legal dogmatics*

The theory of reflexive law has been criticised on the grounds that it passes over the problem of unequal distribution of power in society. According to the critics such problems cannot be solved in terms of procedure; they have to be approached with material regulations (see, e.g., Reich, 1984, pp 283-4). This critique certainly hints at one of the most fundamental problems in the new model. This decisive question, however, is in fact touched upon by Teubner, although rather shortly. The thought of 'simulating' genuine reflexive processes described above is expressly recommended as a solution in cases where 'social asymmetries of power and information can resist institutional attempts at equalization' (Teubner, 1983, p 277). It may be noted that some of the authors proposing theories related to the theory of reflexive law (see the table in part II) in fact seem to think that an equalisation of the power structures in society has taken place. The *social autonomous law* of Eike Schmidt rests on the presupposition that society now is in a state which to a lesser extent is characterised by class antagonism and to an increasing extent by mutual dependence between different social groups (Schmidt, 1980, p 158). One may ask, whether the theory of reflexive law is also implicitly founded on such dubious presuppositions. Some Scandinavian authors have stressed that the significance of the insufficient analysis of power structures in the theory of reflexive law depends on the social perspective in which the theory is thought to function as a Utopia. The development of a real reflexive law would obviously require thorough decentralisation and democratisation of the economic order as a whole (see Eriksson, 1986, p 286). Teubner's model would thus, according to this view, function as a goal only in a *wider*, social philosophical *time perspective* (see also Dalberg-Larsen, 1986, p 19). Its great discursive force seems also to lie primarily in the social and political ideals which are only implicitly contained in the theory. Reflexive law is a social Utopia disguised in the form of a legal Utopia.

As a consequence of this reflexive law seems to have little to offer legal dogmatics which, also in its alternative or critical forms, has to work within a shorter time perspective. An argumentation—even a very critical one—on the basis of the law in force, which has a fundamentally material content, can seldom lead to a realisation of the reflexive or procedural structures which reflexive law strives for.

This assertion, however, shows just one side of the coin. As is noted earlier, the theory of reflexive law also contains a model for application of law in a shorter time perspective: the *simulation* of a reflexive process. Situations in which 'the legal system itself "simulates" processes of social self-regulation' may be interpreted 'as evidence of a reflexive logic within doctrine' (Teubner, 1983, p 277). This possibility is at hand especially when applying certain general clauses.

The question of how such a simulation should be effected in practice, is, however, left open by the theory (Teubner's large alternative commentary to BGB § 242 from 1980 is not yet reflexive in this sense). Different alternatives seem possible: (a) One might take the idea of simulation seriously and try to investigate how all individuals and groups concerned in fact *would act* if they were to solve the problem together in a completely democratic and equal-bargaining situation. Such an analysis would, however, be rather fictional and out of touch with real life. In a world in which the power structures are unequal and the stronger groups may maintain their interests at the expense of weaker ones, our arguments about the possible action of the parties concerned in quite another, equal world would not be very convincing; (b) Another more acceptable way of realising the simulated reflexive process would be to connect the argumentation and decision explicitly to the *needs* and wants of the people involved. The reflexive solution would be the one which on this level would represent the optimal balance between the parties in any given case.

This interpretation of reflexive law lies, however, quite near to the thought of *need-rationality* as a basis of critical legal doctrine. The theory of need-rationality expressly and directly states what is implicitly and indirectly contained in the simulated reflexive logic. The means which reflexive law could offer legal dogmatics, if such means may be specified, are, therefore, easier to describe by using the need-rational model of argumentation. This model contains material as well as methodological guidelines which are directly useful also in the shorter time perspective of legal dogmatics.

The material guideline which may be founded on this theory could be named *need-orientation*. This concept has already proven to be fruitful in Finnish legal doctrine. I have presented an analysis of the emergence of need-oriented concepts in private law (Wilhelmsson, 1987a; some parts of the results are presented in international languages in Wilhelmsson, 1987b and 1989). My work focused on the way the parties are described in the norms of Finnish and Scandinavian contract law and on the changes in this material in a need-oriented direction; these changes could then be taken as a foundation for developing alternative general principles of contract law. The central question was: to what extent is it possible to deviate from the abstract formal way of describing the parties, and consider *the economic and social position of the concrete party* to be a relevant legal fact? The analysis of the concrete legal material, especially from the 1980s, revealed surprisingly many traces of such a need-orientation in contract law: the relevance of the need of housing in the law of tenancy, the possibility to adjust damages in tort and contract law with reference to the low income and low wealth of the liable person, the reference to person-related arguments in applying the general clauses concerning adjustment of unfair contracts and the rules concerning mitigation of sanctions in case of 'social force majeure' may be mentioned as important examples. This rather large concrete material allowed a serious discussion of the question of the extent to which more general need-oriented principles could be created. Poverty, low income and other such concepts referring to the need of the individual party could be pushed more in the foreground as relevant categories in the argumentation structure of private law.

In the dialectic between the existing and the possible which is typical for legal dogmatics, and explicitly adhered to by many of its alternative variants, these new need-oriented principles, created on the basis of existing rules and decisions, represent one aspect of the possible. They provide such courts that want to develop the need-oriented elements of law with new tools for this task.

REFERENCES

Asmund-Bredsdorff Born, Nils-Hansen, Leif-Hansson, Finn ed *Refleksiv ret* (København, 1988).

Gert Brüggemeier, 'Wirtschaftsverfassung und Staatsverfassung', "Mischverfassung des demokratischen Interventionskapitalismus", "Verfassungstheorie des Sozialstaates". Drei Modelle der Verflechtung von Staat und Wirtschaft?—Eine Problemskizze', in *Rechtsformen der Verflechtung von Staat und Wirtschaft,* Volkmar Gessner and Gerd Winter, eds (Opladen, 1982) pp 60–73.

Jørgen Dalberg-Larsen, 'På vej frem mod det gode samfund eller fuld fart tilbage?', *Retfaerd* 32 (1986) pp 6–22.

Lars D Eriksson, 'Utkast till en marxistisk jurisprudens', *Retfaerd* 11 (1979) pp 40–53.

Lars D Eriksson, *Marxistisk teori och rättsvetenskap* (Helsinki, 1980).

Lars D Eriksson, 'Till teorin om den reflexiva rätten', in *Samfunn Rett Retferdighet,* Festskrift til Torstein Eckhoffs 70-årsdag (Otta, 1986) pp 281–92.

Dieter Hart, 'Zur konzeptionellen Entwicklung des Vertragsrechts', *Die Aktiengesellschaft. Zeitschrift für das gesamte Aktienwesen* (1984) pp 66–80.

Håkan Hydén, *Ram eller lag? Om ramlagstiftning och samhällsorganisation,* Civildepartementet, DsC 1984: 12 (Stockholm, 1984).

Juha Pöyhönen, 'Refleksiivinen oikeus—vihreän liikkeen oikeus-ideologiaa?', *Oikeus* 14 (1985) pp 127–38.

Norbert Reich, 'Reflexives Recht? Anfragen an eine neue Theorie von Gunther Teubner', in *Zentrum für Europäische Rechtspolitik Mat* 4 (Bremen, 1984) pp 269–90.

Eike Schmidt, 'Von der Privat- zur Sozialautonomie', *Juristenzeitung* (1980) pp 153–61.

Gunther Teubner, 'BGB § 242', in *BGB-kommentar. Kommentar zum bürgerlichen Gesetzbuch*, Band 2, Allgemeines Schuldrecht, Reihe Alternativkommentare (Darmstadt, 1980) pp 32–91.

Gunther Teubner, 'Substantive and Reflexive Elements in Modern Law', *Law & Society Review* 17 (1983) pp 239–85.

Gunther Teubner, 'Prozeduralisierung', in *Zentrum für Europäische Rechtspolitik Mat* 4 (Bremen, 1984) pp 91–2.

Rudolf Wiethölter, 'Entwicklung des Rechtsbegriffs', in *Rechtsformen der Verflechtung von Staat und Wirtschaft*, Volkmar Gessner and Gerd Winter, eds (Opladen, 1982) pp 38–59.

Rudolf Wiethölter, 'Materialisierungen und Prozeduralisierungen von Recht', in *Zentrum für Europäische Rechtspolitik Mat* 4 (Bremen, 1984) pp 25–64.

Thomas Wilhelmsson, *Social civilrätt* (Vammala, 1987) (1987a).

Thomas Wilhelmsson 'Bedürfnisorientierung im Schuldrecht', *Demokratie und Recht* 15 (1987), pp 175–86 (1987b).

Thomas Wilhelmsson, 'Need-rationality in private law?', *Scandinavian Studies in Law* (1989).

CHAPTER 16

The Possibility of Revolution in Legal Science

Mats Flodin

I *Metaphysics*

The debate concerning the use of the concept paradigm in legal science has been going on for at least fifteen years now, but there are some aspects of the problems involved that have not yet been emphasised enough. Legal science is frequently accused of being overloaded with metaphysics. Metaphysics is however unavoidable in any science, for example as in natural science. It is not likely that a legal scientist considers himself to be more of a positivist than he imagines a natural scientist is. If then unverified statements containing metaphysics are unavoidable in natural science, this should provide sufficient reason to allow them in legal science as well. Popper[1] explains the necessity of metaphysics in the realm of natural science in this way:

> If we wish to avoid the positivist's mistake of eliminating, by our criterion of demarcation, the theoretical systems of natural science, then we must choose a criterion which allows us to admit to the domain of empirical science even statements which cannot be verified . . . not the *verifiability* but the *falsifiability* of a system is to be taken as a criterion of demarcation. In other words: I shall not require of a scientific system that it shall be able to be singled out, once and for all, in a positive sense, but I shall require that its logical form be such that it can be singled out, by means of empirical tests, in a negative sense: it must be possible for an empirical scientific system to be refuted by experience.

But metaphysics can nonetheless be minimised by (1) making universal statements (and theories) falsifiable and (2) attempting to falsify those universal statements. As Popper said:

> . . . it is possible by means of purely deductive inferences (with the help of modus

tollens of classical logic) to argue from the truth of singular statements to the falsity of universal statements.

Such an argument to the falsity of universal statements is the only strictly deductive kind of inference that proceeds, as it were, in the inductive direction; that is, from singular to universal statements.[2]

No matter how the ontology of a particular legal scientist is structured, evaluations and statements concerning facts that cannot be empirically verified are necessary parts of any legal reasoning containing morally or ideologically significant ingredients, whether they can be described as metaphysical or not. This aspect of legal science is also the most controversial and uncertain part of the work, and the inherent problems are crucial for the establishment of the criteria in legal science that would correspond with what is described as scientific *paradigms* in the theory of natural science.

II   *Method, Ideology and Morals in Legal Science*

Kuhn[3] claims that science develops through series of crises and revolutions leading to radical changes and to new paradigms, emanating from the work of mostly new scientists. The perspective of a paradigm is primarily internal retrospection within a scientific field.[4] Kuhn distinguishes between two sets of criteria.

1   A constellation of group commitments; agreement concerning fundamental values, world view, and ideology is required as a prerequisite for the research within the paradigm.

2   Shared examples are models for puzzle solving and constitute the method, logic and classification of the paradigm.

Kuhn emphasises that the two usages of the term are very different:[5]

> ... two very different usages of the term would remain, and they require separation. The more global use will be considered in this subsection; the other [paradigms as shared examples] will be considered in the next.

The concept paradigm is in the first place intended for natural science, primarily physics. An attempt to apply the concept in legal science can, it seems, be only partially successful. Legal science does not fulfil the first criterion of a constellation of group commitments. In legal science there is still disagreement in questions concerning ideology, values, and world view. Statements and theories involving political ideology, judgements concerning morality and the nature of value judgements are unavoidable in legal science, at least as tacit presuppositions. The debate about the very nature of law is still intense and has been going on throughout the whole history of legal science. These facts support the view that the *first* set of criteria for a paradigm is not fulfilled, implying that legal science is still in what Kuhn describes as the pre-paradigmatic phase:[6]

> The pre-paradigm period, in particular, is regularly marked by frequent and deep debates over legitimate methods, problems, and standards of solution, though these serve to define schools rather than to produce agreement . . . Furthermore, debates like these do not vanish once and for all with the appearance of a paradigm. Though almost non-existent during periods of normal science, they recur regularly just before and during scientific revolutions, the periods when the paradigms are first under attack and then subject to change.

Kuhn gives a striking example of the debate in a scientific field during the pre-paradigmatic phase by referring to the history of electrical research in the first half of the eighteenth century:[7]

> During that period there were as many views about the nature of electricity as there were important electrical experimenters, men like Hauksbee, Gray . . . All their numerous concepts of electricity had something in common . . . Yet though all the experiments were electrical and though most of the experimenters read each others works, their theories had no more than a family resemblance.

There are, however, facts that support the view that the *second* set of criteria is fulfilled in legal science.[8] Sources of law, once they are established, are treated in a similar manner everywhere. Statutory rules, precedents, and other possible sources of law, are shared examples as models for puzzle solving,[9] and the central rules of formal logic are accepted. Nevertheless, even if a paradigm is accepted it is not necessarily unchangeable. As Kuhn put it:

> In its established usage, a paradigm is an accepted model or pattern, and that respect of its meaning has enabled me, lacking a better word, to appropriate 'paradigm' here. But it will shortly be clear that the sense of 'model' and 'pattern' that permits the appropriation is not quite the one usual in defining 'paradigm'. In grammar, for example, 'amo, amas, amat' is a paradigm because it displays the pattern to be used in conjugating a large number of Latin verbs, e.g., in producing 'laudo, laudas, laudat'. In this standard application, the paradigm functions by permitting the replication of examples any one of which could in principle serve to replace it. In a science, on the other hand, a paradigm is rarely an object for replication. Instead, like an accepted judicial decision in the common law, it is an object for further articulation and specification under new or more stringent conditions.[10]

It seems appropriate, though, to use the concept paradigm in a somewhat different and narrower meaning in *legal dogmatics*, in accordance with the colloquial language instead of with Kuhn's stipulative definition. This narrower meaning can denote the national or legal-family community of legal scientists: separate paradigms for continental Europe, the common law systems, law in the socialist countries, for example. Paradigms in this sense might be subject to change in a way resembling the changes of paradigms in natural science.

If the concept is used in this way, it follows that there might be large numbers of legal scientists within each nation or legal culture who do not share the dominating paradigm in the sense which Kuhn proposes. Basic divergencies on most important issues concerning legally relevant ideology among the legal scientists prevent the fulfilment of Kuhn's first set of criteria. He demands from a scientific paradigm that its ideology and method must be *universal*, primarily in the relativistic sense that ideology and method factually are accepted within a whole scientific community. This lack of fulfilment is quite appropriate in as much as the very complicated problem of a scientific revolution and the therefore necessary total paradigm change cannot occur in legal science.

The legal scientist has to solve, for his own purposes, epistemological questions concerning, *inter alia*, morality and ideology. A full and mature paradigm in Kuhn's sense requires, as already stated, total or almost total consensus in the whole scientific community concerning morality and ideology. Even if this state of unanimity among legal scientists concerning morality and ideology does not yet exist, there seem to be at least some norms of great moral and ideological import upon which law itself and legal scientists do agree. If the existence of such norms can be established, it will show progress in legal science towards a full and mature paradigm.

III   *Remarks on the Legal Pre-Paradigm*

There are many ways of justifying the existence of legal norms and moral norms: the survival of mankind, the survival of the nation, maximising the good and the right, achieving distributive justice, promoting the interests of a social class, etc. The increasing complexity in society, including the rapid development in technology and natural science, demands continuous adjustment of existing legal norms and also an enormous increase in the body of legal norms. This is especially true for law in the industrialised world, and as the developing countries enter the path of industrialism, this phenomenon will be a reality also for them.

The wide appeal and image of stringency of technology and natural science cannot justify an intrusion into the field of law. It is not possible to derive legal or moral norms from natural science; the complexity of law bases itself on solutions to moral problems. The change and increase as well as the systematic complexity of the body of legal norms, which follow from the regulation of expanding industrialised societies, is mainly a quantitative phenomenon implying little or nothing for the moral complexity of law. The problem whether an act is good or evil, right or wrong remains the same, even though mere causal connections may be more difficult to establish in advanced technology. The technological complexity of modern society is thus foremost relevant primarily to the evaluation of facts. The *justification* aspect of legislation and adjudication is on the other hand not subject to any significant influence from the increased complexity of technology and/or natural science.

It seems plausible that the possibility for individual human beings to comprehend the collective rationality[11] of human societies is as little as, say, the possibility for individual bees to comprehend the rationality of their societies.[12] This problem is also central in social science and for the moral and economical aspects of law and legal science. How can one say anything about what is just and what is good or right without knowing the rationality in human society?

If we assume that there is no collective rationality, it follows that the life of human society is undetermined and developed at random. It is obvious that we have to accept that the collective rationality in human societies is mainly unexplained. However, law consists of norms and man does not let the disagreements in world view discourage him from making rules concerning the actions of other men whose actions are considered to be evil or harmful to society. There is no need factually to prove the nature of the complexity in human society; it is sufficient to be aware of the enormous possibilities of complexity that are hidden in human life. The responsibilities for sensible philosophy and just legal theory for the future development must then be great in proportion to these possibilities, as there are no other relevant scientific means for the construction of legal/moral norm systems.

The fact that the complexity of human society is enormous and incomprehensible will perhaps explain why there is no paradigmatic unity in law and legal science concerning morality and ideology. Then again, if there are norms that are accepted everywhere, this mere fact might be a sign of collective rationality which can provide additional justification to those norms. Such universally valid legal norms would then be segments of a full and comprehensive moral and ideological paradigm.

It seems clear that it is not adequate today to speak about *justice* in a legal system which does not accept the principle of equality between the races or which maintains governmental power. As far as these issues are concerned legal norms throughout the world show almost total unaminity.[13] It is obvious that the technical development, together with the enormous increase in global trade and cultural exchange, presupposes explicit or tacit agreements concerning a necessary foundation of moral values. When this body of universal values increases and makes an impact on law and legal science, the legal paradigm in its full extent will take form.[14] The mature paradigm must, thus also cover the metaphysical elements of legal science which are present primarily on the level of morality and ideology. It seems plausible that, as a continuation of the path already set, the future emphasis in the development of the paradigm will mainly concern legal provinces connected to human rights.

Psychological/sociological explanations of human nature and collective rationality show that there may be an enormous undetectable profoundness in the construction of human society, so great that an attempt at reconstruction by human hands cannot be sufficiently justified. Even a theory of *future* biological evolution of human beings cannot be proven to be correct. That would require standards of measurement for evaluative comparison between human beings. In view of the obviously practically infinite complexity of human beings and human society, attempts to carry out such measurement would have an incredibly small chance of being accurate. Even if they were accurate, which is probably less likely than for someone to sink a battleship by throwing a stone, no one would be able to judge if the standards of measurement really were correct. It may even be that mankind is now biologically perfect, or practically perfect, and to experience the feeling of love in different ways is a meaning of life, intrinsically good, and that the reproductive function thus is only secondary. That statement is not intended as an argument for hedonism, but to point out the possible significance of those feelings in human life.

A quite different matter is that the social conditions and also legal norms are often based on material circumstances which are created by the collective rationality of engineers and natural scientists. The judge or legal theorist cannot totally comprehend these complicated processes; technology and natural science are very divided with many esoteric areas, which make it difficult also for an engineer or a natural scientist to overview the entire development.

There seems to be a lot of room, now as much as ever, for philosophical speculation in the plausibly almost infinite space between the individually thinking capacity and the collective rationality of mankind.

In connection with this one may speculate that there is a distribution of types among mankind, with a disposition for certain roles in society—just as a soccer football team must have different kinds of players (goalkeeper, defence players, forwards)—but much more complex. This distribution of types could be constant, as in the bee colony, even if some type was eliminated temporarily.

One can also speculate that the opponents in the struggle for existence are not other human beings but mother nature herself, who has to be conquered and used, not destroyed; and that all human beings are on the same team in this project. In that perspective the thought of human beings being biological enemies to each other seems horrible, especially knowing that that thought cannot be rationally justified. But far from all writers agree with this view. We might compare this view with Hobbes' view of human society[15] in the prehistorical phase as a war between all individuals (*bellum omnium contra omnes*). According to him all men were egoists without any tendencies to form orderly societies. Grotius also assumed that men were each other's enemies in the phase before the social conract was formed,[16] but he considered this state of reciprocal enmity as a consequence of the emergence of evil into human life. In the very beginning people had an urge towards social life, according to Grotius.

It may be frustrating that the complexity of human society seems to be extremely complex and beyond human comprehension. This problem is also central in social science and the moral and ideological aspects of law and legal science. How can one say anything about what is just and what is good or right, without knowing the rationality in human society? The dilemma is twofold, because if we assume that there is no particular collective rationality, it follows that the destiny of human society is undetermined and developed at random.

In Popper's terminology it is neither possible to verify the existence of moral norms based on natural science nor verify the principles for the rationality in human society. However, Popper did not require that a scientific system should be possible to single out by means of positive verification. But the hypotheses of a scientific theory ought to, according to Popper, withstand attempts to *falsify* the theory.

So I will therefore assume that natural science cannot answer the question of whether there is a collective rationality in human society nor the question concerning an absolute content in law. Natural science can on the other hand serve as a means to show the precipitation in conceptions of social rationality declaring themselves to rely on the laws of nature; that is, it can serve as an analytical means of falsification instead of a constructive one.

It seems, thus, that we have to accept that the rationality in human society is mainly unexplained. The fact that the complexity of human society is enormous and incomprehensible will perhaps explain why there is no paradigmatic unity in law and legal science on ideological and moral issues (the first set of criteria in Kuhn's conception of a paradigm). On the other hand, if there are norms that are accepted everywhere, this mere fact can provide additional justification to those norms, as that might be a sign of collective rationality; the norms are then universally valid, possible parts of a full, comprehensive moral and ideological paradigm.

NOTES

1   K Popper, *The Logic of Scientific Discovery* (London, 1959) pp 40–1.
2   K Popper, op. cit. p 42; see also K Popper, *Objective Knowledge. An Evolutionary Approach* (2nd ed) (Oxford, 1979) pp 12–14 and *passim*.
3   T S Kuhn, *The Structure of Scientific Revolutions* (2nd ed) (Chicago, 1970), pp 43 ff. and *passim*.
4   T S Kuhn, op. cit. pp 174–210.
5   T S Kuhn, op. cit. p 182.
6   T S Kuhn, op. cit. pp 47–8.
7   T S Kuhn, op. cit. pp 13–14.
8   See M Flodin, *On Valid Law and Valid Moral Norms* (Stockholm, 1986) p 22–3 and *passim*.
9   T S Kuhn, op. cit. pp 35–42.
10 T S Kuhn, op. cit. p viii.
11 Collective rationality denotes here the way a social entity is factually structured and functions.
12 The biologist Karl von Frisch's research (K von Frisch, *Binas liv* Stockholm 1973: German original: *Aus dem Leben der Bienen*) on the bee colonies is an instructive example of the complexity of biological heredity. The bee is a primitive creature compared to a human being, especially concerning the intellectual capacity (it has no real brain), but it has a complex language expressed through body motion and buzzing, and is able to communicate information to other bees about the location

of a flower bed or some other source of nutriment, up to distances of around five miles. The bees have an accurate sense of time, and can be taught to have regular meals every day at places far away from the beehive. Further, a group of scout bees can be sent out for reconnaissance of a new location for the bee colony. When they return, their reports, which contain information about light, protection, dampness, etc., are assessed by the bee colony. The bees can then endanger the existence of the entire bee colony by swarming and seeking a new location chosen on the basis of the reports.

The bee colony is arranged in different biologically determined role systems, with a queen (in some phases more than one), workers and drones. The workers, who perform all the work in the hive, such as construction, taking care of larvae, reconnaissance, do not reproduce themselves biologically. The queen, who does not work, lays all the eggs in the colony after fertilisation by one of the drones, a small number of males are also exempt from work.

The bee colonies are furthermore involved in a complex ecological interrelation with plants, transporting pollen from one flower to another. The whole process of fertilisation for certain species of plants is totally dependent on the participation of the bees. It follows from von Frisch's description of the bee colonies that they will survive not by individual biological heredity, but through a complex pattern of collective cooperation aiming at the survival of the bee colony as a whole. It is obvious that this, one may say, collective (or social) rationality, is far above the comprehension of the individual bee. (See also J B Oakley, 'Sociobiology and the law', in *Man, Law and Modern forms of Life*—Proceedings of the Eleventh IVR World Congress, E Bulygin, J-L Gardies, and I Niiniluto, eds (Dordrecht, 1985) pp 44 ff for a comment on the significance of enthymology as a model for sociobiology).

13   Cf. M Flodin, 'On valid moral norms', in *Theory and Systems of Legal Philosophy*—Proceedings of the Eleventh IVR World Congress in Athens 1985, S Panou, G Bozonis, D Georgas and P Trappe, eds) (Stuttgart, 1988) pp 162–8.

14   See T S Kuhn, op. cit. p 185f. Cf. also K Popper, op. cit. p 257ff.

15   T Hobbes, *Leviathan,* in M Oakeshott, ed (Oxford, 1946), pp 81–2.

16   H Grotius, *De iure belli ac pacis* (English translation) (New York, 1964) *passim.*

CHAPTER 17

Obligations to Future Generations: a Revolution in Social and Legal Thought?

H Ph Visser't Hooft

It is impossible today to explore the topic of revolutions in social and legal thought without paying due attention to the issue of our obligations to future generations. Because of the ecological impact of modern technology, with its ever widening temporal horizon, a collective responsibility is felt to exist in growing sectors of public opinion for adopting policies of 'sustainable' development.[1] The question arises whether such a responsibility does not stretch the resources of ethics or social philosophy, such as they have been inherited from our philosophical tradition. The answer may be that this tradition is a very rich one and that all depends on what ethics or what social philosophy are referred to. Hans Jonas, the author of *Das Prinzip Verantwortung*,[2] one of the most stimulating discussions of our subject, is less hesitant: according to him, ethics and political thought have presupposed, until recent times, a self-evident context of reciprocal interaction between individuals which is precisely lacking in our relations with future people. So he tells us that we have to find new bearings. Whether we agree with Hans Jonas or not, this one example already makes it clear that the issue of our obligations to future generations is a very provocative one: it forces us to have a hard look at the fundamentals of our moral and social philosophy. Most elements for such an exercise can already be found in a literature which has been steadily growing in the last twenty years or so. The aim of the present paper is not to offer a systematic account of this body of writing. It is merely to identify the main structural features of the topic. On what levels must the question be answered whether the issue of our obligations to future generations does, or does not, present a revolutionary challenge?

The following preliminary remark may be in order. In our field of inquiry, I consider the task of ethics and jurisprudence to be the clarification and rational criticism of intuitions according to which 'something should be done for safeguarding the life chances of future generations'. I take it that we want to reflect upon such a more or less inchoative moral experience, in which reason and sentiments, principles and moral concern both play a role. Ethics and jurisprudence have to discuss and refine the first element, and be worried about the limitations of the second.

    1   I first want to consider, in a few words, the relevant moral principles. I suggest that we have to stipulate and define three (partly interconnected) ones: responsibility, rationality and justice.

    In asking ourselves whether we should not take care of the interests of future generations, we show ourselves aware of the near certainty, or probability, that present practices will affect these interests. We initiate the moral point of view, so to speak, by tracing in our minds the effects of our present way of life, with their ever greater impact and temporal reach, and in holding ourselves responsible for them. The concept of responsibility therefore is a useful one to start with, if we understand it in a specifically forward-looking sense. In *Das Prinzip Verantwortung*, Hans Jonas quite convincingly insists on the extent to which this forward-looking, anticipating aspect is a novel one within ethics and social thought. Although he finds some analogies for it in traditional concepts and practices, he claims that it is not until present times that we really do witness the entry of the long term into the moral world.[3] One could object that the idea of progress has already caused, since Kant, Hegel and Marx, such a widening of our mental time horizon. But Jonas wants us to differentiate sharply between the moral notion of responsibility and the idea that history is shaped by some teleological process which takes care of the long term. It precisely is the confidence in some inner worth of economic and technological progress which is creating the dangers we are facing now; we must, as it were, take history in our own hand, without the benefit of a guiding star.[4]

    A responsible attitude will then be strengthened, I think, by our becoming aware of a fundamental claim of moral rationality: that the moral relevance of individual or group interests is not affected, *ceteris paribus*, by the spatial or temporal co-ordinates of these interests.[5] It is just as wrong to cause environmental pollution affecting people in the year 2100 or 3000 as it is to cause one affecting our contemporaries (probabilities being presumed to be equivalent, of course). There simply is no justification available for 'après nous le déluge'. Generational egoism cannot be argued for, it can only be practised, by taking advantage of the power one has, as a living generation, over the life chances of future persons.

    The foregoing principles, however, do not tell us what interests we should care for, nor to what sort of standard their valuation should be submitted, in comparison with ours. I suggest that our moral intuitions point in the main at basic ecological interests, and show us to be preoccupied by considerations of distributive justice. Brian Barry offers the following interpretation: '(What) justice requires . . . is that the overall range of opportunities open to successor generations should not be narrowed. If some openings are closed off by depletion or other irreversible damage to the environment, others should be created . . . to make up.'[6]

Now, in presuming that the principles of responsibility, rationality and justice already tend to shape our actual moral experience (whatever its lack of sophistication), and in choosing to be guided by them (as I do), one in effect rejects several conceptual approaches which either make for quite different relations with future interests, or result in there being no moral relations with future generations at all. I am referring, in the first case, to a certain form of utilitarian thought, and in the second, to the claim that there can be no moral community with future generations either because there is no shared conception of the Good, or because the concept of 'justice' cannot make sense outside a context of reciprocity between moral agents.

(a) In his recent and very elaborate argument, Birnbacher[7] starts, just as I do here, by identifying the relevant principles ('*Idealnormen*' as he terms them, in contrast with *Praxisnormen*' which take account of psychological limitations and lack of information). He reminds us at first of the irrelevance of temporal co-ordinates; so far, so good. But he takes a very controversial step when offering a further definition of moral rationality: he then identifies it with a utilitarian maximising policy[8] projected on the intergenerational plane. The ideal observer who embodies moral rationality contemplates all possible futures of humanity in their whole temporal extent and picks out that future which ensures the highest total of utilities (these 'utilities' being defined themselves on a hedonist basis, which only cares for subjective mental states).[9] Justice between generations has no stronger claims than can be justified by the contingent reality of its being wished for by individuals. Birnbacher, indeed, is quite prepared to accept that the interests of one or more generations be sacrificed in order to ensure that a transhistorical maximum be attained.[10] Now, it seems to me that in making a critical estimate of this approach, one has a choice between several strategies. I will not recall in this paper the many objections which can be raised against any utilitarian calculus resorted to in such an all-encompassing manner as Birnbacher's (Birnbacher hardly makes clear how his utilities actually must be computed). A more specific criticism would consist in emphasising the excessively abstract character of Birnbacher's point of view. A first point to be made here is that it scarcely makes sense to envisage a God-like (and philosophically very questionable) knowledge of all possible futures. A second point is that intergenerational 'maximising' is counter-intuitive: Birnbacher explicitly admits this when drawing the consequence that the interests of some generations may have to be sacrificed—but then so much the worse for our intuitions, he says. Putting justice on the forefront would in his view manifest a too 'abstract' spirit:[11] his utilitarian premises, indeed, do not allow him to make room for justice as an independent norm. One may ask on what side abstraction is actually to be found! Who indeed does wish for an intergenerational maximising policy, except, perhaps, some utilitarian God?[12] Birnbacher's premises clearly undermine themselves. What actually is the case is that many people look at the future in terms of a distributive point of view which aims at tolerable living conditions for each successive generation. I suggest that it is this vision which should be chosen as a starting point. The issues we are faced with in real life cannot be put in a strait-jacket by a purely theoretical choice concerning the nature of morality. We need to consult our actual experience in order to know what values we want to affirm. These values, in the present instance, are those of a basic equality between human beings, and of continuity in human history. It must be stressed also that we are under no logical obligation to favour a utilitarian interpretation of moral rationality. As is made clear by Rawls, moral rationality can be specified in terms of a separateness of persons (and generations) which cannot be overridden by an aggregative point of view.[13]

(b) Golding sees a problem in stipulating obligations towards individuals with whom we cannot expect to share a common life. Such obligations, he says, must be derived from some primary duty to produce a desirable state of affairs for future generations.[14] On what condidtions does such a duty depend? Golding argues that people have moral relations with each other when they are members of the same 'moral community'. Such a community, itself, depends on there being a shared conception of the Good, within the context of common life circumstances (there is no abstract definition of the Good). The difficulty with future generations is that the conditions for such a basic recognition of the normative pertinence of the claims of others do not exist: we cannot know whether our own 'social ideal' (let us say: a tolerant society with well-established human rights) will be relevant for them.[15] So, in taking decisions which anticipate presumed long-term interests (based, necessarily, on our present moral conceptions!), we are 'gambling in futures' in an irresponsible fashion.[16] We should be content with caring for our immediate posterity.

I agree with Golding in considering that most of us would scarcely feel obliged towards future generations which we knew would degenerate into robots or howling fanatics. But the point is that we cannot have such knowledge. So the idea of there being some implied condition of basic social or cultural identity can find no application, except through a refusal to care for the long term which would be justified by the mere *possibility* of its housing robots or fanatics. And this, precisely, is Golding's position. A better alternative, it seems to me, is offered by the notion of keeping open basic opportunities for social and cultural choice (by the anticipation of long-term ecological interests), while taking care, at the same time, to transmit our own ideals to our posterity. Golding's views put the future at risk, in so far as they can result in our neglecting hazards, depletions etc. which will especially affect generations located further off in time; must the continuity of human civilisation be endangered because of the mere chance of history taking a wrong turn, which might be temporary anyway?

(c) I now want to discuss in how far the use of the concept of justice in our relations with future generations is obstructed by the notion that it makes no sense outside a context of reciprocity between moral agents—a reciprocity which is obviously lacking in our relations with future people. For Hans Jonas, as I observed already, the answer is clear: our moral conceptions have developed within a framework of relative technological indigence (as compared with present capabilities); there was no need to look beyond the short term (nor indeed was there the scientific knowledge enabling one to do so); accordingly, moral principles were formulated against a self-evident background of individuals and groups living in interactive, broadly contemporaneous relations with each other. Reciprocity at the core of traditional moral thought: there is much to be said for such a view, one merely has to recall the famous 'golden rule' (*quod tibi fieri non vis, alteri non feceris*), which was and still is considered by many to reflect the quintessence of morals. For Hans Jonas, ethics therefore have to start from scratch when dealing with our present problems.

A less intransigent position is taken by Brian Barry in his important essay on 'Justice as reciprocity'.[17] It certainly is the case that the framework within which we ordinarily discuss questions of justice among contemporaries is that of justice as reciprocity. Again, Rawls' *Theory of Justice* is built around a contractualist conception of equality as reciprocity.[18] Barry here wants to identify the sub-concepts of justice as requital, justice as fidelity, and justice as mutual aid. He then observes that on the face of it, there is room for none of these usages between people who are not alive at the same time. 'Since posterity cannot do anything for us, there can be no obligation arising from justice as reciprocity to do anything for posterity.[19] But Barry argues that there is another conception of justice, also deeply rooted in our common ideas, which can give us a grip on intergenerational justice: the conception of justice as 'equal opportunity'.[20] Justice as reciprocity is silent about initial distributions:[21] it places fair exchange at the centre, but it does not tell us what people should start trading with. It is justice as equal opportunity which gives us a criterion for the initial allocation of natural resources (Barry's argument here refers to justice between nations). Now, Barry claims that this notion of fair access to resources can also be deployed beyond the context of justice of reciprocity: unfair distributions can occur over time as well as over space.[22] I already quoted the formula for intergenerational justice which Barry proposes as a result.

I think Barry is right when claiming to find, in our common ideas about justice, such a ready conceptual access to justice between generations. I even want to argue that justice as equal opportunity can then rely on firmer foundations than Barry himself seems to suggest. The notion I am thinking of is social justice, as usually understood. This notion implies that society must see to it that its members enjoy the minimum material and educational conditions for the exercise of individual liberty. If it is true, perhaps, that 'proportionality between investment and profit lies at the heart of distributive justice',[23] the point of social justice is to make sure that 'investment' (i.e. contributing to the common enterprise) can rely on starting positions which are as equal as possible, and in any case, to guarantee that such 'investment' is humanly possible at all. One may object that this still presupposes a framework of reciprocity, for it precisely is 'starting' positions which one is concerned with, in other words, with initial conditions for the operation of justice in its 'mutualist' form. So how can this usage make sense in our relations with future generations? Well, I think that the suggested dependence on a context of reciprocity is not a stringent one. One may very well take an interest in people enjoying a just share of the opportunities for self-realisation, without making it a *condition* that they contribute in some way to social exchange. There is such a thing as wanting people to lead decent lives, just because of the human condition one shares with them (social justice then flows into the channel of unconditional human rights). And wanting no more than that may already commit us to fight, in the most various surroundings, for protective measures or policies of some sort. Future generations need special protection because of their obvious powerlessness.

However, a clear perception of the fact that we can find, in our common ideas, the requisite formula for tackling the issue of justice between generations is not yet quite good enough for our present purposes. We still have to shore up that perception by resisting or qualifying the philosophical proposition that 'justice' can have no meaning except when certain circumstances actually exist 'which make human cooperation both possible and necessary'.[24] According to John Rawls, who largely follows Hume's account, these circumstances can be divided into two kinds: (a) objective conditions—individuals co-exist together at the same time on a definite geographical territory, are roughly similar in physical or mental powers, are vulnerable to attack, and live under conditions of moderate scarcity; (b) subjective circumstances—'while the parties have roughly similar needs and interests, or needs and interests in various ways complementary, so that mutually advantageous cooperation among them is possible, they nevertheless have their own plans of life'; this leads them 'to have different ends and purposes, and to make conflicting claims on the natural and social resources available'.[25] It is clear that if no meaningful use of the concept of justice can be contemplated unless these circumstances are held to be actually present, relations with future generations cannot be 'just' or 'unjust'. There is no co-existence with future people; these people, being as yet non-existent, are in a position of structural inequality with us; no co-operation, no mutually advantageous arrangement can be envisaged with them. Strictly interpreted, the circumstances of justice prevent us from looking beyond the context of justice as reciprocity i.e. they foreclose any departure from con-temporaneity. It is clearly in that strict sense that Rawls makes them a part of his theory. As a result, he must stipulate that the parties in the original position are contemporaries, and know it.[26] But is there any intrinsic need to consider the circumstances of justice as conditions which have to be fulfilled in actual fact? There is if we cannot imagine, because of some theoretical veto, that justice may find employment, as a concept, beyond the sphere of 'rational co-operation', i.e. of mutual benefit. Such a veto, I think, is strongly supported by the contractualist tradition in moral and social philosophy. According to Bernard Williams, the beginnings of this tradition can be traced to the theory offered by Glaucon and Adeimantus in Book 2 of Plato's Republic, which represents the conventions of justice as a contractual device of the weak to protect themselves against the strong. 'This theory . . . is the prototype of many which view public norms as the solution of a problem which would now be expressed in the language of games theory.'[27] As considered by these theories, the desires which are served by the institutions of justice and generally, the practices of morality are in the first instance self-interested desires: morality is represented as a device for promoting egoistic satisfactions which could in principle occur without it, but which are as a matter of fact unlikely to do so because of everyone's weak position in an amoral state of nature.[28]

This, of course, again puts reciprocity in the centre. No justice or injustice can exist, says Epicurus, between beings which cannot enter into agreements for mutual security. In Hume's argument, rules of justice arise and are maintained only when and so long as they are mutually advantageous to the parties; the circumstance of approximate equality, insisted upon by Hume, in effect identifies the parties: '(Only) those who are in a position to cause trouble unless they are cut in on the deal qualify for a seat at the bargaining table.'[29]

Now, I feel that the claims of moral experience have to be defended in this particular context (as they also did in an earlier one) against those of a too rigid or ungenerous moral philosophy.[30] It simply is a matter of fact that we do deploy the concept of justice beyond the sphere of mutual advantage: I observed so with regard to the idea of justice as equal opportunity. Taken strictly, Hume's argument would prevent us, for instance, from condemning as 'unjust' any strong, man-made inequality like apartheid. Enslaving people would paradoxically make sure that their treatment could not be subjected to such a censure any more. Moreover, it can be observed that law and morals often require from us that we respect the interests of others without personal interests of ours being served thereby (the thief cannot justify himself by saying that because of a lack of personal property, he has no interest in other people respecting the norm 'thou shalt not steal'). Should the notion of 'circumstances of justice', with its contractualist backing, therefore be utterly rejected? I do not think so. Brian Barry suggests that we admit its explanatory power for purposes of social history: focusing on Hume's argument again, he remarks that it may well be that the idea of justice could arise only among approximate equals, and that it is still true that justice is more likely to be realised among approximate equals.[31] It may be interesting to notice the analogy between such views and Bergson's well-known conception of the history of morals according to which society evolves from a '*morale close*' to a '*morale ouverte*'. In the first-mentioned stage, the idea of justice is still very much linked to notions of equality, proportion, reciprocity;[32] in the second one, justice has broken with its mercantile origins in order to affirm, in an unconditional way, the inviolability and incommensurability of the individual.[33]

However, one could still claim that there is, all the same, no problem of justice, and no room for the application of that concept, unless individuals have interests which make them compete for the means of satisfying them. That is Kant's position: the concept of justice is redundant where no possibility of conflict exists.[34] An identical claim is a constituent part of Rawls' 'subjective' circumstances of justice, which were quoted above. In that quite general sense, the relevance of justice could indeed be held to depend on certain circumstances existing in actual fact (competitive relations). This claim, surely, is a strong one; but I am not sure that it has an impact on my argument. There is no reciprocity with future generations, but one may readily admit that there is a 'competition' between our interests and theirs, created precisely by our decision to respect their anticipated interests; the whole issue of our obligations to future generations is one of sharing resources, that is of finding a just solution for the conflict between their probable needs and our present wants.

2   I suggested that an interpretation of our moral intuitions which concentrates on the notion of justice as equal opportunity can hold its own on the conceptual level. But there is more to our topic than concepts, reasons, principles. There also is the problem of moral concern: what makes us care for the future at all, what 'interest' do we have in it? The 'moral distance'[35] which already accounts for massive indifference towards the sufferings of people remote in space is compounded, within the time dimension, by the structural anonymity of our would-be moral partners (we cannot bring their sufferings home by television). I think Hans Jonas is right, on the other hand, when he says that the risks created by technological civilisation are such that it is a moral duty in itself to be fully aware of them and to let them incline us to action. We have to ask ourselves very insistently whether we can overcome the limitations which characterise our attitudes.

A first point to be made here is that the sort of ethics which concentrates on self-interest when discussing basic motivations can find no room for future-oriented concerns. (The objection that when having such a concern, it is in our interest that the future is taken care of, quite evidently fails. The question is, whether we should be concerned, and not whether we happen to be.) In criticising the idea that a meaningful application of the concept of justice is limited to social settings of mutual advantage, as was done in the former paragraph, one in effect attacks or qualifies such a conception; self-interest cannot make us look beyond justice as reciprocity—although we certainly do look in that further direction in actual speech and practice (consider for instance the efforts aiming at a long-term protection against radiation caused by nuclear waste). Moral experience itself demonstrates that a merely prudential approach to morality must fail; that approach may be successful to a certain extent, but disinterested concern must enter in at a certain point. In consequence, the treatment of our whole topic must be linked to criticism of a too timid view of moral phenomena.

Self-interest quite evidently falling short, what other-directed interests give us a stake in the future? This of course is a very complex, and mostly psychological field of investigation, which Birnbacher has admirably dealt with in his book.[36] I will only venture a few remarks.

The sentiments connected with parenthood quite naturally come first. But how far do these sentiments make us look into the future? Interest in the continuity of one's group, nation or culture would seem to be the next major candidate. The psychology of future-orientation, a subtle enough matter as is apparent already, is further complicated by general cultural factors, two instances of which I want to give here. (i) The strongly individualistic character of modern society makes it more difficult to propagate a forward-looking stance. We cannot easily find room for such an eminently collective good as the protection of the interests of future members of society. When thinking about future generations, one is tempted therefore to wish for some more communitarian perspective, which would allow us to repeat what Burke said about society—that it is a partnership between the dead, the living and the unborn. This surely is one of the great challenges to which our topic subjects social philosophy: to conceive society, so to speak, within the time dimension. Traditional social patterns may offer us some inspiration in that respect. For instance, the notion that certain basic resources must be considered to be a 'common heritage of mankind' (which has been embodied in the recent treaty on the law of the sea) can find its ancestry in the institution of the village commons, which was destroyed in former times by the process of capitalistic enclosure, and which carried, through an in-built veto on overgrazing, a sense of responsibility for the future. (ii) Another interesting cultural dimension (but a more ambiguous one as I see it) is the way in which modern shapes our experience of history. I already mentioned that for Hans Jonas the idea of progress is, so to speak, the great enemy; in his view, it in effect replaces responsibility by uncritical belief in a Utopia. It precisely is a global confidence in the benefits of technological development that we should be suspicious of. One can agree with that. But the question arises, at the same time, whether the idea of progress (in some more qualified sense, perhaps) does not very much strengthen an awareness of continuity between the past, the present and the future; it makes future generations share with us some definable common destiny, some definable meaning of human history, and so brings them, in a sense, closer to us.

I have not mentioned as yet, among the different ways in which psychology or a philosophy of culture can expect people to be committed to the interests of the long term, the feeling that 'humanity should carry on'—or, in Brian Barry's words, the feeling that we would be guilty of a 'cosmic impertinence' in taking risks with the survival of our species. These are deep waters indeed. I do not know for sure how widely such a feeling is shared, but I suspect that it is embedded, as a latent one, in our most unsophisticated concerns, and that it underlies, more specifically, the channels of future-orientation which I have just been talking about. There probably is an 'obscure instinctual scheme'[37] which makes us care for the continuation of the human adventure as such. As Dante puts it in his Inferno:

You may understand, therefore
that all our knowledge shall be a dead thing from that moment on
when the door of the future is shut.[38]

Now, it is very interesting to observe that Hans Jonas' main argument, in *Das Prinzip Verantwortung,* precisely is an attempt to justify on the philosophical level that concern for the future as such which I just described tentatively as an instinctual one. According to Jonas, it is the basic claim of Man in 'being there' at all on this planet which should prompt us to take action. The gist of his argument is squarely metaphysical. I already said that Jonas puts forward a principle of responsibility which prescribes that we must anticipate the consequences of our actions in their full material and temporal extent. This principle is explained by a still higher norm, which also directly works as a source of moral concern: the responsibility we bear consists in having to respond to the moral requirement that the *Dasein*, the existence of Man on this planet, must not be endangered. It is this fundamental norm which governs our duty to secure future living conditions compatible with human dignity—a norm which does not aim at a mere biological reproduction of the race, but conceives Man as a free moral agent, who should be able to exercise his freedom. The doors of history must be kept open, so to speak. Because of these high stakes, we are morally bound to realise clearly what risks we are creating through the continuous extension of our powers (i.e. how much our powers have extended beyond our capacities for judgement!) and we are under a moral obligation, also, to let ourselves be inclined towards effective action by the picture we thus have built up in our minds.

I have no room to discuss the manner in which Hans Jonas justifies his fundamental norm on a still higher level of thought. Let me remark, merely, that he does it by reading an ontological implication in the idea of Man: this idea, he says, intrinsically calls for its embodiment in reality (it denies the separation of 'ought' from 'is'). Jonas is quite aware that such a line of argument is contrary to the spirit of modern philosophy—but then, he says, so much the worse for that philosophy, the actual issues we are faced with cannot be taken seriously except through some sort of heroic argument. The merits of this claim will have to be discussed elsewhere; I only want to observe here that Jonas himself acknowledges that religion could, at first sight, be held to be a better candidate for grounding his fundamental norm; but then, everybody will not be sensitive to an argument based on religious belief.

3   I have limited my short discussion of the subject to the structural features I consider to be the most important ones. A more elaborate argument would, of course, have to delve into many other problems of a conceptual or normative nature. One may ask, for instance, what specific issues arise on the level of legal concepts and institutions. Would it make sense to translate justice towards future generations, and the concomitant idea of future people having a moral right upon a liveable earth, into the conceptually and operationally more rigorous language of legal rights, or would that be a superfluous or, in any case, quite impractical exercise?[39] Should future people be represented by an 'ombudsman' whose duty it would be to speak on behalf of their interests? What can be expected in the future from the 'common heritage' concept adopted in the recent UN treaty on the law of the sea?

4   What answer must be given to the question formulated at the beginning of this paper: whether the issue of our obligations to future generations does, or does not, present a revolutionary challenge to social and legal thought? I am tempted to give one along the following lines. (i) A principled relation with the future is asked for by the concept of moral rationality itself. An impact on current philosophy occurs at the next stage of definition, where the concept of justice comes in. Options like utilitarianism or like a prudential perspective on

human institutions then have to be rejected or qualified. This, however, does not yet amount to a 'revolutionary' challenge: the options I just mentioned are quite controversial already. (ii) It is on the level of motives rather than that of principles that a revolutionary challenge exists: although our moral intuitions do point at intergenerational justice, there still is a long way to go before the reasons and concerns which underlie that inchoate experience can overcome the 'moral distance' between the present and the long-term future. We have to make ourselves see, and treat as our equals, persons which we cannot give a name to, and whose way of life is beyond conjecture. The question is, whether such a formidable step does not necessitate a fundamental change in our conception of society (which basically still is a contractual one). Whether that step also presents a metaphysical challenge, as it is suggested by Hans Jonas, depends upon the views one has concerning the possible ambitions of philosophy.

NOTES

1　See *Our Common Future* (WCED, Oxford, 1987) p 4: 'We came to see that a new development path was required, one that sustained human progress not just in a few places for a few years, but for the entire planet into the distant future.'

2　*Das Prinzip Verantwortung* (Frankfurt, 1979).

3　Ibid. ch 1.

4　Ibid. ch 5.

5　Cf. the exclusion of 'time preference' in John Rawls, *A Theory of Justice* (Oxford, 1972) p 293.

6　Brian Barry, 'Circumstances of justice and future generations', p 243 in *Obligations to Future Generations* Barry and Sikora, eds (Philadelphia, 1978). Cf. *Our Common Future*, op. cit. p 43: 'Sustainable development is development that meets the needs of the present without compromising the ability of future generations to meet their own needs.'

7　Dieter Birnbacher, *Verantwortung für künftige Generationen* (Stuttgart, 1988).

8　Ibid. pp 56–7, 103.

9　Ibid. p 87.

10　Ibid. pp 111, 117.

11　Ibid. pp 124, 130–1.

12　H L A Hart, 'Between utility and rights', in *Essays in Jurisprudence and Philosophy* (Oxford, 1983) p 201: '. . . The modern critique of utilitarianism asserts that there is nothing self-evidently valuable or authoritative as a moral goal in the mere increase in totals of pleasure or happiness abstracted from all questions of distribution. The collective sum of different person's pleasures . . . is not in itself a pleasure or happiness which anybody experiences.'

13　Rawls, op. cit. p 190: utilitarianism mixes up impartiality with impersonality. It should be mentioned here that one cannot detect any strong impact of Birnbacher's 'ideal' norms upon his *Praxisnormen*. The practical context, according to him, is quite convincingly one of solving conflicts of interest between the present and the future in conditions of strong uncertainty and of weak moral concern; and the main directive he wants us to accept is the widely recognised one of ensuring 'sustainability'.

14   Martin P Golding, 'Obligations to future generations', *Monist* 56(1972) pp 87-8.
15   Ibid. pp 95ff.
16   Ibid. pp 97-8.
17   Ibid. 'Justice as reciprocity', in *Justice (Ideas and ideologies)*, Kamenka, ed (London, 1979).
18   Ibid. p 51.
19   Ibid. p 69.
20   Ibid. p 51.
21   Ibid. p 73.
22   Ibid. p 78
23   Ibid. p 52, note 8.
24   Rawls, op. cit. p 126.
25   Ibid. p 127.
26   Ibid. pp 138ff, 292. As a consequence, Rawls must introduce a specific 'motivational assumption' of concern for one's descendants in order to deploy his concept of justice within the time dimension i.e. in the relations between generations.
27   Bernard Williams, 'Philosphy', in *The legacy of Greece* (Oxford, 1981) p 244.
28   Ibid. p 245.
29   Barry, 'Circumstances of justice', loc. cit. p 220.
30   I am indebted to G A van der Wal, 'De zorgen voor lateren: van later zorg?', inaugural lecture, Rotterdam 1979.
31   Barry, op. cit. p 223.
32   Henri Bergson, *Les Deux Sources de la Morale et de la Religion* (Paris, 1932) p 68.
33   Ibid. p 71.
34   Otfried Höffe, *Zur vertragstheoretischen Begründung politischer Gerechtigkeit, in Ethik und Politik* (Frankfurt, 1979) pp 209-10.
35   See the stimulating (last) chapter on 'moral distance' in Jonathan Glover, *Causing Death and Saving Lives* (Penguin, 1977).
36   Birnbacher, op. cit. chs 5 and 6.
37   George Steiner, *In Bluebeard's Castle (Some notes towards the redefinition of culture)* (Yale UP, 1971) p 71.
38   Ibid. p 73.
39   See Joel Feinberg, 'The rights of animals and unborn generations', in *Rights, Justice and the Bounds of Liberty* (Princeton UP, 1980), for an argument which dismisses conceptual objections against the idea of future generations having rights. A plea for constitutional rights of future generations, which also deals with difficulties of a doctrinal nature, is to be found in Peter Saladin and Christoph Zenger, *Rechte künftiger Generationen* (Basel/Frankfurt, 1988).

Index of names